It Ain't Necessarily So

It Ain't Necessarily So

HOW MEDIA MAKE
AND UNMAKE
THE SCIENTIFIC PICTURE
OF REALITY

By David Murray, Joel Schwartz, and S. Robert Lichter

ROWMAN & LITTLEFIELD PUBLISHERS, INC.
Lanham • Boulder • New York • Oxford

ROWMAN & LITTLEFIELD PUBLISHERS, INC.

Published in the United States of America
by Rowman & Littlefield Publishers, Inc.
4720 Boston Way, Lanham, Maryland 20706
http://www.rowmanlittlefield.com

12 Hid's Copse Road
Cumnor Hill, Oxford OX2 9JJ, England

Distributed by NATIONAL BOOK NETWORK

British Cataloging in Publication Information Available

Library of Congress Cataloging-in-Publication Data
Murray, David, 1946–
    It ain't necessarily so : how media make and unmake the scientific picture of reality /
    David Murray, Joel Schwartz, and S. Robert Lichter.
        p. cm.
    Includes bibliographical references and index.
    ISBN 0-7425-1095-6 (alk. paper)
        1. Journalism, Scientific. 2. Journalism—Objectivity. I. Schwartz, Joel (Joel B.), 1950–
II. Lichter, S. Robert. III. Title.

    PN4784.T3 M87 2001
    070.4'495—dc21   00-066464

Printed in the United States of America

∞™ The paper used in this publication meets the minimum requirements of American
National Standard for Information Sciences—Permanence of Paper for Printed Library
Materials, ANSI/NISO Z39.48-1992.

CONTENTS

Prologue   vii

Introduction   MAKING NEWS AND MAKING SENSE
                The News That's "Fit to Print"   1

PART I   THE AMBIGUITY OF NEWS

Chapter 1   THE NEWS THAT ISN'T THERE
                Stories That Are—and Aren't—Covered   17

Chapter 2   MUCH ADO ABOUT LITTLE
                Making News Mountains out of Research Molehills   35

PART II   THE AMBIGUITY OF MEASUREMENT

Chapter 3   BAIT AND SWITCH
                Understanding "Tomato" Statistics   57

Chapter 4   THE PERILS OF PROXIES
                Is There a There There?   71

Chapter 5   IS THE GLASS HALF EMPTY OR HALF FULL?
                A Look at Statistics from Both Sides Now   85

Chapter 6   POLLS APART
              The Gertrude Stein Approach to Making Sense
              of Contradictory Surveys   97

Chapter 7   THE REALITY AND RHETORIC OF RISK
              Telling It Like It Is—and Isn't   115

Chapter 8   DISTINGUISHING "REPORTS" FROM REALITY
              Confusing the Map with the Territory   133

PART III   THE AMBIGUITY OF EXPLANATION

Chapter 9   BLAMING THE MESSENGER, IGNORING
              THE MESSAGE
              Do Motives Matter?   147

Chapter 10   TUNNEL VISION AND BLIND SPOTS
              The Danger of Hedgehog Interpretations   163

Conclusion   HARD TO TELL
              Journalism, Science, and Public Policy—
              An Inherent Conflict?   175

Notes   197

Bibliography   233

Index   241

About the Authors   249

PROLOGUE

I t would be a tough October day for a typical male American waking to his morning paper and cup of coffee in the year 2000. He would face a world of apparent danger and vast uncertainty. Take that steaming cup of coffee. According to recent health news, it might be beneficial— or it might be dark-brewed death. At least, so suggested some recent medical research.

Not only that, Halloween would fast be approaching. Should our typical American parent allow his children to go out trick-or-treating, when the news has been full of dire warnings about malicious strangers who threaten children with booby-trapped apples and poison-laced licorice?

If our typical parent is also a Texan, he must be very confused about the quality of his children's schools. Though some recent research made a case for Texas school achievement, a blockbuster news report just announced a Texas school debacle. A new RAND study that appeared in the midst of the presidential election campaign appeared to undermine one candidate's showpiece educational policy.

The woman of the household likewise has grounds for concern. She has heard a television address by the current president, warning of the severity of domestic violence in America. Seeking reauthorization of a bill directed toward lessening violence against women, the president repeated some truly alarming numbers identifying the risks a woman might face from her putative beloved.

So much danger so early in the morning would be very unsettling indeed. Would, that is, if each of the fears and risks were actually true. But what if the news reports were inaccurate, or at least, very partial in their accounting? What if the magnitude of our daily dangers has been considerably overblown? What if, in fact, neither the underlying science nor the overlying headline that occasioned each of these fears was quite what it seemed to be?

Let's examine the coffee cup first. All that science had actually shown was a correlation between coffee consumption and various states of health. Was coffee being declared guilty through a mere association with illnesses? In 1981 the *New England Journal of Medicine* (*NEJM*) reported that coffee "might account" for cases of pancreatic cancer.[1] Further, a 1998 study linked coffee to difficulty getting pregnant, miscarriages, and even low infant birth weight.[2] But then the tables turned. Based on a study in the *Journal of the American Medical Association*, a news headline claimed "Coffee Might Prevent Parkinson's" (*Dayton Daily News*), while other papers chose verbs like "Repel" or "Deter" to characterize the effect.[3]

The clear sense is that coffee has been convicted of doing something—in one case, something negative, in the other, something positive. But what did we really learn? In the first place, we don't know what it is about coffee that does the trick—the caffeine or something else in the bean. Nor whether it might matter that the population in the *JAMA* Parkinson's study was 8,004 Japanese American men drinking Hawaiian coffee. Would it work for 8,004 Norwegian American women drinking a Minnesota blend? Have we been jived with java?

And what causes Parkinson's, anyway? According to a *New York Post* headline, "Bug Spray Could Lead to Parkinson's," home pesticide use was said to cause the disease.[4] If one sprayed the aspidistras while holding an open Starbucks mocha grande, would he or she come out even? What's the verdict on coffee—a Parkinson's panacea, or the pathway to a pancreatic pandemic? What exactly has been demonstrated by all these studies? Cause? Cure?

In fact, it's neither. Epidemiology, the science of looking for risk factors by comparing populations, is never able to establish "causation" in either direction. All that it can show is "association," a much-misunderstood term. The biggest single problem is that few people—including journalists—understand how health risk studies actually operate. We mistake correlation for causation, and coincidence for conviction. Hence, we are continually fooled into thinking that we know something when we really don't. When all goes well in an epidemiological study, one finds an association between two things. No more, no less. And that's true even of the best of studies, those that are methodologically rigorous and carefully constructed.

Moreover, it's clear that we haven't hit the health dregs yet. No sooner had the Parkinson's study been digested when a July 25 report from the Associated Press appeared, headlined "Coffee, Rheumatoid Arthritis Linked."[5] This article mentioned a Finnish study published in the *Annals of the Rheumatic Diseases* that followed 19,000 people over fifteen years. The researchers found that among people who drank more than three cups a day, 0.5 percent got the disease, as opposed to only 0.2 percent of those who drank three cups a day or less. While the effect is not large and the study was criticized by several scientific commentators (particularly for not controlling for confounding factors that may affect the development of the disease), the AP stressed that the study was important because "it is the first to produce evidence of a possible link" between coffee and rheumatoid arthritis.

That should perk us up, for once again we are witnessing the alacrity with which journalists and policymakers move from evidence of "possible links" to assumptions of demonstrated causality. But isn't discovering and then publicizing "possible links" a public health service? It would seem so, at first blush. But while much of science depends upon coming up with good ideas by finding new connections, it depends at least as much on sorting out and defeating bad ideas. Too much is connected already to too much, and nearly everything is instantly connected to the media. The challenge is to discriminate between valuable connections and the mirage of mere coincidence.

We are rapidly arriving at a dilemma. With the development of supercomputing capability, our searching, connecting, and data-dredging associational power grows exponentially (the computations are cheap, fast, and fun to watch). Yet with the postulation of "possible links" proceeding at a gallop, the need for an adequate disabling mechanism becomes ever more imperative, lest perception of risk keep us up all night. Coleridge once said that poetic faith depended on the "willing suspension of disbelief." Perhaps good science depends, at least in its first stage, on the opposite. But what to make of coffee? Is having another cup a matter of Russian roulette? We simply don't know, no matter how many news reports we scan. The only lasting message has to be *caveat lector*—that is, "let the reader beware."

Halloween is a time for scary stories: tales of ghouls, ghosts, Hookhand, and the Boogeyman. At least our typical adult knows these stories are not true. But in recent years we've been spreading a myth that even he or she believes—that homicidal strangers are regularly poisoning trick-or-treat candy. Every year, newspapers and television programs warn parents about these "threats," usually including grave reminders to check apples for razor blades and needles. In recent years, hospitals and airports have taken to X-raying children's trick-or-treat bags as a community service. In fact, this time-consuming and expensive practice has become so widespread that a controversy arose in St. Louis a few years ago when a local hospital decided to stop offering the service. Why would a hospital be willing to risk children's lives to save a few dollars? Because their experience has been consistent with the national data: Halloween candy-tampering is a myth. Joel Best, a professor of sociology and criminal justice at the University of Delaware, has studied national criminal data going back to 1958 and found only seventy-six reports of any kind of tampering. Almost all of these have turned out to be mistaken or fraudulent.

In all that time, there have been only three incidents of children dying in what were reported as cases of tainted candy. But even these had nothing to do with homicidal strangers. A case in 1970 involved a child from Detroit who had stumbled upon, and eaten, his uncle's stash of heroin. The child's parents, not wanting the uncle to go to jail for possession, concocted the tainted candy story. In 1974, a Houston boy was intentionally poisoned by his father, who then made up the story about contaminated candy. The third case, in 1990, concerned a Los Angeles–area girl with a congenital heart condition. The girl had a fatal seizure while trick-or-treating, and even though her parents immediately notified the authorities about their daughter's heart condition, television, radio, and newspapers blared shocking news reports of yet another incident of poisoned Halloween candy. Needless to say, no evidence of tampering was ever found. Professor Best emphasizes that "It is not the number of cases; it is the fact that there aren't any cases that involve death or injury."

There is one undetermined case. In 1982, fifteen children and one adult fell ill after eating candy and cakes supplied at a New Jersey school Halloween party. Some observers were suspicious, although there did not appear to be any tampering. Regardless, no one died.

The lack of evidence is such that Mt. Holyoke College criminologist Richard Moran could "not uncover a single case of child murder that could be attributed to Halloween sadists." He dubs them "mythical." So why do we persist in scaring ourselves this way? Strangely enough, the reason may lie in how safe our society is for our children. If our children are not subjected to the real horrors of disease, starvation, and war that have been major worries for parents throughout history, we still feel a need to protect them from something. The figure of the murderous candy-poisoner fills the vacuum very well. But, in protecting children from an unproven threat, parents may not just be taking some of the fun out of childhood but also raising children in an atmosphere of paranoia, which cannot be good for them.

The trail of Halloween "incidents" almost always leads to crimes directed at specific individuals or misdiagnosed illnesses or fatalities. The news media, however, rarely retract frightening stories as prominently as they sound the initial alarm. Perversely, repeating myths like these every year may ultimately elicit a "copycat" effect, inspiring deranged individuals to carry out previously nonexistent crimes. To paraphrase some useful advice: Be careful what you warn about—you might just get it.

How about the Texas schools? If the new RAND report on education had landed on November 8, 2000, the day after the presidential election, it likely would have gained small media attention. It was, after all, a brief (eighteen pages total) "Issue Paper" that offered modest insights on the dangers of state testing when compared to standardized national measures. Unfortunately, a research contribution to legitimate issues fell victim to inauspicious timing. The RAND paper appeared just in time to be injected into election news, causing media to inflate a footnote study into an educational juggernaut.

Typical of media coverage was the October 24 *CBS Evening News*, which claimed the report "dropped like dynamite on the so-called Texas miracle."[6] *CBS* further termed the news "explosive" and a "shot to the heart." Newspapers from the *Baltimore Sun* to the *New York Times* followed suit.[7] But a careful reading of the actual record shows these claims to be hyperbolic. For those primed for revelations of malfeasance, it was anticlimactic to encounter the actual document. The RAND paper argued that of two measures of educational performance by Texas school children, tests showing dramatic improvement were probably not as reliable as other tests showing only modest improvement. Laudably, *USA Today* stood apart from other media with its more sober account: "A report Tuesday asserted that Texas schoolchildren have not demonstrated as much improvement in national tests as they have in the high-stakes, state-administered tests."[8]

Why did most media overreact? To tell the full story requires some background. This is a story of three research results: RAND I, issued in July, an extensive analysis of National Assessment of Educational Progress (NAEP) state-by-state comparison scores; an analysis of Texas children using only the Texas Assessment of Academic Skills (TAAS); and then the "blockbuster," RAND II, a brief evaluation of why the state test and the national test results differed. All results agree that Texas did well—but they differ as to how well. One can indeed read the latest report (RAND II) as a challenge to assertions about the "Texas miracle." The TAAS results showed dramatic improvement not matched by the national comparison NAEP test. It is possible not only that the test is too easy but that Texas teachers have been training students to the TAAS task without imparting general learning skills. Moreover, a key component of the "Texas miracle" has been that TAAS shows minority students closing the performance gap with white students. But the NAEP scores show no such progress in Texas; in fact, by some measures the gap appears to be widening. Is the "miracle" a mirage?

Virtually ignored by the media was the fact that undisputed NAEP results continued to show Texas at the top of the heap among states in some grades, while at the national average in others. TAAS scores showed a much brighter picture. But are they necessarily less reliable than the NAEP scores? It's simply not clear. As RAND II notes, the two tests "assess different skills and knowledge." Moreover, the report notes that "divergence of trends does not prove that NAEP is right and the state assessment is misleading, but it does raise important questions about the generalizability of gains." In fact, the report continues, "Understanding the source and consequences of the impressive score gains on the TAAS would require an extensive independent study. We have not done that."

Moreover, it is common to find state assessments showing more dramatic improvement than national assessments in many states besides Texas. For instance, Virginia recently posted an amazing 230 percent increase in just one year in the number of schools passing its state-mandated tests. Such improvement might result from requirements that tests such as the TAAS must be passed in order to graduate. Thus state assessments, unlike the NAEP, receive "high-stakes" status. That is, their accountability features might "concentrate the mind" in just the same way as the prospect of being hanged in the morning focuses the prisoner's mind on redemption, whether it be through physical escape or religious belief.

Further, the NAEP results showing a widening of the gap between minorities and whites were not particular to Texas, but were a dismaying nationwide trend. Nevertheless, even given the national trends, RAND II acknowledges, "within racial or ethnic group, the average performance of Texas students tends to be about six percentile-points higher than the national average for that group." Finally, the NAEP and the TAAS are really not comparable in a number of ways. NAEP tests are not administered every year, not every subject is included, only a few grade levels are tested, and individual school and district scores are not available. The test simply doesn't measure what the TAAS does. Nor does it measure the same students; the NAEP analyzed the period 1992 to 1996, the TAAS 1994 to 1998. Several positive policies were initiated in Texas by his predecessors, but since Republican presidential candidate George W. Bush became governor in 1995, if there were to be a "policy effect," it could only have affected a single year (out of four) in the NAEP performance, while conversely affecting the TAAS three out of four years. No one really knows the impact.

Domestic violence is a serious subject. President Bill Clinton underlined this during his Oct. 28 radio address when he said, "In America today, domestic violence is the number one health risk for women between the ages of fifteen and forty-four. . . . Every twelve seconds, another woman is beaten. That's nearly 900,000 victims a year." A dreadful state of affairs, if true. The trouble is that all three of these statements are untrue. Furthermore, most of them were untrue when the president first made them in 1995. In fact, the White House was forced to retract the original statement after the inaccuracies became a public issue.[9] But now that the dust has settled, these fraudulent figures have resurfaced again, despite the fact that a few moments' thought will show how unsound they remain.

Let's start with the "every twelve seconds" figure. Most obviously, this doesn't even square with the "900,000 a year" figure. If five women are beaten a minute, 60 minutes an hour, 24 hours a day (you get the idea), the sum would be over two and a half million, not "nearly 900,000." But even without this arithmetical carelessness, the figure still doesn't add up. The *total* number of violent incidents recorded by the FBI in 1999 was 1,430,693. That's about one every 22 seconds. Domestic violence is underreported to the authorities, certainly. But can it really be so underreported as to make it more common than the total number of *all* violent crimes?

Presumably, this is why White House Press Secretary Michael McCurry acknowledged its inadequacy the first time the president used it in March 1995. "We want to take back that statistic," he said. The 900,000 figure is also five years old. It is actually a survey estimate for violence against women by intimates from 1995. In itself, that figure had shown a substantial decline from the figure of over a million that had been posted in 1993. But violent crime has declined dramatically since the heights of the early 1990s. In fact, according to the survey figures, violent crime against women by intimates has declined almost 30 percent since 1995.

The third figure being misused is the claim that domestic violence is "the number one health risk" for young women. The official backing for this figure derives from a statement by a badly briefed Surgeon General Antonia Novello. In actuality, the primary source was an extremely small study of one emergency room, which simply suggested that domestic violence *may* be a more common reason for visiting the ER than car accidents, rapes, and muggings combined. The Centers for Disease Control, often cited as the source of this factoid, have disowned it, telling journalists that it is neither theirs nor reputable.

So how could the White House repeat its mistake? Did someone merely pull a five-year-old briefing document out of a dusty file and recycle it without bothering to check any of the figures? To paraphrase Oscar Wilde, to be badly briefed once may be regarded as a misfortune; to do it twice looks like carelessness. The last word on the seriousness of this matter should, however, be left to *The New Republic*, commenting on the first incident: "The statistics are bad enough as they are. Why inflate them, unless you don't think [the real numbers] warrant a response?"[10]

At least our hypothetical couple could take comfort in one assured fact—the upcoming presidential election in November would be a calm, orderly process of choosing the leader of the free world based on democratic voting. Indeed, they could take a certain pride in the fact that as Americans, they were the envy of the world for the stately and definitive way that they settled their politics by the simple expedient of counting the majority. And they were reassured by the vision of the whole process being relayed through measured and accurate media reports on election night, guided by the best statistical projections. Certainly there could be no ambiguity of measurement, absence of clarity, wild surmises, or disputing of the final outcome. Of course, back in October the word "chad" was associated by most Americans with, if anything, a poor, landlocked African nation. The prospect that the detritus of machine counting in Palm Beach County, Florida could shake American democracy to its core was about as likely that a chad, whatever it was, could be either swinging or hanging, much less dimpled or pregnant.

We, on the other hand, who are now older and wiser than our typical couple (if not sadder as well), find ourselves facing, in addition to our routine concerns, a new set occasioned by the examples set out above. Can we trust media reports of reality? Just how solid is the research that we use increasingly to guide our personal lives as well as our public policy? Can it really be that things aren't always what they seem, even though the news was reported in an authoritative manner through a responsible media outlet? Do we have any protection, or are we simply at the mercy of the information explosion, constantly blown hither and yon with each new blast of data? There is hope. No, it ain't necessarily so, those things that you're liable to read, even in the reliable press. But there are ways that the forewarned can be forearmed and means by which savvy news consumers can defend themselves.

INTRODUCTION

MAKING NEWS AND MAKING SENSE
The News That's "Fit to Print"

Scientific research may at first glance sound specialized or even forbidding as a topic, but in fact it is research results—of a remarkable variety, from health news to environmental alarms to the latest findings on child-rearing practices—that increasingly construct the public agenda. And acting as a catalyst is the news, that urgent, insistent, up-to-the-minute breakthrough establishing how you and your world are doing. But what is news, and how does it work?

Until we learn the intricacies of media culture and the processes by which news is made, we are vulnerable to a daily dose of misunderstanding contained in each morning's headlines. Indeed, we are at risk of perpetually misdiagnosing our modern world and the role we play in it. This book not only sets the record straight on an intriguing variety of contemporary issues but also strengthens and empowers the news consumer by providing a new and deeper understanding of the "reality industry" whose product defines our daily agenda.

The primary goal of this book is to reveal the inner workings—the choices, judgments, arrangements, spinnings, deletions, and framings—of the news process as it engages with research-based portraits of our world. Organized as a series of detailed case studies of journalistic practice, the book reveals to the news consumer the process that constructs news about who we are and what we know about ourselves.

While we correct many surprising misapprehensions that have become "conventional wisdom," the larger task is that of demystification (or even disillusioning). We show the news consumer how the magic trick, as it were, was done: how the lighting was placed, where were the mirrors, wires, and struts, what sleight-of-hand was employed. Yet our purpose in demystifying the news is not cynical dismissal. Rather, we appreciate news as a manufactured, even theatrical, artifact, as much as it is an engagement with reality. Watching research results go through the prism of media and get thereby refracted into multiple colors and shadings is valuable. It doesn't mean that the process is fraudulent or misleading. But it does reveal the action of the prism. We can for the first time answer the question of what can and cannot be known and proclaimed with confidence.

A book of careful case studies detailing the perilous misadventures that befall research results as they are transformed into daily headlines should become a staple of both science education and the journalism curriculum. Media studies, communications programs, political science and environmental programs as well as public policy think tanks will likewise find this book a valuable guide, as will university public information officers, legal and lobbying domains, corporate public affairs offices, and the formal institutions of the scientific community. In short, this book contains cautionary tales and sound guidance for anyone concerned with the intersection of science, media, and public policy.

A wider audience of interested parties will benefit from these arguments as well. This is a book for anyone interested in or affected by the news. That is, anyone who reads a newspaper, wouldn't miss the early and late evening broadcasts, catches the talk radio show, subscribes to a newsweekly, or connects to the Internet, that constant news stream for the information junky.

Rationale, Scope, and Aims of This Book

It is commonly agreed that we stand, as never before, on the brink of a vast new world of information, with data becoming more and more immediate as news sources proliferate. Images, numbers, narratives, charts, charges, and action advice burgeon before our eyes. But can we handle the flow?

Paradoxically, the more data stream our way, the less meaningful information we seem to be able to abstract and manage. The situation has been compared to trying to get a drink of water from a fire hydrant: the water is there in abundance, but the pressure nearly takes your head off. So it is with the search for news. The chatter, reports, analyses, updates, evaluations, commentaries, and digests that offer to guide us can themselves barely keep their head above the incoming tide of events and representations.

If raw data only become meaningful information that is usable when they are processed and organized, categorized and compared, then we need new management resources for understanding the news. There are abundant chances for things to go awry. At a minimum, we stand at risk of missing the significance of some new development. Perhaps more consequentially, we stand at risk of being actively misled by misunderstanding. We can come to know or believe some "information" about ourselves or our world that directly contradicts the real state of affairs.

Have we misunderstood the latest health report, which led us to eat precisely the wrong thing? Did we truly comprehend the research result that transformed our sense of poverty, altered the relations between the sexes, or heralded an urgent environmental doom? Or have we understood very clearly what we were told, when unfortunately the source itself was corrupted, rendering the knowledge we gained about nature, society, the economy, politics, or even matters of intimacy entirely erroneous? Surely some of the causes of misunderstanding are attributable to innocent mistakes. Others, however, may be more directly intended.

Perhaps we require "gatekeepers" in order to avoid the misdirection, embarrassment, or improper action that results from our misapprehension (or our simple incapacity to keep up on "breaking developments"). These experienced third parties could intervene between the news consumer and the source. They would monitor, condense, evaluate, and recast information for us, sparing us the trouble and guiding us past pitfalls. Perhaps the gatekeepers might even have a "value-added" role, not only transmitting data but framing its significance and ensuring that we don't miss the "moral of the story."

Certainly there is a need for such figures in the information landscape, and when the role is properly played, we are all served thereby.

But reservations and suspicions still lurk. Just how wise is it to yield control over information upon which we may have to act? After all, "who shall guard the guardians" is a question that stands perennially near. How can we be assured that our gatekeepers have sound judgment, share our values, or even operate in good faith? For that matter, how do we even know who they are, or just what their effect might be, once they are cloaked behind the information curtain? In fact, aren't developments like the Internet, cable news networks, and alternative publications driven by the quest for more "immediate" and reliable news untouched by unreliable narrators?

In reality, no news other than that in which we directly participate can ever really be "immediate"; it cannot come to us in an "un-mediated" fashion, without passing first through the hands of another. We must perpetually rely on some mechanism of mediation. Is there a solution? Perhaps we may supersede the "unseen hand" of the gatekeeper (or at least complement it) by becoming savvy, empowered consumers of news, capable of gate-keeping the gatekeepers, as it were. Or at least knowing when things are going awry, and why.

How well do we understand what we've been told? In the *Washington Post* on April 12, 2000, a front-page above-the-fold story (its very position indicating that the *Post* intends us to regard this news as important), follows this headline: "U.S. Plans to Pay for Ills from Radiation: Government Shifts Policy on Workers at Bomb Plants."

That certainly sounds important, and we learn soon enough that it will be an expensive policy shift, as well, with costs expected to exceed 520 million dollars. What are we to make of this circumstance? Is it an example of justice being done, with nuclear workers who genuinely suffer from work-related maladies properly being compensated? Or is this a story of a government capitulating to pressure politics from a combination of anti-nuclear activists, trial attorneys, and needlessly frightened workers who are really about as healthy as anyone else?

To choose between those alternative scenarios, we need reliable information, such as how the health circumstances of nuclear workers compare to those of others in the population. Since the major radiation-related concern is cancer, it would be helpful to know something about worker cancer rates. The story did provide some medical guidance, but only in a single short paragraph. Here is the information the *Post* considered both pertinent and sufficient: "Government-funded medical surveys since 1960 have shown higher rates of at least one type of cancer—varying from thyroid tumors to leukemia—at most of the major facilities that produced nuclear weapons."

But a second look reveals that this statement is actually a candidate for the least-meaningful health-risk paragraph of the month. Cancer rates for workers are "higher," assuredly, but higher than what? Higher than that of the general population? Higher than that of people of the same age, sex, and background? Higher than workers at nonnuclear industries? Higher than nuclear-power workers at facilities that didn't produce weapons? Higher than the *Washington Post* thinks that they should be? There is no answer; we are simply left hanging.

Moreover, what does it mean to say that there are higher rates of "at least one type of cancer"? There are several types of cancers mentioned, and apparently the case is that some one of those will be found higher at some plant (while presumably the others are found at either the same or even lower rates among the workers). At another facility a second, separate type of cancer will be found that exceeds some (as yet unspecified) standard, while the rates of other cancers (including apparently the first elevated one) are found to be normal, and so on through the list of "major facilities." What of "minor" facilities? And why is it "most" and not "all" facilities, if workers at all facilities faced the same causal conditions? It is not uncommon to find that incidents of a given disease will be higher at one place than it is at another, for no more compelling reason than the law of averages. Why should we expect that all cancers will be found at rates "lower" (again, than what?) at each of the facilities?

Such a scenario begins to sound like Lake Wobegon, the mythical place where all children are above average and presumably all workers are healthier than average. Yet it is not altogether inconceivable that lower rates for all cancers is what we should expect, since nuclear plant workers are, surprisingly to some, actually healthier than the general population, even when it comes to cancer rates.

But the point is that this story, even though it appears in a major U.S. metropolitan daily and was written by an environmental journalist who specializes in this theme, fails to tell us any of these simple but necessary facts. The unwary reader is vulnerable to accidental (or otherwise) confusion. Was the absence of facts a result of simple negligence, or were the facts "gate-kept" away, on the assumption that readers either didn't need to know them or wouldn't grasp their significance anyway? As it is, the implicit message of the *Post* story is "you'll just have to trust our conclusions, that we're telling you the way it is." We acknowledge that the *Washington Post* employs very accomplished science writers, as competent as those of any American newspaper. What went wrong in the reporting of nuclear hazards to workers?

The answer to that question takes us down many pathways, which this book will explore in depth. To begin with, it is worth remembering the old Russian lament about the two major newspapers under Communism, *Pravda* and *Isvestia*. Pravda is Russian for "truth," and Isvestia means "news." In the gibe that circulated during the last days of the Soviet Union, we learned that "*Isvestia nye Pravda, y Pravda nye Isvestia.*" That is, "The news isn't the truth, and the truth isn't news." Without charging that our newspapers convey only propaganda, we can nevertheless learn an important lesson from this ironic Russian commentary: newspaper reports on scientific research are constructs, "news," that result from selections and choices about the facts themselves.

"It's absolutely correct to say that there are objectively occurring events," says Cole Campbell of the *Virginian-Pilot*. "Speeches are made, volcanoes erupt, trees fall. But *news* is not a scientifically observable event. News is a choice, an extraction process, saying that one event is more meaningful than another event. The very act of saying that means making judgments that are based on values and based on frames." The news clearly has a relationship to the truth, but it is never simply equivalent to it. Likewise, that which is scientifically true is often complex and hedged with qualifications. Consequently, scientific research may not make for satisfying "news": it may not attract public attention by (for example) scaring news consumers about the dangers that confront them.

Michael Schudson, professor of Communications and Sociology at UC San Diego, wrote in *Forbes MediaCritic*,

> What produces news in this country . . . is a strategic ballet, a form of political action in itself. But the news as such is a cultural product. . . . News as a form of culture incorporates assumptions about what matters, what makes sense, what time and place we live in, what range of consider-

ations we should take seriously. A news story is supposed to answer the questions "who, what, when, where, and why" about its subject. But to understand news as culture requires asking of news writing what categories of persons count as a "who," what kinds of things pass for facts or "whats," what geography and sense of time is inscribed as "where" and "when," and what counts as an explanation of "why."

While we must attend to the "who, what, when, where, and why" that affect our daily lives, we must also remember not to treat them as self-evident "found objects" of our experience. Rather, they are constructed objects, rendered in a particular place and time, shaped by particular questions and assumptions, and produced by particular persons. Coming to a fuller understanding of this process of construction should not make us cynics or doubters of media portraits, but lead us to be more savvy and accomplished in making our own and society's choices.

The Reality Industry and Its Discontents

Why are we so often anxious about the state of our world? Do we encounter dramatic research findings whose significance troubles us but also perplexes us? Do we suspect that we are in some measure captive to a largely hidden process that shapes our "conventional wisdom"? How, we may begin to wonder, did we ever get this particular though fuzzy picture of our assumed reality?

Everyone is familiar with the observation that the closer we are to an event that makes the news, the less satisfied we are with the coverage. Reality observed firsthand is always filled with complexity and room for doubt, while news coverage tends to present us with simple and conclusive portraits of what "really" happened. Yet we tend more readily to accept accounts from outside of our immediate personal experience.

But what are we to make of events so distant from our daily lives that any direct grasp of them becomes nearly impossible? When we hear of global climate change, falling sperm counts, spiraling rates of violent crime, or threats from emerging infectious diseases, we discover that our choices are reduced to two—remain in a state of perpetual bewilderment, or place a measure of trust in those who convey the accounts.

Unable to gain immediate knowledge, we learn to accept *mediated* portrayals of the world around us. And mediation puts us in a bind, for it allows what journalist Jonathan Rauch has termed the "reality industry" to take some of our most important decisions hostage. The reality industry is made up of those people and institutions that gather, interpret, and transmit to us information that we expect to be accurate and pertinent to our lives. While we cannot do without the reality industry, we can perhaps learn to watch their doings with a bit more skepticism.

We are bombarded daily by news stories that purport to portray the state of the world. The press and electronic media pass along accounts that are generated in sites such as university laboratories, government agencies, and policy think tanks. These accounts, most commonly based on research findings about phenomena that lie beyond our personal experience, represent highly specialized knowledge affecting our personal lives, our society, or the fate of the natural world. When any one of these sites produces findings, information begins to flow through a circuit that shapes, prunes, and finally transmits the resulting picture of reality so that it arrives as consumable "news." This pathway from institution to headline entails a regular process of evaluation and decision making that is very often opaque. The task of our book is to make this process more transparent.

How accurate is the transmission of information, and how much may we trust in the conclusions? Recent criticism of the media suggests that our trust may be misplaced and that some features of the reality industry are obscuring our perception. Thus it is high time for a behind-the-curtains look at the vital process by which knowledge of "the way things are" is created and brought home. By uncovering and analyzing the process by which knowledge is made, transformed, and delivered to our attention, we aim to forearm the news consumer. What we will discover by examining specific cases of research reports gone awry are the potential missteps in the passage of events to our attention, missteps involving simple error, honest misunderstandings, subtle spin, or outright mendacity at virtually any stage in the process that daily drives our personal decisions and our public policy.

How can we as citizens judge responsibly when we are so dependent upon the fidelity of transmission from the laboratory or government agency to our morning headlines? Consumers of knowledge, understandably enough, demand clarity and certainty. And their understanding of events feeds back into public policy, since government officials quickly learn to respond to research findings with a certainty that may be unwarranted. As the recent mad cow disease episode in Great Britain showed, confusion and conflicting statements of risk prove disastrous not only to herds of cattle but to herds of politicians as well.

The press has heeded our demands, and it tends to provide us with reports that are dramatic and unlikely to be hedged with doubt or complexity. We want answers to our questions, and it is in the interest of journalists to give them to us. The more stark and unexpected the findings, of course, the more compelling they seem. And the more the findings are dressed up with the appearance of certainty, the more fidelity we imagine we are getting. Statistics, percentages, graphs, and enumerations accompany the stories we regard as reliable, adding concrete elements to conclusions that are more often carved in mere newsprint than in stone.

The research community, however, operates by a different set of rules than do journalists. For researchers, certainty is often an illusion, since knowledge is developing and liable to change with tomorrow's results. In the mind of scientists, "reality" is held inside a frame of contingency, an expectation that every number and conclusion is provisional. Scientists know perfectly well that many difficulties condition their findings and cause them to hedge their conclusions; they are well aware just how hard it is to count in the most elementary way many of the things that they study.

When they publicize their research, however, their findings are still a long way from the consumer's breakfast table. Research must cross many barriers on its way to the morning's headlines. Advocacy groups consciously shape and prune the results. Government agencies put political pressure on the interpretations. And journalists bring to bear not only their professional interests but also their sometimes limited scientific capacities. At every step in the transmission process, room for error increases.

We will examine in detail how the uncertain and shifting world of research becomes congealed into the various firm, though often premature, convictions of conventional wisdom. Do we *really* know what we think we know? To find out, we will analyze media reports and portrayals of research affecting our lives, comparing the results to the actual findings themselves.

Writing a book about news is a perilous venture, since it is assuredly out of date from the start of the first paragraph. Yet there are compensations for standing back from the process and not being overwhelmed by the swirl of today's events. News is that which is novel, the events that "just happened." But news is also a process perpetually in the making. Nothing is as stale as yesterday's newspaper; but on the other hand, tomorrow's headlines will almost certainly be constructed according to the same recipe as today's—and will make not a few of the same errors.

We believe that by examining specific cases in depth one can acquire enough of an understanding of the news process to become a forewarned and forearmed news consumer. By grasping the general lessons found in this examination, tomorrow's stories need not be so surprising. Just as important, our hope is that misleading, alarmist, or partial accounts will lose some of their power to cloud or lead astray the necessary judgments of public policy.

Scientific findings of all kinds comprise a topic of huge scope. It should therefore be obvious that an analysis of the totality of scientific reports would be an impossibly broad undertaking. Accordingly, we have limited the scope of our enterprise in a number of ways.

First, our quarry is any information generated by scientific investigation that seeks to affect or has an impact upon a public-policy outcome (court decisions and liability awards, regulatory initiatives, the development of programs addressing perceived social ills, the setting of government research agendas), where that impact is substantially energized by media attention to the findings. That is, all three components (research generated, media attention to the data, policy engagement with the findings) have to come together in order for us to consider the scientific claims to be appropriate grist for our mill. We principally examine media coverage of studies of health and statistical accounts of the state of society, since the science that drives public policy mostly deals with these two domains. Research in these areas also purports to be relevant to our common experience, hence to be more accessible and pertinent to the educated public that must grapple with its claims.

Our examination of scientific research is also narrowed because it particularly concerns questions of measurement. We consistently ask how we know what we think we know—or what we are told by experts and the headlines—about the extent of various problems that confront us. That is, we examine the methodological bases for various quantitative portraits of the world that are offered for our consumption.

Just as we have limited ourselves to assessing particular types of scientific reports, we have also restricted our focus on the media that transmit the findings. We attend most carefully, though not exclusively, to print media, principally concerning ourselves with news accounts in major newspapers and magazines. This decision is partly a function of the difficulty of analyzing electronic media such as television, radio, and increasingly the Internet. The presence of a dominant visual component in most electronic media necessitates an enormously complex method of capturing and analyzing content, a problem that is minimized with respect to print media. But more importantly, we believe that the print media still retain a more definitive standing in public policy circles and even in society at large. Published news in the newspaper is still regarded as more authoritative and is therefore more commonly cited by policy figures than are broadcast news accounts or even television science specials. A comprehensive treatment detailing how all of science is covered by all of the media must remain a task for another day—but at least we have made an important start.

Another necessary disclosure on our part involves our own status as examiners. Though all three of us have had extensive training in the social sciences and are current or former university professors (two of us, Lichter and Schwartz, have doctorates in political science, while Murray holds a Ph.D. in social anthropology), and while each of us has had varying degrees of exposure and training in science in the strictest sense, none of us is a graduate-trained expert in laboratory sciences—either physical or biological—or a medical doctor. By the same token, none of us is a working journalist (though again, each of us has undertaken either an intensive study of journalism in its cultural and institutional practices, or served in journalistic capacities, writing and editing news accounts).

These characteristics are admittedly limitations on our vision, but we believe that they also endow us with a certain virtue, that of interested and observant outsiders, able to perceive and question the practices and assumptions of both science and journalism from an objective position that is sometimes referred to as the "immaculate perception." We have chosen to adopt as a deliberate stance a perspective on scientific and journalistic practices and institutions that is most appropriately termed ethnographic.

As interested outsiders, we are able to function as anthropologists do in approaching a foreign culture—in this case, two cultures (media and science) and their engagement with one another and the wider society. While the cultures are in some sense sufficiently alien to us that we can step back and ask about their fundamentals, they are also cultures whose language and behaviors are sufficiently familiar to us that we can operate as semi-natives. We claim for ourselves the status of outsider observers whose position is in a sense privileged. Our contention is that we are able to convey to an audience of readers, who are also outsiders who might benefit from ethnographic reports, an "account from the field" of great utility.

We present, then, a book about science and how it is made, one that is especially concerned with the complexities of measurement. Our reports focus on such things as the measuring and reporting of crime statistics, AIDS deaths, breast cancer risk, causes of infant mortality, and potential nuclear disaster. Our effort is to teach a few principles of data gathering and to encourage a healthy skepticism that accompanies clear thinking and engagement with the evidence.

But this is also a book about journalism and how it is made. Our strong belief is that the best way to explain journalism is to focus on its choices and predilections. As the editor and media critic James Fallows has written, "The simplest daily reminder that the news is the result of countless judgment calls, rather than some abstract truth, is a comparison of the front page of the *Wall Street Journal* with that of almost any other major newspaper. The 'news' that dominates four-fifths of most front pages is confined, in the *Journal*, to two little columns of news summary." In keeping with that spirit, what we present here are concrete examples of the media's doings. We argue that journalism can best be grasped through a careful examination of cases, concrete and specific stories that can be made to yield general understandings when they are compiled, digested, and evaluated.

The book is divided into three sections, devoted to the ambiguity of news, the ambiguity of measurement, and the ambiguity of explanation. Arrayed under each are accounts of specific research findings: how they were generated and came to public attention; how journalists received, parsed, selected, and conveyed them; and how they could have been portrayed differently while still being faithful to the same facts. Each chapter has three overriding goals: to educate readers about specific controversies regarding data; about specific choices in the newsmaking process; and about general principles of measurement, data, and the likelihood of evidentiary claims. It is our hope that these case studies will generate a broader understanding of facts and arguments that can make readers more discerning consumers of the news. It is time to begin our inquiry.

PART I

THE AMBIGUITY OF NEWS

CHAPTER 1

THE NEWS THAT ISN'T THERE
Stories That Are—and Aren't—Covered

When the Centers for Disease Control and Prevention (CDC) found that AIDS deaths increased in 1994, that story was covered by the *New York Times*—as it should have been. But two months later, the CDC announced that the number of AIDS diagnoses fell in 1995. An interesting and important piece of news, you might think, yet the *Times* effectively ignored it.

In April 1996 the federal government released figures from the National Criminal Victimization Survey (NCVS) showing that violent crime dropped slightly between 1993 and 1994 and that sexual assaults and rapes declined by an impressive 13 percent. That story, however, received almost no news coverage. But in October 1996, when the FBI's Uniform Crime Reports (UCR) showed that violent crime had dropped by 4 percent between 1994 and 1995, the story made front-page news— even though the UCR's figures are generally thought to be less reliable than those of the NCVS.

A Federal Reserve study showing that minority applicants for mortgages fared worse than white applicants was big news in the summer of 1995, but in the same month Federal Reserve figures pointing to a 55 percent increase in mortgages for black applicants were mostly ignored.

In May 1996 the media appropriately alerted readers to a World Health Organization (WHO) report calling attention to a worldwide resurgence of familiar infectious diseases like tuberculosis. But in the same month, the media failed to cover data released by the CDC showing that tuberculosis cases had declined to an all-time low in the United States. In the fall of 1996 front-page stories were devoted to a report from the National Center for Health Statistics (NCHS) that showed a decline in illegitimate births in 1995. Only a few months earlier, though, the media ignored an NCHS finding that illegitimate births had reached an all-time high in 1994.

As these examples illustrate, some stories make it into the newspapers, while others don't—and it's not always because the stories that make it are inherently more newsworthy. If a story isn't covered, is it "news"? Almost by definition, no, just as some philosophers like to argue that a tree falling in the forest doesn't make a sound unless someone is nearby to hear it. News, in this view, is what appears in the newspapers.

But even if uncovered stories aren't news, one can still argue that they should have been news. Not, of course, from the standpoint of the occurrences themselves; we don't mean to attribute human feelings to uncovered data, imagining them conversing with other data that do make it into the newspapers, insisting (as Marlon Brando does in *On the Waterfront*) that "I coulda been a contender." Instead, of course, we adopt the standpoint of news consumers when we say that some stories should have been covered, even if they weren't. Often news consumers would be better informed if they learned of research findings that go unreported even in our best and most comprehensive papers.

Uncovered potential news stories are reminiscent of the nursery rhyme about the "little man who wasn't there": "Last night I met upon the stair/ A little man who wasn't there/ He wasn't there again today/ Oh, how I wish he'd go away." Our purpose is to account for the phenomenon of the little (and sometimes big) story that wasn't there, because it escaped the attention of reporters.

Why don't we learn about some developments, even though they seem to be of genuine importance? To answer this question, we'll begin by looking at individual stories. Our procedure here will necessarily differ from what it is elsewhere in our examination of what's right and what's wrong with news coverage. We can't examine nonexistent coverage, but we will explain the importance of the various ignored research findings and document the fact that they were ignored. So as to set a standard of newsworthiness that in our view was met by the uncovered story, in each case we'll pair an uncovered story with a related (and not obviously more significant) story that did receive media attention.

An Untold AIDS Story

In February 1996 the *New York Times* appropriately and responsibly reported the CDC's finding that in 1994 deaths from AIDS had increased by 9 percent from the previous year; AIDS actually became the leading cause of death among American women aged twenty-five to forty-four. As the article explained (summarizing the views of CDC scientist John Ward), "death rates for AIDS [are] only one way to measure the epidemic. Another measure is the number of people in which AIDS has been diagnosed. . . . The measure that gives the most up-to-date measure [sic] of the continuing spread of H.I.V. is the number of new infections" that have not yet developed into full-blown AIDS.[1]

Among these various AIDS statistics, death totals in effect track the epidemic's past; AIDS deaths provide a coda to tragedies that may have occurred ten or fifteen years earlier, when individuals first were infected with the virus that until recently was thought to lead inexorably to their doom. Diagnoses of AIDS and reports of HIV infections, on the other hand, track the epidemic's future: HIV infections become AIDS diagnoses, and AIDS diagnoses (it was believed, before the promising development of anti–AIDS drug "cocktails") culminate in AIDS deaths. In principle the number of HIV infections offers a better guide to the future than the number of AIDS diagnoses, but in practice the number of new infections is harder to pin down (since all AIDS diagnoses, but not all reports of HIV infections, must be reported to the CDC).[2]

All of this is to say that the yearly total of new AIDS diagnoses is an important statistic: it enables us to judge whether or not the disease is likely to do even more damage in the future. For that reason, the CDC's news about 1995 AIDS diagnoses was surprisingly encouraging: in April 1996—two months after releasing the information about AIDS deaths—the CDC reported that the number of AIDS diagnoses had fallen 7 percent between 1994 and 1995 and that diagnoses of AIDS in children had dropped by 23 percent. The CDC learned of 79,897 people who were diagnosed with AIDS in 1994 (including 1,034 children), whereas the number fell to 74,180 in 1995 (including only 800 children).

Thus the CDC offered on-the-whole encouraging news, indicating that the horrific toll taken by AIDS promised to decrease in years to come. And particularly because so much of the news about AIDS over the years has been so grim, one might have thought that newspapers would eagerly seize on the small glimmer of encouragement offered by the CDC as evidence that things were finally becoming less dire. In the months preceding the first successes of the promising drugs known as protease blockers, an "AIDS-is-becoming-less-bad-than-you-think" story would really have been new—and should really have been news.

But it wasn't, at least as far as the *Washington Post* and the *New York Times* were concerned. To be more precise, the *Post* and the *Times* chose to treat the story as local (and discouraging) news, rather than national (and somewhat encouraging) news. The *Post* ignored the story in its news columns but published an editorial focusing on the fact that the District of Columbia has a higher proportion of AIDS cases than any state. The editorial also argued that the CDC figures don't "necessarily mean the disease is on the wane," because "the definition of AIDS was changed in 1994," when "many more cases were moved from HIV-positive status to full-blown AIDS. The number of 'new' cases reported that year included thousands that wouldn't have been counted at that stage under the old guidelines," which means that the perceived "drop" in the 1995 numbers is "exaggerated."[3]

Thus the *Post* attempted to explain on its editorial page why it failed to cover this particular bit of basically encouraging AIDS news. But the explanation happens to be wrong: the CDC's redefinition of AIDS took place in 1993 (when the number of AIDS diagnoses surged to 105,828) rather than 1994. Consequently, the 74,180 AIDS diagnoses in 1995 are in every respect comparable to (and represent a genuine decline from) the 79,897 AIDS diagnoses in 1994.

The *Times*, by contrast, did not attempt to explain away the encouraging CDC report; it simply ignored what was encouraging about it. The report was covered by the *Times* metropolitan desk, for which the only relevant news was that Jersey City, New Jersey, had attained the "grim distinction" of being "second only to Washington in numbers of AIDS cases per 100,000 population." Almost in spite of itself, however, the *Times* story (which was all of eighty-four words) conveyed to the attentive reader that even for Jersey City the news was not unrelievedly "grim." The *Times* noted that "Jersey City's rate in 1995 was 138.1 cases [per 100,000 people], down from 148.7 in 1994." Thus the Jersey City rate declined by 7.1 percent, which almost exactly replicates the decline in the national rate.[4] The decline in the national rate went unmentioned in both the *Post* and the *Times*.

As we have argued elsewhere, the media's coverage of AIDS has tended (to reverse the words of songwriter Johnny Mercer) to "accentuate the negative" and "eliminate the positive." As a result, many inherently newsworthy findings about AIDS have not in fact become actual news.[5]

What's Not Reported Can Be Criminal

In October 1996 the *Washington Post* published a front-page story documenting an encouraging drop in the nation's crime rate.[6] The UCR, the FBI's survey of crimes reported to almost all American law-enforcement agencies, showed that violent crime fell 4 percent between 1994 and 1995; crime overall dropped to its lowest level in a decade.

In some ways the attention given to the release of the UCR data was surprising. To begin with, as the *Post* article pointed out, the drop in serious crime had already been documented back in May, when preliminary data from the UCR were first made available. The preliminary data had not been covered by the *Post* but did receive attention in, for example, the *Chicago Tribune*. More than five months before the *Post* article appeared, *Tribune* readers learned that crime had fallen for the fourth straight year in 1995, with particularly impressive drops in the number of murders, robberies, and rapes.[7] In that respect, the *Post* accorded front-page status to something that was arguably not "new" but instead a confirmation of what was already "old."

The attention lavished on the UCR is also surprising because the report isn't thought to give a particularly accurate reading of America's crime problem: the UCR counts only crimes that are reported to the police (and then reported by the police to the FBI), while many crimes are committed but never reported to the police. With good reason, the

FBI's count of rapes in particular is thought to be unreliable, since we know that a great many rape victims never report the crime to the police. To be sure, the UCR may offer useful information about the crime rate's trend, since its limitations are the same, year in and year out;[8] nevertheless, its data aren't considered all that reliable.

For this reason, the government's more accurate survey of crime is thought to be the NCVS, which surveys a large and representative sample of ordinary Americans to get a sense of the total amount of crime, both reported and unreported. NCVS findings (admittedly for 1994 rather than 1995) were released in April 1996. Although they offered data that are thought to be more informative, data that actually track the UCR numbers reasonably closely, they received virtually no media attention.

The NCVS offered only slightly less encouraging news about our crime problem. The rate of violent crime dropped slightly between 1993 and 1994, falling from 51.3 to 50.8 victimizations per thousand people, a decrease of 1 percent. The rate of property crime dropped substantially, going from 322.1 to 307.6 victimizations per thousand people, a decrease of 5 percent.[9]

But the one arguably big piece of news in the NCVS was ignored by the media. As we will see in our discussion of surveys in chapter 6, the NCVS was substantially redesigned in 1992, with the aim of obtaining a more accurate count of the total number of rapes, attempted rapes, and other sexual assaults. Between 1993 and 1994, the survey showed, the victimization rates for rape and attempted rape held steady—but the rate for other sexual assaults plummeted by 38 percent. As a result, the combined rate for all sexual assaults fell by 13 percent.[10]

On the face of it, this would seem to be very big news. In our subsequent discussion of surveys we see that the media attentively—and appropriately—covered the redesign of the NCVS, emphasizing that the survey was now likely to be able to count incidents of sexual violence against women more accurately. But in only the second year of the redesigned survey, its findings received next to no attention, even though the supposedly more accurate count showed that sexual violence against women had declined significantly.

The NCVS findings should have been big news, then. Amid a mass of contentions that an epidemic of sexual violence was being directed against American women, a survey that feminists had rightly hailed for its improved capacity to detect such violence had uncovered a notable decline. Again, if "news" is understood to be what is unexpected, the NCVS findings on sexual assaults should undeniably have been news. But they weren't. The NCVS results were wholly ignored by the *New York Times* and the *Washington Post*; to our knowledge they were covered most extensively in a ninety-four–word report in the *Pittsburgh Post-Gazette*.[11] Thus a report that should have been big news turned out to be no news.

Do Minorities Get Mortgages?

In 1985 the *New York Times* paid great attention to a study conducted by the Federal Reserve Bank of Chicago, which found disparities in the treatment of minority and white applicants for mortgages. Among those with bad credit ratings, 90 percent of the white applicants—versus only 81 percent of the minority applicants—received mortgages.[12] The *Times* placed its 902-word story on the first page of the business section—even though the study was little more than a rehash of 1992 research carried out by the Federal Reserve Bank of Boston. Because the Chicago study was derivative (and because it didn't address criticisms leveled at the Boston study), reporter David Andrew Price of *Investor's Business Daily* has argued that "the Chicago Fed study really didn't warrant press coverage."[13] Nevertheless, it got it.

But the media paid much less attention to a second set of Fed findings, released the same week, that was arguably more illuminating. Between 1993 and 1994, the Fed found, home loans to black applicants rose by an impressive 55 percent; loans to Hispanics went up 42 percent. Native Americans received 24 percent more loans, and loans to Asians rose some 19 percent. Trailing the pack were white mortgage recipients, whose numbers rose by 16 percent.

These encouraging findings were covered most extensively in the *Wall Street Journal*.[14] They were not wholly ignored by the *Times*, but it is fair to say that the *Times* coverage was far less extensive than that accorded the Chicago study: the 215-word story appeared on page 6 of the business section. Of greater importance, the *Times* story made the good news sound more like bad news. It led by announcing that "black and Hispanic mortgage applicants remain much more likely than white applicants to be turned down for loans to buy homes but the gap is narrowing."[15] The fact that loans to black applicants "soared" by 54.7 percent was treated as an afterthought, relegated to the third paragraph of the four-paragraph story.

The *Times* coverage evidently presupposed that the continued (although lessening) disparity in the rates at which minority and white applicants received mortgages was more important than the sharp rise in the number of loans awarded to minority applicants. The *Times* seemed to explain away the increase in loans to blacks, noting that "more applications were filed" by black applicants.

The alternate view, though, is that the disparities in denial rates are not very meaningful; as the *Journal* article pointed out, denial-rate disparities "don't take into account such factors as disparities in net worth, assets or credit history." If, as seems likely, white applicants have higher net worth and more assets, the disparities hardly indicate that minority applicants are treated worse than white applicants with comparable qualifications.

But the larger point was made by economist Lawrence Lindsey, at that time one of the seven governors of the Federal Reserve Board. Speaking in September 1995, Lindsey complained that the dramatic increase in home loans to minorities was "the great underreported news story of the summer." He argued that the 54.7 percent increase in loans to black applicants was "a staggering, or at least a newsworthy, economic statistic"—and that, unlike the disparities in rejection rates, it received virtually no attention from newspapers. Lindsey observed that the media had never refrained from "printing negative stories" about the obstacles faced by minority mortgage applicants—so he wondered why many media outlets ignored or played down the good news represented by the huge increase in home loans to blacks.[16]

In short, the increase in loans to minority applicants was not obviously less newsworthy than the disparate treatment of white and minority applicants, yet the latter story received far more attention from the press.

All Quiet on the Tuberculosis (News) Front

In May 1996 the WHO published its annual report, which highlighted grave difficulties in the worldwide battle against infectious diseases—a battle that had seemed easily winnable a generation earlier. The report spoke of "ominous trends on all fronts."[17]

This report was undeniably newsworthy, and it received extensive attention from the press. The advent of AIDS and the danger posed by an outbreak of Ebola in Africa had focused popular attention on the threat of infectious diseases. Additionally, an influential article in the *Journal of the American Medical Association* (*JAMA*) had pointed to a large upsurge in American deaths from infectious diseases since 1980.[18] The WHO report added an important international perspective to buttress the concerns.

Nevertheless, coverage of the report may have been a bit unbalanced by a tilt toward the negative. Consider, for example, the story published in [New York] *Newsday*, written by Laurie Garrett. In her *Newsday* article Garrett correctly declared that "a host of diseases that were once thought controllable are now taking record tolls worldwide—including tuberculosis, malaria and cholera." But she went on to argue that several diseases once thought almost eradicated in the United States had "surged, notably tuberculosis." The story appeared on May 20, 1996. Exactly ten days earlier, the CDC published a report showing that in 1995 reported TB cases were at the "lowest rate" ever, "since national surveillance began in 1953."[19] In short, Garrett's claim makes sense only if you think there are downward surges.

Lest it seem that we are unfairly picking on Garrett, we note that she stands at the top of her profession: she has served as president of the National Association of Science Writers and is the author of a massive and well-received study of infectious diseases, *The Coming Plague: Newly Emerging Diseases in a World Out of Balance*. But despite her deserved eminence, Garrett did not cover the CDC report on tuberculosis. Nor did almost anyone else. In fact, as far as we can tell the only report of the CDC's encouraging findings appeared in the *Orange County Register*.[20]

In this case we do not argue that the CDC tuberculosis study was more important than or even as important as the WHO report. Still, the fact remains that the WHO report basically did nothing but confirm a sense of pessimism about infectious diseases that was already, and in some respects justly, widespread. The CDC report, on the other hand, had all the makings of a great contrarian story. Amidst all the lamentations about the unchecked resurgence of infectious diseases, here was striking evidence that at least one notable infectious disease was very much under control—at least in the United States, the country of greatest interest for almost all American newspaper readers.[21] If ever there was a "man bites dog" story, this would seem to be it. Imagine the headline: TB Is Not To Be: Tuberculosis Cases Way Down. Yet the story received almost no attention anywhere in the United States.

When Are Illegitimate Births Legitimate News?

In October 1996 the National Center for Health Statistics (NCHS) issued data showing that the rate of births to unwed mothers had declined in 1995—the first decline after almost two decades of consecutive rises. The rate dropped by 4 percent, falling from 46.9 births per thousand unmarried women in 1994 to 44.9 in 1995.[22]

This finding was treated as big news, as indeed it should have been. It made the front page of papers like the *New York Times*[23] and the *Los Angeles Times*.[24] Analysts offered competing explanations for the encouraging news. Perhaps predictably, President Clinton tried to take credit in his weekly radio address, mentioning a 1996 executive order that required young mothers to stay in school or live with their parents so as to receive welfare benefits. It is hard to see how that order could have affected women who did or did not become pregnant in 1994 and early 1995. Liberals said the drop proved that sex education was resulting in increased use of birth control, while conservatives took it as a sign of increasing sexual abstinence among the young and unwed.[25]

Whatever else was responsible for the downturn, the good news also resulted in part from a methodological improvement. As the *New York Times* reported, "About half of the decline in the out-of-wedlock birth rate stemmed from changes in reporting births in California, so that children whose parents had different surnames were no longer automatically considered to have been born out of wedlock."[26]

Less than four months earlier, the NCHS produced a second set of natality findings, which pertained to 1994.[27] Though these findings were also of great interest, they were ignored by newspapers, surfacing only when policy analyst Charles Murray called attention to them in an article in the *Weekly Standard*.[28] As Murray noted, "in 1994 the percentage of children born out of wedlock logged its largest one-year increase since national figures have been kept. The new figure, 32.6 percent, was up from 31.0 percent in 1993. . . . The percentage of black births out of wedlock passed 70 percent, marking the largest increase since 1973."[29] Yet no newspaper whatsoever covered this alarming story; instead, newspapers covering the 1994 findings reported a drop in the birth rate for teenagers.[30]

The first decline in illegitimate births in twenty years was (and should have been) a huge story. Still, the twentieth consecutive rise in illegitimacy should have been big news as well, especially since, as Murray argued in his *Weekly Standard* piece, there was every reason to predict a downturn. The illegitimacy ratio (especially among blacks) was already so high in 1993 that there seemed to be little room for further increases. In addition, a consensus had finally developed, among liberals as well as conservatives, blacks as well as whites, that illegitimacy was wrong; it was not unreasonable to expect that this would have some impact on the behavior of the man and woman in the street (and between the sheets).

For these reasons, the decline that did not occur in 1994 should have been newsworthy. Just as it was significant when the dog in a Sherlock Holmes story did not bark during a nighttime intrusion, it's generally noteworthy when predictable things don't take place. Thus the continued rise in the illegitimacy ratio in 1994 should have made headlines; instead it didn't even make it into the newspapers.

Journalistic Pessimism?

How can we make sense of the fact that some stories become news, while others that are often intrinsically of equal interest don't? Our five case studies don't offer anything like an exhaustive—or statistically representative—sample. Still, it may be helpful to begin by comparing the stories that made the news with those that didn't. Crudely categorizing the stories as either optimistic or pessimistic, we can say that in three instances (AIDS, mortgages, and tuberculosis) pessimistic news was covered and optimistic news ignored (or, in the case of mortgages, downplayed). In one instance (crime), optimistic news was covered and more or less equally optimistic news ignored. In the final example (illegitimacy), optimistic news was covered and pessimistic news ignored. These findings appear to suggest at least a modest bias in favor of bad news. Because there is no reason to believe that our sample is representative, the bias that we detect here could safely be ignored—except for the fact that many other observers agree that there is indeed a media bias in favor of bad news.

That view was advanced forcefully in 1984 by columnist Ben Wattenberg, in a book entitled *The Good News Is the Bad News Is Wrong*.[31] Wattenberg argued that a great many statistical indicators pointing to improvements in Americans' lives—as manifested in things like better health, increased life expectancy, cleaner air and water, greater prosperity, and decreased poverty—were unknown to an unreasonably pessimistic American public, because they had mostly been ignored by the unreasonably pessimistic American media. As he put it (in words that apply to our enterprise as well), "sooner or later [readers would] have to make a choice" whether to believe the "media—or [the] data."[32]

Wattenberg notes that judgments about what is newsworthy often reflect three invalid criteria: "1. Bad news [e.g., 'the carcinogen-of-the-month'] is big news; 2. Good news [e.g., the dramatic increase in American life expectancy] is no news; 3. Good news is bad news [e.g., this 1983 *New York Times* headline: Longer Lives Seen as Threat to Nation's Budget]."[33]

For our purposes, of course, the question is why bad news might tend to be emphasized. Wattenberg points to four causes.[34] He argues first that there is a *"commercial negative tilt"* to the news, in that bad news appeals to readers and viewers: "Bad news is exciting: scandal, war, murder."

Secondly, he spoke of a *"left-of-center tilt* in the news-gathering establishment." Most reporters at the most prestigious newspapers are politically liberal, and contemporary liberals "believe that accentuating the negative will let . . . others see the problems and this . . . will engender further progress." He denied, though, that any journalistic tilt toward the left was "typically a conscious decision," emphasizing instead that "we all see reality through a filter." For liberal journalists, what tends to make it through the filter is "a set of severe problems, subject to solution through aroused concern, often through the instrumentality of government."[35]

In addition, Wattenberg hypothesized that there is an *"adversarial* tilt to the media,"* in that "journalists are, almost by definition, *antistatus quo*," dedicated to criticizing "a corrupt, dissembling, and heartless establishment." Lastly, he spoke of the self-righteousness of reporters who "believe that only their vigilant eyes can keep the nation from international adventurism, political skullduggery, and corporate corruption."

Wattenberg's observations about the proclivities of the press are provocative, and they may help account for the stories that did and didn't make the news in some of the case studies that we've looked at. Still, if journalists are pessimists, they are also professionals. Why would they ignore potentially big stories that are worthy of coverage (and might also advance their careers)? To answer this question, we need to look at some other factors.

The "Template" Theory

Wall Street Journal Atlanta bureau chief Amanda Bennett offers a compelling theory to account for what does and doesn't make it into the press. She contends that only stories conforming to a governing "template" tend to appear—the template being "what editors and other people who are not on the ground have decided is The Story."[36] Bennett derived her theory from her experience covering China. Prior to the Tiananmen Square uprising, she argues, the received wisdom governing editorial news judgments about China was that The Story was positive: "Editors only wanted good stories about happy little children, beaming peasants, friendly people. They didn't want to hear about businessmen who were getting hassled or beaten up." Thus the template was that post-Mao China was a good country that was getting better. So stories inconsistent with that widely shared premise did not often or easily make it into the papers, even though (actually, because) they challenged the conventional wisdom. After Tiananmen Square, on the other hand, the template was reversed. "Now it was impossible to get a story in that said anything *good* about China. All anyone wanted to hear about was human rights abuses. And again the reporters who were actually there were complaining."

In other words, in theory "Man bites dog" is news, and "Dog bites man" is not. In practice, however, it often works just the other way. If you are a reporter who assumes that it is dogs who bite men, you will tend to be skeptical of a story that has a man biting a dog: you will question it, you will demand corroboration, you will want to talk to sources who deny that men bite dogs. Often you (or your likeminded editor) will end up killing the story. Initially we tend to disbelieve things that are inconsistent with the way in which we see the world; as Wattenberg's filter image suggests, often we do not even see them at all.[37]

Bennett's "template" theory helps account for many of the news judgments that earlier puzzled us. If the template is that AIDS is a catastrophic illness causing stupendous damage (and AIDS was and still is a catastrophic illness causing stupendous damage), one will tend to gloss over evidence suggesting that it may be abating rather than worsening. If the presupposition is that AIDS can only get worse, news to the contrary (like the CDC report of a 1995 decline in AIDS diagnoses) will simply be ignored, or, as in the case of the *Washington Post* editorial, explained away.

Templates can also explain the nonappearance of stories on the tuberculosis decline and the decrease in sexual assaults and the de-emphasis on the story of the increase in mortgages going to minorities. If the template is that infectious diseases, sexual assaults, and mortgage discrimination each pose severe (and possibly worsening) problems, evidence to the contrary will often be ignored or rejected. This is the case even though, again, the media are ostensibly and sincerely interested in telling us news stories that teach us something new—not simply those confirming what we may perhaps wrongly think we already know.

Still, we are left with the interesting exception of the nonreport of the 1994 illegitimacy numbers and the contrasting front-page emphasis accorded the 1995 illegitimacy numbers. Pessimism can't explain that contrast, since good news was trumpeted and bad news ignored. It's not clear that any sort of obvious template would explain the decision, either. Furthermore, it seems too simpleminded to suggest that liberal journalists (anxious to avoid seeming to "blame the victim" by calling attention to yet another increase in black illegitimacy) engaged in some sort of cover-up to hide the bad news in the 1994 numbers. What else can have been going on?

Press-Release Journalism

In fact, almost certainly, reporters did not tell us about the 1994 rise in illegitimacy because they did not realize that it had taken place.[38] The NCHS press release accompanying the statistics on 1994 births emphasized the drop in teenage births—which, not all that surprisingly, turned out to be the focus of the newspaper coverage. The rise in illegitimate births was not mentioned until the second page of the press release, and only in a four-line paragraph, which said no more than that "in 1994, nearly one out of three births were to unmarried women."

In short, reporters did not tell the illegitimacy story because the NCHS chose not to highlight it—a decision that itself raises interesting questions. Still, the startling dimensions of the news about illegitimacy would have been apparent to journalists who examined the tables of the NCHS report, but not those who relied on the press release. Unfortunately, no reporter seems to have waded through the tables and realized the implications of the data; anyone who did would have had a nice scoop.

A similar story could be told about all of our other "no news" stories. The CDC did not emphasize the possible significance of the 1995 drop in reported AIDS cases or the continued decline in tuberculosis; the numbers were by no means hidden, but reporters would still have had to figure out for themselves why both bits of data would have been newsworthy. The Bureau of Justice Statistics (BJS) did not highlight the dramatic decline in sexual assaults shown by the 1994 NCVS—perhaps because the BJS itself was unsure how to make sense of the sharp decline in a statistic that began to be compiled only in 1992.[39] And the Federal Reserve report on 1994 mortgages (unseen by us) was presumably also matter-of-fact in tone; we doubt that it trumpeted the importance of its findings. In other words, journalists can easily fail to understand the significance of data when that significance is not pointed out to them by the researchers who compile and issue the data. And they might be particularly likely to miss the significance when the data challenge an unquestioned template.

By contrast, in the cases when news stories were written, the significance of the data was abundantly clear to journalists or did not need to be made clear. For perfectly understandable political reasons, the Clinton administration took pains to publicize the 1995 declines in crime and illegitimacy. The WHO report on infectious diseases was clearly designed to arouse concern and succeeded in doing so. The Chicago Fed study on lending disparities and the CDC study of AIDS deaths were seen as newsworthy, we suspect, because they neatly fit a reigning template.

This discussion is meant to offer what high school teachers often call "an explanation, not an excuse." In our view, the causes that we've identified help explain why reporting is sometimes less good than one would wish; but better reporting is still what we should hope for and expect.

Coming to Terms with the News That Is Not There

Of what use is it for a news consumer to know that there may be important news that is not there? In one sense, it's not at all useful. Elsewhere we are able to offer suggestions that may alert you to reasons for doubting the authenticity and importance of some of the news that *is* there. But by definition we can offer no suggestions for how to read nonexistent news stories.

In another sense, though, it is useful to be aware of the news that is not there. First, it's important to realize that even the best newspaper imaginable could not possibly offer anything like an accurate reproduction and distillation of reality. "News" is not an altogether objective reality; instead, it is brought to you through the subjective decisions of reporters and editors who necessarily have blind spots, because they are only human and therefore fallible. Even with the best will in the world, they would tell us some things that are false or unimportant, and they would fail to tell us of other things that are both true and important. Being aware of the category of news that is not there helps drive home that all-important lesson.

In some sense everyone knows what we've just said, but like many things that everyone knows, it's too often taken for granted; its importance is too seldom acknowledged. Consider, for example, the claim with which Walter Cronkite used to conclude his news broadcasts: "And that's the way it is." But it wasn't, and it couldn't have been; reality simply can't be reproduced in a half-hour newscast. Nor, by the same token, can the *New York Times* possibly convey "all the news that's fit to print." If it did, each issue (and not just the Sunday edition) would resemble a tome that made *War and Peace* look like a minimalist short story.

News that is not there exists, because the news is brought to us by people who make choices. Some of their choices, inevitably, are better than others. In the jargon of the contemporary academy, the news is "socially constructed" by the reporters and editors who produce the papers. This realization does lead to a practical recommendation. Because news is the product of editorial and reportorial decisions, you're more likely to encounter news that does not make it into one paper if you read others as well. Thus the news that was barely there in the *New York Times* about the increase in mortgages to minorities received far better coverage in the *Wall Street Journal*. In some cases, as we have seen, the news that is not there is literally nowhere (or in only one or two places); but in others, your odds of finding it increase when you cast your net more widely.

It's not generally realized how greatly newspapers—even the prestige newspapers—differ from one another. The size of that difference was established in an interesting experiment conducted some years ago by David Shaw, the media critic of the *Los Angeles Times*. Over a five-month period Shaw looked at the front page of the *Los Angeles Times*, the *New York Times*, and the *Washington Post*. Sixty percent of the time, he discovered, the three front pages had no more than one or two of their eight or ten stories in common.[40] Shaw concluded that the American press is anything but a monolith: to speak of "'The Press'—as if it were a single, mammoth, national newspaper with more than 1,700 slightly varying regional editions—is a glaring misconception."[41]

Instead, Shaw argued, even the three prestige papers offer their readers disparate representations of the world.[42] The news coverage in paper A will not resemble that found in paper B, because editors and journalists inevitably have "different, even conflicting, views of the same information." Stories will appear in one paper but not in another, because they "are the product of individual initiative by one reporter or one newspaper. Or a newspaper may decide not to play a given story . . . because the competition already had it. Or because a reporter did so poor a job on it that his editors do not deem it worthy. . . . Or because a reporter, or the paper, did not have access to the story."[43]

The news is a result of subjective decisions, so one paper's version of "the news" may well have little to do with another's. "There is no blueprint, no grand design, no formula or quota; just different editors—all human, all capable of error—viewing the world through the prisms of their different life experiences and making decisions on a daily basis for different readerships in different historical, cultural, and geographical contexts."[44]

Our focus on uncovered news stories has pointed to uniformities among journalists—reigning templates, a widespread bias toward negative news, a general overreliance on press releases. Those cautions remain important. But at the same time, it is worth remembering that newspapers and journalists also differ among themselves. Some news that is not there appears nowhere, but other stories are treated in one paper though not in another. In still other cases, different stories, revealing biases of different sorts, will appear in different papers; comparing them may give a perceptive reader a better grasp of what's going on than would any single story taken in isolation.

Thus news that is not there presents the news consumer with a problem that isn't always soluble. But simple awareness of the problem is important in itself. And the problem can often at least be mitigated by consuming news from several different sources.

CHAPTER 2

MUCH ADO ABOUT LITTLE
Making News Mountains out of Research Molehills

A front-page *New York Times* story spoke of a possible nuclear explosion at the repository for nuclear wastes to be created in Nevada. Was the explosion theory credible? Almost all scientists dismissed it, but the *Times* still highlighted it.

Many newsweeklies prominently reported the worrisome finding that male sperm counts had declined by almost 50 percent worldwide between 1940 and 1990—a conclusion publicized in a popular environmentalist tract. Why were the flaws in the sperm count research downplayed or ignored?

Front-page newspaper stories reported on research showing that the bond between mothers and babies is not weakened when a baby is placed in childcare. Is it the finding's innate significance or the implicit political message that explains the prominent coverage?

Newspaper articles treated the northward movement of a type of butterfly as biological confirmation of the reality of global warming. How much media attention did this finding really deserve?

If newsworthy stories are sometimes ignored by the media, it's also true that what's not very newsworthy sometimes makes headlines. Too often, research that is either preliminary or inconclusive (or both) receives almost reverential treatment in the press. Preliminary findings are the product of "premature" science—that is, scientific research that hasn't yet been critically examined by other scientists. Such findings often are treated as big news but then turn out to be no news at all. Scientists, after all, can advance interesting theories that would be important if they were true. But if, as often happens, the theories are proven to be false, they're of no importance whatsoever, a corollary that is occasionally forgotten in media coverage.

The classic example of non-news that was hyped as big news is the alleged discovery in 1989 of the means of achieving nuclear fusion at room temperature. Two University of Utah chemists, Stanley Pons and Martin Fleischmann, wrongly claimed to have achieved this result. Until it became clear that the two scientists had claimed vastly more than they had actually accomplished, they became instant media celebrities.[1]

It's easy to see why the media made much of Pons and Fleischmann's claim. Unlocking the secret of nuclear cold fusion would have been a discovery of incalculable importance, guaranteeing an ample supply of energy at virtually no cost, either economic or environmental. All that means, though, is that Pons and Fleischmann would have made a great discovery if they had actually discovered it; but of course they didn't. To say that something is "interesting, if true" is also to acknowledge that it's trivial if false, as the claim to have achieved cold fusion proved to be. The coverage of premature science can err, in other words, by focusing on the "interestingness" of a scientific claim and downplaying or ignoring questions about its truth.

The same danger presents itself regarding even "mature" (that is, peer-reviewed and published) research. Too often, scientific research is made to appear less equivocal than it is. First, a set of scientific findings can be made to seem more important than it really is, if it's not understood that the data can perhaps be interpreted in other ways that would support a less dramatic conclusion. In addition, one set of scientific findings may be contradicted by a second, equally valid set; if attention focuses on Finding A (while Finding B, which tells a different story, is ignored), it may be accorded more significance than it really deserves.

In short, reports on research, like testimony in a trial, should offer "the truth, the whole truth, and nothing but the truth." Coverage can easily mislead when reporters don't make it sufficiently clear that premature science may well not offer the truth. Furthermore, coverage even of mature science can mislead if reporters don't acknowledge the existence of alternate interpretations or rival data sets; if they don't, readers can understandably confuse a portion of the truth with the whole truth.

Legendary movie mogul Sam Goldwyn is reported once to have told an associate, "Don't confuse me with the facts." In this chapter we'll look at some examples of stories that became bigger than they should have been when reporters did not confuse their readers (or, perhaps, themselves) with some of the relevant facts.

The Bombing of the Yucca Mountain Explosion Theory

Early in 1995, reporter William J. Broad of the *New York Times* was told about a report prepared by two physicists at the Los Alamos National Laboratory (Charles D. Bowman and Francesco Venneri) who were arguing against the plan to bury nuclear waste materials in a repository (scheduled to open in 2010) deep beneath Yucca Mountain in the Nevada desert. Bowman and Venneri contended that the waste materials might explode. The *Times* made much of this speculation, broadcasting the scientists' concerns far and wide. It published a front-page story about the feared explosion on March 5, 1995 (as well as three follow-up stories that same month).[2] Significantly, no other paper followed the *Times*'s lead; other journalists evidently regarded the controversy as a nonstory rather than a scoop.

The *Times* front-page story on Yucca Mountain began by noting that a "debate ha[d] broken out among Federal scientists over whether the planned underground dump for the nation's high-level atomic wastes in Nevada might erupt in a nuclear explosion, scattering radioactivity to the winds or into ground water or both." According to the story, the concerned scientists hypothesized that wastes buried at Yucca Mountain might detonate in a nuclear explosion. In response, the *Times* added, "lab managers [had] formed three teams with a total of 30 scientists to investigate the idea and, if possible, disprove it."

What was the rationale for the blow-up theory? Bowman argued that the steel canisters in which the waste plutonium would be stored might dissolve after thousands of years; the plutonium might then disperse into the surrounding rock beneath the mountain, which could then conceivably set off a chain reaction resulting in an explosion. Bowman's critics, on the other hand, altogether rejected his scenario, contending that only a miracle (as opposed to the forces of nature) could bring it about. They claimed that the plutonium would disperse more slowly than Bowman suggested (if it dispersed at all), the reaction would slow down and stop (if it began at all), and any reaction that occurred would be too slow to cause an explosion.

Should this story have been front-page news? Note first of all that Bowman and Venneri were decidedly in the minority: their view was vehemently opposed by the other researchers involved in the Los Alamos internal review, as well as the lab administration. Although the *Times* article was scrupulous in noting that Bowman's thesis was strongly disputed, the story nevertheless suggested that the two sides were fairly evenly matched. But as Gary Taubes reported in *Science*,[3] the article understated the virtual unanimity of opinion rejecting Bowman's thesis; in this respect it was flawed and unbalanced. By according front-page status to Bowman and Venneri's hypothesis, the *Times* arguably (and in hindsight, undoubtedly) granted an idiosyncratic view more credibility than it deserved.

The front-page placement of the initial story was also inappropriate for a second reason. Even if Bowman's thesis had been right, it isn't as though the *Times* had stumbled upon a scientific prediction that another Three Mile Island or Chernobyl was just around the corner. If Bowman thought an explosion was possible shortly after the repository was scheduled to open in 2010, that should have been front-page news; but Bowman himself, as we have seen, argued (in the words of the *Times* article) "that serious dangers would arise thousands of years from now."

It is true that environmentalism rightly encourages us to consider the plight of our posterity; nevertheless, an explosion that might occur (according to a hotly disputed thesis) in the year 5000 or 10,000 does not seem to be obvious front-page news in 1995. Nor should the fact that the hypothetical danger was expected only thousands of years from now have appeared in the eighteenth paragraph of the *Times* story—long after it had referred to "a nuclear explosion" (first paragraph), "buried waste . . . [that] might eventually explode" (third paragraph), and "buried wastes [that] might detonate in a nuclear explosion" (fourth paragraph). In other words, the *Times* story did some burying of its own. Its account was misleadingly alarmist, in that it took too long to convey important information about the timing of the anticipated danger that would have placed that danger in context.

Finally, it's important to realize that the Bowman–Venneri hypothesis was premature science; it hadn't yet been reviewed by other scientists, so it was unclear whether it should have been considered at all credible. For that reason, once again, putting the story on the front page seemed to accord it more prominence than it really deserved. In this context it is significant that the *Times* reporter first learned of Bowman's paper through a leak. When the *Times* article appeared, no one outside the Los Alamos scientific community was supposed to be privy to the Bowman–Venneri hypothesis; the Los Alamos administration did not want to spread what might prove to be a groundless alarm spurred by a theory that had yet to be critically examined by competent scientists.

Why did the *Times* get the story? Most likely, the leaker was motivated by precisely the opposite of the concern that led Los Alamos to want to keep Bowman's theory under wraps. In other words, the Bowman–Venneri hypothesis was probably leaked to Broad because of a desire to publicize a possible danger, even if it should later turn out to be unfounded. An opponent of the waste disposal plan might have reasoned as follows: construction of the Yucca Mountain repository could be halted if the public were to learn of the danger hypothesized by Bowman, even if scientists were subsequently to conclude that the danger did not really exist.

In addition, Broad was the obvious person to receive a leak pointing to future disasters at Yucca Mountain. He was the right choice, not only because of the *Times*'s prestige and influence, but also because he had previously published a lengthy story in the *New York Times Magazine* casting doubt on the safety of a Yucca Mountain repository ("Within two decades [Yucca Mountain] could hold the most dangerous nuclear facility in the world") and lionizing another dissident scientist (geologist Jerry S. Szymanski of the U.S. Department of Energy), who argued that depositing nuclear wastes at Yucca could "prompt a calamity of vast proportions."[4] For these reasons it seems plausible that Bowman's report was leaked to Broad because someone wanted to publicize a message about the dangers of nuclear waste disposal—regardless of whether scientific reviewers would later find the message at all credible.

In fact, when the scientific reviews appeared, they turned out to be remarkably dismissive. Within a year after the initial flurry of stories appeared in the *Times*, the scientific reviews completely rejected Bowman's argument for a nuclear explosion on Yucca Mountain. First the Lawrence Livermore National Laboratory released its report: according to Gary Taubes, it found "six significant errors and shortcomings in the Bowman–Venneri paper," concluding that the explosion hypothesis did not " 'make a useful contribution to the literature.' "[5]

A second review of the doomsday scenario was conducted by the nuclear engineering department at the University of California, Berkeley. As a subsequent *Science* article informed its readers, the Berkeley engineers concluded that there was absolutely no cause for alarm. In the words of study leader William Kastenberg, "At the Yucca Mountain site there don't appear to be any geochemical or geophysical mechanisms" that could precipitate an explosion: simple engineering fixes could therefore reduce whatever minimal risk there might be to zero. As Kastenberg observed, "The crux of the matter is, by the time you accumulate the necessary plutonium for an explosion—about 250 kilograms—most of it has decayed."[6]

What is most remarkable about this story is not that the *Times* exaggerated a threat perceived by a minority of scientists; after all, scientific minorities sometimes turn out to be right. Far worse is that neither of these follow-up studies received any coverage in the *Times*—even though they allayed a concern that the *Times* had previously chosen to highlight. The decision not to report on these studies seems truly indefensible: if Bowman's original thesis was newsworthy, its subsequent refutations should also have been newsworthy. The Berkeley and Livermore reviews determined that there would be no nuclear bang; but the *Times* ignored these important follow-up stories, not even according them a whimper.

In this case, then, a leak of premature science was played into a big story; once the science was thoroughly investigated, though, the big story turned out to be a nonstory. With the benefit of hindsight, we can see that the *Times*'s competitors, who ignored the Yucca Mountain controversy, turned out to be right. In this instance, the *Times* offered its readers not only all the news that's fit to print but (as an added bonus) some that wasn't as well.

Sperm Counts Are Falling—Unless They're Rising

In the space of a few weeks in early 1996, many media outlets raised an alarm about declining sperm counts, casting their reports in remarkably apocalyptic terms. For example, in a *Los Angeles Times* op-ed piece, Dartmouth scientist Donella H. Meadows observed that chemicals, the presumed cause of the declining sperm counts, "have ways of getting back into us, or into our children. As long as we are able to have children, anyway."[7] Not to be outdone, *U.S. News & World Report* warned that "in the not too distant future, men may have a difficult time upholding their end of the biblical bargain" to be fruitful and multiply.[8] And *Business Week* spoke of the "fear that the latest endangered species could be us."[9]

It would be an extraordinary coincidence if this herd of independent journalistic minds all raised the same alarm simultaneously, without the benefit of any sort of coordination. Instead, design rather than chance seems to explain this flurry of stories. All of these accounts and a great many others resulted from a masterly public relations campaign designed to promote the findings of a book written by environmentalist activists: *Our Stolen Future: Are We Threatening Our Fertility, Intelligence, and Survival?—A Scientific Detective Story*, coauthored by zoologist Theo Colborn, foundation executive John Peterson Myers, and science journalist Dianne Dumanoski.[10] No less a figure than Vice President Al Gore took part in the publicity campaign: he wrote the book's foreword, in which he heralded it as the "sequel" to Rachel Carson's environmentalist classic, *Silent Spring*.[11] *Our Stolen Future* was a godsend to the environmentalist movement, offering new grounds for concern about environmental hazards to human health; and journalists were largely receptive to spreading its message.

All of the stories cited above testify to *Our Stolen Future*'s success in popularizing, publicizing, and (as we will see) glossing over the weaknesses of scientific studies pointing to a decline in sperm counts. All of them alluded to Colborn's work and used it as their hook to account for why they were telling the story just then. In the book Colborn and her colleagues contended that man-made chemicals, which mimic estrogen (a female hormone), harm the development of male babies still in their mothers' wombs—and that this chemical attack on natural masculine development is arguably to blame for a decline in sperm counts, a rise in infertility, and increases in testicular cancer and assorted birth defects.

In general, the initial media accounts clearly followed the lead offered by *Our Stolen Future* by failing to convey that the findings of lowered sperm counts are hotly disputed. Colborn's book did not suggest that the reports about falling sperm counts are at all dubious: it compared skepticism about the decline to the initial skepticism about a hole in the ozone layer. It also brushed aside criticisms of the methodology of one study pointing to a decline (which we will examine below). It did mention other studies that report a decline but ignored those with empirical data pointing in the other direction.[12] With the notable exception of the *New York Times*,[13] journalists by and large uncritically accepted Colborn's contention at first.

For example, the *Business Week* article spoke of "an apparent drop of as much as 50% in sperm counts during the past few decades" and gave every reason to believe that the apparent drop was real.[14] A more thorough exposition appeared in *U.S. News & World Report*, which raised this question: "Why are sperm counts falling so precipitously?" As evidence, it pointed to "a 1992 Danish study . . . reporting that the average sperm count had plunged. . . . The research covered men from around the world and was intensely controversial."[15]

Why was the Danish research controversial? The *U.S. News* article offered no explanation of the controversy, perhaps because it was thought to have been resolved in favor of the research. According to *U.S. News*,

> Two subsequent reports have confirmed the gist of the Danish findings. Last year, in a survey of 20 years of donations to the same Paris sperm bank, French researchers found that the average concentration of sperm in semen has slipped 2 percent a year over the past two decades, while the fraction of deformed sperm has risen steadily. Two weeks ago, scientists also reported sperm count declines of 2 percent a year in a study of nearly 600 Scottish men with the youngest men exhibiting the lowest sperm counts.[16]

Overall, it is fair to say that the media coverage did a much better job at first of trumpeting potentially alarming findings than of explaining what is questionable about them. Journalists were evidently receptive to spreading an alarm that activists wished to publicize.

Was the alarm justified? To answer this question, let's turn to the crucial study itself. The Danish findings appeared in a 1992 article,

"Evidence for Decreasing Quality of Semen during [the] Past 50 Years," by Elisabeth Carlsen and colleagues.[17] Carlsen and her colleagues produced a meta-analysis, a study compiling and analyzing other studies. They reviewed sixty-one scientific papers published between 1938 and 1991, in which a total of 14,947 men had their sperm tested: their statistical analysis showed "a significant decline in mean sperm count,"[18] from 113 million sperm per milliliter of semen in 1940 to 66 million sperm per milliliter of semen in 1990. On the face of it, that would seem to be persuasive evidence of a genuine (and troublesome) decline.

But how reliable is their evidence? Consider some of the problems with the data that led to their findings, as reported in a methodological critique published in 1995, that is, before *Our Stolen Future* had publicized them.[19] For Carlsen's conclusions to be reliable, roughly comparable numbers of men would have had to be tested in the early, middle, and late years of the study. In fact, forty-eight of the sixty-one studies were from after 1970. Only 596 of the subjects (4.0 percent) were tested before 1950, only 1,184 (7.9 percent) were tested between 1950 and 1970, and 13,167 (88.1 percent) were tested after 1970. In other words, not enough data were available from before 1970 to make possible a persuasive comparison with the post-1970 data.

Furthermore, only four studies, with a total of 184 subjects, were available for the years 1952 to 1970—38 percent of the years in the relevant time span. And a single 1951 study accounted for a thousand of the 1,780 subjects in the pre-1970 studies. Carlsen and her colleagues have acknowledged that "this early paper is . . . responsible for a considerable part of the observed decline" in sperm counts.[20] Significantly, a coauthor of the large 1951 study subsequently published a 1979 paper (not included among the sixty-one studies examined by Carlsen) that found no decline in mean sperm counts between 1951 and 1977.[21]

And when the more voluminous post-1970 data are examined by themselves, they show an actual *increase* in sperm counts between 1970 and 1990[22]—precisely the years when synthetic chemicals would have been expected to do their damage (if the thesis advanced in *Our Stolen Future* were correct). In fact, Carlsen and her colleagues themselves granted that their "study does not provide evidence for a *continuing* decrease in mean sperm concentration."[23]

Thus the evidence for the decline in sperm counts—as popularized first by the Colborn book and then by the various media accounts—was actually far more ambiguous than it was made to seem. In addition, making the case for a global decline in sperm counts required that much contrary evidence be ignored. In fact, just as the hysteria about the supposed decline was peaking, a number of studies appeared presenting evidence against any decline whatsoever.[24] In short, the sperm count data, examined in their entirety, were less conclusive and more ambiguous than was suggested by the media representation, which was influenced by the public relations campaign on behalf of *Our Stolen Future*.

Finally, there is good cause to be dubious about sperm count data altogether. As researchers recognize, a man's sperm count can vary from sample to sample by as much as 200 to 400 percent even under identical circumstances. For this reason, any study that relies on a single sample (such as the Paris research mentioned in *U.S. News & World Report*) is unlikely to be very reliable. As one would expect, sperm counts also vary dramatically among individuals, depending not only on their age, but also on how recently and frequently they have ejaculated. Since evidence about sexual abstinence depends on the self-reports of the study subjects, it is hard to be altogether confident about its accuracy. People who are on diets, after all, have occasionally been known to lie about when they last sneaked a piece of chocolate cake.

Of still greater importance, it is hard to generalize from study samples to the entire mature male population. Getting your sperm counted isn't like getting your blood tested, which almost everyone does routinely. Instead, men whose sperm is tested tend to be potential sperm donors, candidates for vasectomies, or men with infertility problems.[25] In other words, sperm counts will tend to have data on those with reason to believe that their counts are high or low; it isn't altogether clear how representative their results are for the large majority of men whose sperm is never tested.

In retrospect, it is easy to see why the sperm count story took hold: it had everything. Not only did it raise the specter of the world coming to an end, it also involved sex. (*Our Stolen Future* made it possible for journalists to speculate about the possible significance of decreasing penis size among alligators, as an indication of the baleful effects of man-made chemicals.) Finally, the supposed sperm count decline could be interpreted as a sign of cosmic if not divine retribution—some writers hypothesized that lower sperm counts represent a sort of payback for the damage done by humans to the environment.[26] Screenwriters have received enormous sums for scripting Hollywood blockbusters with less box-office potential.

Nevertheless, the fact remains that the orchestrated campaign to highlight a decline in sperm counts aimed to popularize findings that were (a) ambiguous in themselves; (b) contradicted by other, equally relevant, findings; and (c) of questionable relevance altogether. All in all, a classic case of a journalistic mountain made out of a research molehill.

Caring Too Much about a Day Care Study

In April 1996 the *New York Times* published a front-page, above-the-fold story about the results of a study of day care's effect on the relationship between mothers and infants.[27] The study was also covered extensively by papers like the *Los Angeles Times* (again on page one)[28] and the *Washington Post* (where it was relegated to page three).[29]

The media focus on this research was surprising in a number of respects. For one thing, the research itself was preliminary; it had not yet been peer-reviewed or published in a scientific journal. Instead, journalists were covering a synopsis (presented at a scholarly meeting organized by the International Conference on Infant Studies) of a study prepared by researchers supported by the National Institute of Child Health and Human Development (NICHD).

We do not suggest that the research should have been ignored; it was the most comprehensive study ever undertaken to measure the impact of childcare on infants (in relation to their mothers), and a number of eminent developmental psychologists took part in it. Nevertheless, because of the importance of peer review, research released at professional meetings is generally, and deservedly, viewed more cautiously than research appearing in scholarly publications. Yet this study made it onto the front page of two major newspapers.

In addition, the topic of the research is not obvious front-page news. Despite the fact that the personal is increasingly the political, page-one stories generally reflect the more traditional view that the political is the political. The study did not deal with pressing issues related to national security or economic security, concerns that are more commonly addressed on page one.

Day care is, admittedly, an important issue in its own right; but by the researchers' own admission, the study did not offer anything like a comprehensive evaluation of it. Instead it examined just one aspect of day care, its impact on the bond between mother and infant. To be sure, that bond is significant in itself; furthermore, some research argues that an insecure bond between infant and mother foreshadows future emotional and behavioral problems for the child. Nevertheless, the study did not address any of the other obvious important questions regarding the impact of day care on children's intellectual, social, and physical development. Again, the limited character of the study would suggest that its results should not have made it onto page one.

Furthermore, by the nature of things, all research findings in this area should be viewed with a certain skepticism, simply because it's not easy to interpret infant behavior. The NICHD Study of Early Child Care examined the behavior of some 1,201 infants (when they were fifteen months old) to see whether they had developed secure attachments to their mothers. The obvious difficulty is that the behavior of fifteen-month-olds is anything but self-explanatory and must accordingly be interpreted by researchers, who have differing views on how to understand it. Researchers can't, after all, interview these youthful study subjects, so the researchers' determinations must inevitably be based on their own subjective—and questionable—decisions.

In the NICHD study, researchers evaluated the mother–infant bond by examining the behavior of infants in what is known as the "Strange Situation"—whose strangeness is perhaps reflected in the decision to capitalize it. In the Strange Situation, an infant encounters brief episodes of increasing stress, including two mother–infant separations and reunions. The rationale for the Strange Situation is that the infant will be distressed by its mother's departure and calmed by her return; an infant with a secure attachment to its mother will be comforted by her and able to resume playing. An insecure-avoidant infant, on the other hand, would not be distressed by the mother's departure and would ignore the mother on reunion. Based on their behavior, infants can also be assigned three other classifications.[30]

The results yielded by a study of infants' reactions to the Strange Situation, it should be clear, depend on the investigators' classification of the behavior that they observe. That classification is necessarily subjective if not altogether arbitrary; different investigators will draw the line between secure and insecure-avoidant at different places along the continuum. There is also a theoretical objection that may be more serious. It can and has been argued that an infant labeled as insecure-avoidant may actually be quite secure—so secure that it is not distressed by the departure of its mother, hence in no need of being comforted by its mother upon her return.[31] Our point is not that the Strange Situation is clearly invalid;[32] instead we raise a broader concern, suggesting that all research on infant behavior needs to be viewed cautiously.

The NICHD study in particular should have been viewed cautiously, because several of the individual findings were perplexing. For one thing, the study found that baby boys were most likely to be insecurely bonded to their mothers when they were in day care for more than thirty hours a week but that baby girls were most likely to have insecure bonds with their mothers when they were in day care for less than ten hours a week! Thus, if the study is to be believed, too much day care is dangerous for boys, and too little is dangerous for girls. Perhaps this counterintuitive finding of an infant gender gap makes sense: one of the researchers, Jay Belsky, hypothesized that "separation might prove stressful for boys, but girls who are home with mothers extensively may become almost too close and enmeshed."[33] Then again, perhaps the finding confirms the suspicion that all research in this field needs to be taken with several shakers of salt.

It also seems odd that the quality of day care (as evaluated—obviously subjectively—by the researchers) had no evident impact upon the security of the mother–infant bond. Nor, for that matter, did the amount of time spent in day care, the age at which day care began, or the frequency with which day care arrangements were changed. The only factor found to matter was the most obvious one: the mother's sensitivity and responsiveness to her child (as determined, once again, by the researchers' subjective decisions). Perhaps this finding is correct; still, one would think that poor day care might harm the security of an infant's attachment to all adults, including its mother.

Finally, it turns out that the NICHD study did not do much to evaluate day care as day care is ordinarily understood. One of the study's principal strengths is that it is an ongoing, longitudinal examination of its subjects beginning with their births—before any decisions about day care had been implemented. As a result, the NICHD study evaluated infants who received care in many different ways. In some cases, the mother was the primary caregiver; in others, it was the father or another relative. Other infants were looked after at their own homes (by nonrelatives), in childcare homes, and in childcare centers.

Of all the infants aged fourteen months, close to 60 percent were primarily looked after by mothers, fathers, or other relatives; an additional 9 percent were cared for at home by a nonrelative. Thus, less than a third of all the children were recipients of day care in other people's homes (21 percent) or in childcare centers (12 percent).[34] If day care is understood broadly (to include care by anyone other than the mother), 70 percent of the infants were in day care; but if it is understood more narrowly, the figure is far smaller. For that reason the study actually had little to say about day care as it is offered in childcare centers—perhaps the most contentious and important day care issue. In sum, we have argued that the NICHD study offered questionable findings in a preliminary setting in answer to an important but nonetheless narrow question about day care. So why was it covered so extensively?

The central question is whether the study would have received so much attention if it had concluded that day care did indeed pose problems for the mother–infant bond. A finding of that sort would have been equally important for parents to know (though also, in our view, equally dubious, because research in this field is so fraught with uncertainty). But would it have been featured so prominently?

Our guess is that it would not. If, as we think possible, the media decided to play up the NICHD study because its results were reassuring to working mothers, that decision is in one way defensible. The NICHD research counteracted earlier studies suggesting that day care does indeed place the mother–infant bond at some risk, and several of the NICHD investigators (in particular Jay Belsky) had previously published research along these lines.[35] In that sense, the NICHD finding that day care does not pose a risk—put forth by these researchers in particular— amounted to a "Man bites dog" story; whereas an additional confirmation that it does pose a risk, emanating from the same group of researchers, would have been more like "Dog bites man."

Still, one can wonder. Day care is a highly charged issue, such that researchers like Belsky who have raised concerns about its impact on children have been subjected to harsh attacks as opponents of women's entry into the workforce.[36] It is certainly conceivable that newspapers chose to highlight the NICHD study, despite the many limitations and uncertainties that we have pointed out, because they were eager to publish findings that would reassure working mothers and provide ammunition against a perceived backlash from the antifeminist right. In any case, we cannot prove motive; but we can observe that the NICHD study was accorded more prominent coverage than it really deserved.

Of Butterflies and the Temperature Rise

In August 1996 Camille Parmesan, a biologist at the University of California at Santa Barbara, published a brief discussion in the British science journal *Nature* recording her observations of the movements of a butterfly, the Edith's checkerspot, found in the American West.[37] Parmesan observed that overall the butterfly had moved north by about one hundred miles; she suggested that the northward movement resulted from climatic warming. She also found that the butterfly was now extinct in a number of more southerly locations in which it had previously been found: "Sites where previously recorded populations still existed were on average 2° [Celsius] further north than sites where populations were extinct. Populations in Mexico were four times more likely to be extinct than those in Canada."[38]

Parmesan did not make outlandish claims for the significance of her finding about one sort of butterfly. Instead, she declared that "conclusive evidence for or against the existence of the predicted biological effects of climate change will come . . . from replication of this type of study with additional taxa [that is, varieties of animals] in other regions." On the other hand, she did argue that the evidence to which she pointed "suggests climate change as the cause of the observed range shift [of the checkerspot]." And she concluded by declaring that "the evidence presented here provides the clearest indication to date that global climate warming is already influencing species' distributions."[39]

In short, Parmesan made an interesting and provocative claim about the possible implications of the movement of a single species of butterfly.

Still, the attention that her study received is surprising. *Nature*, in whose pages her research finding appeared, is a weekly offering an excellent overview of developments throughout the scientific world. Every issue contains many interesting and provocative claims, the vast majority of which is never reported on by major news outlets. Parmesan's communication, however, was covered in a lengthy story (lengthier, in fact, than the communication itself) in the *New York Times* weekly Tuesday science section.[40] And her finding was also reported in newspapers like the *Atlanta Constitution* (in a front-page article),[41] *Baltimore Sun*,[42] *Los Angeles Times*,[43] and *Washington Post*.[44]

In other words, major news outlets heavily publicized a suggestive finding that by the researcher's own admission needed to be replicated to be at all conclusive. If one swallow does not a summer make, it is at least as true that one butterfly does not a global warming prove. Nevertheless, Parmesan's preliminary finding became an important news story.

Furthermore, Parmesan's finding was not only preliminary, but also questionable. Most notably, she took it for granted that the climate had warmed in the locales in which the checkerspot was now extinct. In fact, however, West Coast temperatures do not appear to have warmed at all between 1909 and 1994, once one adjusts for growing urbanization: a temperature increase resulting from the construction of pavement, heated buildings, and night-lights is not attributable to greenhouse gases. Thus a recent communication in the *Bulletin of the American Meteorological Society* concluded that "the apparent 'global warming' is in reality urban waste heat affecting only urban areas" in California, Oregon, Washington, and British Columbia.[45]

It should be clear that these temperature records squarely contradict Parmesan's interpretation of the evidence. For regardless of whether Edith's checkerspot thinks globally, it must act locally. So even if warming is occurring on a global basis, it cannot explain the butterfly's range shift unless it has also taken place locally: a warming that has not affected rural southern California cannot explain the butterfly's departure from sites there. It cannot, that is, unless we assume that the Edith's checkerspot is an avid newspaper reader; in that case, perhaps media reports of the reality of warming convinced it to ignore the evidence of its own senses.

Furthermore, it is not clear that warming—assuming for the moment that it occurred—would be the factor responsible for the butterfly's range shift. In Parmesan's understanding, warming is the proximate cause of the butterfly's range shift; but the direct cause is the alteration of suitable plants, caused by warming, that had formerly hosted it.[46] Thus Parmesan took pains to exclude from consideration sites from which the butterfly had departed when the host plant had disappeared as a result of "human activities such as land-clearing construction, overgrazing and introduction of exotic plants."[47]

But human activities (rather than warming) could arguably still be responsible for much of the range shift in the sites that Parmesan did consider.[48] Even if development did not harm the host plants, changes in air quality or the impact of agricultural chemicals might still account for the butterfly's extinction in sites that were being developed. It is at least suggestive that many of the southern sites from which the checkerspot has departed are adjacent to San Diego and Los Angeles.

Finally, it is hard to know what to make of Parmesan's findings, because her communication did not include anything like a baseline for the number of extinctions that would be expected in the absence of any warming—assuming once again that warming actually took place. Was warming responsible for many of the local extinctions? It's hard to be certain, unless we have a sense of how many extinctions would have occurred normally, even in the absence of warming.

For all of these reasons, Parmesan's conclusion about the impact of warming, while interesting, is eminently debatable. Yet preliminary research subjected to a debatable interpretation was unquestioningly reported in major newspapers. Although a few of the stories explained that some scientists were unsure of the impact of the climate on the checkerspot,[49] for the most part the media raised no doubts while publicizing Parmesan's finding widely.

The interesting question, of course, is what would have happened had Parmesan's findings called into question, rather than seeming to confirm, the impact of global warming. Suppose that Parmesan had found that the checkerspot was shifting southward rather than northward. That would have been an equally important observation. Would it have been covered in the *New York Times*? For that matter, would her research have appeared in *Nature* in the first place? We obviously cannot answer those questions conclusively, but they are still worth raising. Certainly one can suspect that research conforming to the global warming scenario is greeted more favorably in many newsrooms than research contradicting it. Be that as it may, disproportionate coverage of a preliminary research finding is always unwelcome—no matter what belief the finding may seem to bolster.

Why Big News Emerges from Small Findings

On one level, the four case studies that we have examined differ greatly from one another. The Bowman–Venneri hypothesis of a nuclear explosion at Yucca Mountain emerged from an internal Los Alamos document, not yet peer-reviewed, that was leaked to a reporter; whereas the Carlsen meta-analysis of previous studies of sperm counts appeared in the *British Medical Journal*, a prestigious, peer-reviewed publication. The NICHD analysis of childcare, a product of government funding, united twenty-five researchers who jointly undertook "the largest and most comprehensive ongoing longitudinal study of child development and of the effects of childcare on such development";[50] whereas Camille Parmesan, a solitary investigator acting on her own, began to study the movements of the checkerspot in 1992 by driving around in what she has described as a "ratty old" 1977 four-wheel-drive vehicle.[51]

Nevertheless, in every one of these cases findings that were either preliminary or inconclusive received more attention than they really deserved. What accounts for the excessive coverage? The important factors are the same ones that emerged when we explained why inherently newsworthy findings are sometimes ignored. Everything else being equal, findings will get more attention if their significance is stressed by the researchers or by those individuals (who include publicity agents and leakers) who bring the findings to the attention of journalists. Everything else being equal, findings will also get more attention if they fit the template that journalists use in making sense of the world.

Thus, the Yucca Mountain was leaked to the *New York Times* journalist William J. Broad by someone who presumably had grave concerns about nuclear waste disposal. It would not have been hard for the leaker to argue that a possible nuclear explosion was a bad thing, and important news. And Broad, whose previous reporting evidenced skepticism about the safety of disposal plans for nuclear wastes, would not have been a hard audience to convince.

The research on declining sperm counts, as tendentiously summarized in *Our Stolen Future*, benefited from what seems to have been a highly effective public relations campaign managed by David Fenton, whose communications firm had previously spearheaded the campaign that resulted in the banning of the preservative Alar used by apple growers.[52] As we have seen, the NICHD study on childcare and Parmesan's research on the checkerspot were covered extensively right after the research was released, which again suggests that both were effectively publicized.

And in the three latter cases it seems plausible (though it cannot be proven) that reporters were more receptive and less skeptical than they might have been, because the stories fit the template. If you assume that man-made chemicals are degrading the environment, you may be inclined to believe the claim that they are lowering sperm counts. If you wish to support women who work outside the home, you may be inclined to publicize research that eases the perceived tension between mother-hood and such work. If you are convinced that global warming poses a serious threat, you may be inclined to make much of a finding that appears to confirm its reality.

Should these stories have been ignored by the media? Not necessarily, but clearly the coverage should have been more balanced than it was. The *Times* stories should have made it clearer that a Yucca Mountain explo-sion was a long way away at worst and an impossibility at best. The newsweeklies' sperm count stories should have followed the *New York Times*'s lead and surveyed all of the evidence—not just the evidence high-lighted in *Our Stolen Future*. And the coverage of the NICHD study and Parmesan's communication should have emphasized the limits of the research and the manifold uncertainties.

Would stories like these have made for less exciting reading? Conceivably. Would they have been more accurate? Undoubtedly. But news accounts, as we stated above, should aim for the truth, the whole truth, and nothing but the truth—not the excitement, the whole excite-ment, and nothing but the excitement.

Since news accounts are unlikely to focus altogether on truth to the exclusion of (spurious) excitement, how can readers cope? In many cases, surprisingly well. Skeptical and attentive readers would have noted that the *Times* chose to highlight a doomsday scenario for Yucca Mountain that was disputed by many scientists. Such readers would also have realized that Parmesan was studying a single butterfly and that the

NICHD study addressed only one of many important questions about day care. In these cases, at least (though perhaps not in most of the sperm count stories, in which contradictory evidence was brushed aside by reporters, as it had been in *Our Stolen Future*), the evidence that was presented sufficed to enable readers to suspect that a mountain story was perhaps being made out of a research molehill.

Thus the question of the template—reporters' greater receptivity to stories that "fit" and greater wariness toward those that don't—is less worrisome with respect to research that is overplayed than research that is ignored. A story that is at least reasonably faithful to the research that it summarizes will indicate to the alert reader that there may be less here than meets the eye; but when a news story never appears at all, the reader cannot realize that there is more here than meets the eye—because nothing meets the eye at all.

Coverage of research that is proportionate to its actual importance would obviously be welcome. But in its absence, readers often can and should decide for themselves whether something journalists depict as a mountain is actually only a small pile of dirt.

PART II

THE AMBIGUITY OF MEASUREMENT

CHAPTER 3

BAIT AND SWITCH
Understanding "Tomato" Statistics

Jane and Richard Stevens are a married couple who are having an argument. As their tempers heat up, she slaps his face; he responds by shoving her. Is Jane a victim of spousal abuse?

Mary Smith and Peter Jones are college students out on a date. At dinner (for which they split the bill) each drinks a whole bottle of wine. They then return to her apartment and smoke a stash of marijuana that she had hidden away. Their inhibitions lowered by the alcohol and the drugs, they have intercourse. The morning after, Mary is sorry that they had sex and decides that it happened only because she drank too much and smoked dope. Has Mary been raped?

Bob Patterson and Cindy Smith, who were married for fifteen years, divorce. Cindy gets custody of their twelve-year-old son Billy. Bob and Cindy agree that Billy will spend a week of his summer vacation visiting his dad (who lives a hundred miles away). But at Billy's request Bob decides to take him camping, so Billy returns to his mom a day late. Has Bob abducted Billy?

Answers of "yes" to questions like these helped create the frighteningly high numbers cited in the following news reports: a *Washington Post* summary of the results of the Commonwealth Fund's survey of women's health, which showed that "3.9 million women who were married or living with a man as a couple were physically abused in the past year";[1] a *New York Times* account of the results of a second survey, conducted by psychologist Mary P. Koss on behalf of *Ms.* magazine, which found that "27.5 percent of college women reported having been raped at some point since age 14";[2] and a third story, in which the *Times* summarized the results of yet another survey (the National Incidence Studies of Missing Abducted, Runaway, and Thrownaway Children, or NISMART), declaring that "about 350,000 children are abducted every year by family members."[3] All three of these stories conveyed bad news; all three of them accurately (but selectively) informed readers of the results of scientific surveys. But none of them informed readers that the terms "physical abuse," "abductions by family members," and even "rape" can cover a multitude of different offenses, some of which are far more serious than others.

Because of that omission, readers, perhaps unaware of the range of incidents that can be squeezed to fit under the definitions of these terms, might well have supposed that the alarmingly high numbers referred to the narrow definitions that apply only to the most serious incidents. When you read that 3.9 million women are victims of domestic abuse, that more than a fourth of female college students have been raped, and that 350,000 children have been abducted by family members, it's easy to assume that those numbers count incidents that reflect a commonsense understanding of these offenses.

But as we saw above, that assumption turns out to be false: all three of these numbers are large precisely because they reflect loose definitions unexplained in the news reports. Readers ignorant of the operative definitions would have misinterpreted the results to make them seem worse than they really were; thus they would have been victimized by manipulation of the numbers. We're all familiar with the unscrupulous sales technique known as "bait and switch." A store will advertise one product at a very attractive price to get shoppers in the door; but then you're told that the item is "out of stock," and a salesman tries to get you to purchase an inferior item at a higher price.

Imagine, for instance, a supermarket advertising tomatoes at three for a dollar. A very attractive price, you might think, assuming that they were beefsteak tomatoes. So you head to the produce section, where a stockboy tells you that they're out of beefsteak tomatoes, but they'll be pleased to sell you three cherry tomatoes for a dollar. Suddenly it doesn't seem like such a good deal—at least not for you, the shopper. The important thing to realize, of course, is that all tomatoes are not created equal: some tomatoes are much bigger than others, even though a common term describes them all.

In this chapter we'll look at what you might call "tomato" statistics: cases in which news reports call attention to alarmingly high numbers of criminal incidents by obscuring the crucial differences that make a few of the incidents far worse than the vast majority of the others. If someone has a hundred tomatoes, it matters if ninety-five are beefsteak tomatoes and five cherry tomatoes, or the other way around. Similarly, when you read statistics about large numbers of rapes, domestic assaults, or abductions of children, you need to realize that those terms are often used to describe incidents that many people would characterize differently. The individual incidents that make up the sum total will always differ in gravity; the composite ordinarily includes a comparatively small number of the most serious incidents and a notably larger number of less serious ones. A news report that doesn't convey that information (and most news reports don't) can be misleading.

What makes the bait and switch possible? We noted above that a common factor linking the three newspaper stories is that all of them reported results of surveys. For most crimes other than murder (where the victim can't speak, and there's hard physical evidence in the form of a corpse), surveys are thought to be the most reliable way to assess how often they are committed. Police reports are thought to be less reliable, because many victims won't take the trouble to report a crime to the police if they think the criminal is unlikely to be caught. (If you left your house unlocked and someone entered and stole a radio, would you bother reporting it to the authorities, or would you just forget about it, move on, buy a new radio, and try always to lock up in the future?)

Underreporting is thought to be particularly common when it comes to rape, domestic violence, and family abductions. Fear and shame would be obvious factors that might lead victims to keep silent. People are understandably reluctant to air messy family disputes in public, which could account for underreporting of domestic assaults and family abductions. And rape victims have often been stigmatized (to the point where it was the victim rather than the perpetrator who felt that she was being put on trial); those raped by acquaintances might be particularly reluctant to press charges.

For this reason surveys of representative samples of people are thought to be more likely to get at the true totals than are reports to the police. But surveys, of course, can have problems of their own. You can obviously wonder whether the respondents will tell the truth to the investigators; if not, there could well be either an overcount or an undercount. But the investigators' criteria are just as important (though less frequently noted). You might also wonder: On what bases do they decide that a given incident should (or should not) be classified as a rape, a domestic assault, or an abduction?

Thus it's the investigators' leeway in deciding upon a definition that creates a major difficulty. If their definition is broader than yours would be (and you don't know that, because the news story doesn't tell you), you'll assume that spousal abuse (or rape, or child abduction) is more common than it actually is—and that our society is in worse shape than it actually is. We can illustrate the difficulty by looking briefly at the three surveys discussed in the news stories with which we began.

Defining Domestic Assault

The Commonwealth Fund conducted a telephone survey of 2,500 women to determine the state of their health.[4] The survey measured domestic abuse of women by asking a series of eleven "yes or no" questions, in which women were asked whether, in the past year, their spouse or partner had ever done the following things: (1) insulted you or swore at you; (2) stomped out of the room or house or yard; (3) threatened to hit you or throw something at you; (4) threw or smashed or hit or kicked something; (5) threw something at you; (6) pushed, grabbed, shoved, or slapped you; (7) kicked, bit, or hit you with a fist or some other object; (8) beat you up; (9) choked you; (10) threatened you with a knife or gun; or (11) used a knife or gun on you.

Those questions are taken from a survey designed by the leading academic researchers on domestic abuse, Murray A. Straus of the University of New Hampshire and Richard J. Gelles, now at the University of Pennsylvania. In 1975 and 1985, Straus and Gelles conducted two large-scale national surveys of domestic abuse. They found that assaults by women upon men were more common than assaults by men upon women (though women were far more likely to be injured than men). They also found that assaults by men upon women decreased between the first and second surveys even though methodological differences between the two surveys "should have led to higher, not lower, rates of reported violence."[5] In their 1985 survey Straus and Gelles found an 11.6 percent rate of any violence by men against women, but that figure chiefly reflects the more common, less dangerous sorts of violence asked about in questions 3 through 6 above. Their figure for the more dangerous but rarer sorts of violence (indicated by positive answers to any of the questions from 7 through 11) was 3.4 percent, which works out to about 1.8 million women overall.

So how did the Commonwealth Fund use the same survey to arrive at much higher, more worrisome numbers? It simply ignored the common-sense distinction that Straus and Gelles made between serious acts of violence that might cause injury, and minor acts. The Commonwealth Fund total of 3.9 million women physically assaulted by their male partners reflects the fact that 5 percent of the women respondents answered question 6 affirmatively—they said that at least once in the past year they had been "pushed, grabbed, shoved, or slapped" by their partner.

Some of these incidents were conceivably quite serious, but others (think of the case of our hypothetical Jane Stevens) were surely not. The survey made no attempt to determine whether the violence was mutual or directed exclusively by the male against the female, no attempt to determine whether the woman was physically injured or genuinely frightened, and no attempt to determine whether such an incident occurred once during the year or more frequently. Nor, finally, was any attention paid to the finding that, if the respondents are to be believed, the most serious acts of violence simply never occurred: not a single respondent answered "yes" to questions 8 through 11 about beatings, chokings, or threatened or actual violence with knives or guns. Instead, just as an unscrupulous grocer might try to substitute cherry tomatoes for beefsteak tomatoes, the Commonwealth Fund survey treated very different sorts of acts (performed under very different circumstances) as though they were all equivalent, all equally indicative of the brutality of American males.

Reporting Rape

Mary Koss's Ms. Foundation survey found that "one in four female respondents had an experience that met the legal definition of rape or attempted rape."[6] Legal definitions vary from state to state, but generally the definition involves sexual penetration against a person's will. It must take place through the use of force or the threat of force, or when the victim cannot consent (because she is mentally ill, developmentally disabled, or the recipient of intoxicants or anesthetics administered with the intent to incapacitate her).[7]

How did Koss arrive at her alarming figure? She conducted a survey of 6,159 college students (3,187 of whom were women) to determine the incidence of rape, defined as sexual behavior involving penetration. Her frightening findings were that 15.4 percent of the female respondents had been raped, and 12.1 percent were victims of attempted rape, which together is more than a quarter of the surveyed population. But Koss's research described much behavior as rape that would not be seen as rape by many people.

One of the questions she asked women was as follows: "Have you had sexual intercourse when you didn't want to because a man gave you alcohol or drugs?" But as Berkeley social scientist Neil Gilbert has observed, this question is problematical: "What does it mean to have sex when you don't want to 'because' a man gives you alcohol or drugs?" A positive response to this question would "not indicate whether duress, intoxication, force, or the threat of force was present; whether the woman's judgment or control was substantially impaired; or whether the man purposefully got the woman drunk in order to prevent her from resisting his sexual advances." The wording would apply to cases where "a few drinks lowered the respondent's inhibitions and she consented to an act she later regretted," as in the case of Mary Smith with which we began. The question "could have been clearly worded to denote the legal standard of 'intentional incapacitation of the victim'"; but as it was asked, "there is no way to detect whether an affirmative response corresponds to the legal definition of rape."[8]

Moreover, would Mary Smith consider herself a rape victim? If not, should that matter to the investigator or to those interpreting her work? We raise these questions because most of the women whom Koss labeled as rape victims did not regard themselves that way. Eleven percent of the women in question said that they "d[id]n't feel victimized"; 49 percent labeled the experience "miscommunication"; 14 percent labeled it "crime, but not rape"; and only 27 percent said that it was "rape."[9] (For that reason, the *Times* account of Koss's research was somewhat misleading. The women did not "report having been raped"; they recounted experiences that Koss herself labeled as rape.)

In addition, 42 percent of the women who were said by Koss to have been raped went on to have sex again with their supposed rapists. Reporters for the *Toledo Blade* have calculated that if women given drugs or alcohol (as well as women who did not think that they had been raped) are subtracted from Koss's totals, the one-in-four figure for rape and attempted rape "drops to between one in twenty-two and one in thirty-three," depending on the amount of overlap between the two groups.[10]

In short, Koss chose to characterize many sexual experiences as rapes, even though the experiences would not be seen as rapes by many observers and in fact were not seen as rapes by the participants themselves. Young women (and also young men) are often of two minds about whether to have sex—but the confusion and ambiguity that they feel was disregarded by Koss, who imposed her own characterization of the behavior. And Koss's figures become still more incredible when one compares her "one in four" figure with the actual findings from college campuses, where very few rapes are reported to either the police or campus rape crisis centers.[11]

Feminist researchers, like Koss, state forthrightly that victims' subjective perceptions should be disregarded: "Rape victims frequently fail to realize that their victimization qualifies as a crime and often avoid choosing the label 'rape' to conceptualize their experience."[12] In fairness, researchers ought not to rely simply on women's self-identification as rape victims: since women's individual definitions of rape would undoubtedly differ, relying exclusively on self-reports (in the absence of interviewers offering a definition of rape to guide the respondents) would produce arbitrary and therefore unreliable conclusions.

But at the same time, simply ignoring respondents' views, as Koss does, is also problematic. It is odd to see a feminist researcher who presumably believes in women's autonomy simply discounting women's views; the decision to ignore them has Orwellian overtones of Big Sister knowing best. Note also a disturbing implication of Koss's findings: she presents women as helpless victims who do not understand that they have been raped, who return to have sex with their rapists, and who are easily incapacitated by drinking or psychological coercion. Koss has also written that "women are socialized to be passive, good-willed, and compliant, and to assume the status of property":[13] these views, expressed by a supposed defender of women, might fit in perfectly well at a meeting of the International Brotherhood of Male Chauvinist Pigs.

The more important, more general point, though, is methodological: Koss's high numbers derive from a loose definition of rape. If an investigator chooses to place more and more sorts of incidents beneath the rubric of rape, it is not surprising when she finds that rape is more common than people believe. In short, the number of rapes can increase because rape is occurring more often; because it is occurring as often (or even less often), but victims are more willing to acknowledge what has happened to them; or because an investigator chooses to categorize more things as rape, regardless of whether the victims (or anyone else) would agree.

There may well be a case for expanding the definition of rape; and there may well be a case for classifying some incidents as rapes that the victims, who may be in denial, would not categorize in that way. But there is no case for trumpeting an alarming increase in the number of rapes without explaining that the increase results from a broadened definition that disregards the alleged victims' views. Again, how many incidents you count will depend greatly on the sorts of incidents that you think should count. If Mary Smith is counted as a rape victim, rape can indeed be shown to be more common. But the important question is *whether* she should be counted—not what the total is if she is counted.

Analyzing Family Abductions

In the early and mid-1980s many Americans believed that tens of thousands of children were being abducted by strangers, as they extrapolated from a small number of well-publicized incidents. But because no scientific study of the problem had yet been undertaken, estimates of the problem's size were largely guesswork. In order to get reliable figures, the federal government commissioned a series of studies designed to count the number of missing children in various categories: How many children were abducted by strangers? By family members? How many children ran away from home? How many were kicked out of the house by a parent or guardian?

The NISMART findings, released in 1990, provided the first set of numbers with scientific credibility. The two major NISMART findings were that the number of children abducted by strangers came nowhere near the figures (in the tens of thousands) that earlier had been advanced and that the number of kidnappings by family members was far higher.

Relying primarily on a nationally representative sample of records from eighty-three law enforcement agencies, NISMART researchers estimated that in 1988 there were only 200 to 300 "stereotypical kidnappings" and 3,200 to 4,600 nonfamily abductions according to a strict legal definition. To fit the definition of a stereotypical kidnapping, one or more of the following had to occur: either the perpetrator had to show an intent to keep the child permanently or the child must have been gone overnight, been transported more than fifty miles from the point of abduction, or been killed or ransomed. As the researchers concluded, "the number of these serious . . . cases is no more than 200–300 a year."[14]

But as the report observed, controversy can arise when "abductions are *counted* using a legal definition, but the results are *interpreted* using the popular stereotype."[15] The researchers noted that the legal definition of nonfamily kidnapping is surprisingly broad. It applies when a child is forcibly transported for as little as twenty feet, when he is detained for only an hour, and when the perpetrator is an acquaintance (a babysitter or neighbor) as well as a stranger.[16] About two-thirds of the legal-definition kidnappings actually involved sexual assaults on teenage girls who were then released by their assailants—horrifying crimes, but quite different from the stereotype of children who were kidnapped and kept incommunicado for long periods before being ransomed or killed.[17]

The report's major surprise, though, was not the low number of nonfamily abductions but the high number of family ones. Extrapolating from the results of their survey of a nationally representative sample of over 10,000 households (including more than 20,000 children), the NISMART researchers estimated that over 350,000 had been abducted by family members;[18] previous guesstimates, the report noted, had ranged between 25,000 and 100,000.[19] Remarkably, NISMART detected between three and fourteen times as many incidents as had previously been thought to occur.

Since most family abductions occur in the context of disputes over custody between separated or divorced parents, the NISMART figures may not be implausibly high: ten million children live with a mother or father who is separated or divorced, and 10 to 15 percent of custody arrangements are contested by one party or the other.[20] In addition, the figure of 350,000 cited in the *New York Times* story (the precise figure was 354,100) derives from a broad definition of family abduction, in which a family member takes a child in violation of a custody agreement or decree, or a family member violates a custody agreement by not returning a child at the end of a legal or agreed-upon visit (and the child is away at least overnight).[21] According to this broad definition, our hypothetical Billy Patterson was abducted by his father.

The NISMART researchers also used a stricter definition, in which the abductor must attempt to conceal the child or prevent contact with him, transport him out of state, or have intended to keep the child indefinitely. This stricter definition yielded a subset of 163,200 family abductions—still an impressively high number, even if it can be questioned.[22]

Its specific findings, though, may not be what's most important about the NISMART report; its decision about how to report those findings is arguably more interesting. As we have seen, the report provided two figures for both family and nonfamily abductions—a higher number applying to a broader definition of the phenomenon, and a lower number applying to a stricter one. Two numbers were also given for the other sorts of incidents covered by the report: episodes in which children ran away from home; were "thrown away" (told to leave by a parent or guardian); or were lost, injured, or otherwise missing (without being abducted).

Why two definitions? As the report explained, the "Broad Scope" definition "generally defines the problem the way the persons involved might define it. It includes more minor episodes that may nonetheless be alarming to the participants": to say this, of course, is also to say that the broad-scope definition may include episodes that did *not* alarm the participants. The stricter "Policy Focal" definition, on the other hand, "generally defines the problem from the point of view of police or other social agencies. This category is restricted to episodes of a more serious nature, where without intervention a child may be further endangered or at risk of harm."[23]

Writing with Tracy M. Thibodeau, University of Delaware sociologist Joel Best has described the dual-definition strategy as "an apparent effort to placate both activists (who preferred to define categories of missing children broadly) and their critics (who tended to favor narrower definitions)."[24] For their part, the NISMART researchers contended that two definitions "satisf[ied] the need for an incidence estimate of the problem that includes most of what is colloquially thought of as runaway, family abduction, or lost, [sic] for example, and at the same time a figure that shows the portion that policymakers and the public believe is the cause for alarm."[25]

The researchers' argument on behalf of two definitions is not altogether persuasive, though. The claim that a "colloquial" understanding of what it means to be a missing child is a broad one that incorporates many less serious incidents appears to be at odds with the statement that the "popular stereotype" of stranger abductions focuses narrowly on crimes in which total strangers snatch children, transport them far away, and keep them for a long time.[26] This popular stereotype, then, suggests that in reality the public is chiefly concerned with the more serious, less common crimes (policy-focal cases)—not the more typical broad-scope incidents. And as we just saw, the NISMART researchers themselves declared that the policy-focal incidents are the ones that "the public believes is the cause for alarm."

Nor is it clear that a broad-scope amalgamation of serious and less serious incidents provides particularly useful information. By analogy, a medical researcher might report an alarmingly high number of respiratory infections nationwide, but what should truly concern us is presumably the small number of cases of pneumonia and bronchitis requiring hospitalization, not the large number of common colds that boosted the sales of Contac and Nyquil.

The policy-focal numbers would also seem to be more relevant in that the NISMART study was commissioned by a government agency (the United States Department of Justice), in response to a federally legislated mandate (contained in the 1984 Missing Children Act), presumably with the intent to guide government agencies in the formation of public policy. This is the context in which the *New York Times* coverage of the NISMART data must be understood. The *Times* highlighted the broad-scope number of 350,000 abductions of children by family members each year and did not even mention that the report offered a second and substantially lower figure. A *Times* reader would thus have been unaware of the NISMART distinction between broad-scope and policy-focal numbers.

On the other hand, the *Boston Globe* took the opposite tack, citing only the policy-focal numbers while ignoring the higher broad-scope figures. It reported that "more than 160,000" children are abducted by family members every year.[27] Thus both papers were accurately summarizing results from the same study—even though the figure offered by the *Times* more than doubled that printed in the *Globe*. But because both the *Globe* and the *Times* chose to report only one of the two figures (without explaining that the other existed), someone reading both papers would have been puzzled; readers of only one would have learned the truth but not the whole truth conveyed by NISMART.

Numbers Don't Speak for Themselves

In some ways the missing children episode is the most revealing of the three that we have looked at. The Commonwealth Fund seems to have wanted to report that large numbers of American women were physically abused by their husbands, and the Ms. Foundation surely wanted to assert that rape is far more prevalent in America than people assumed: both groups presented journalists with a high (hence newsworthy) figure, without in any way suggesting that a narrower definition would have yielded a substantially lower one. Journalists might have questioned their numbers, but in each case reporters simply digested the numbers that they themselves received from the investigators. In other words, it would have taken a certain effort to determine that a "bait and switch" tactic had been employed.

In the case of missing children, however, the NISMART researchers were commendably honest about their enterprise, explicitly stating that they were providing two figures for each category (and why they were doing so). Yet here, too, readers were effectively prevented from realizing that the *number* of missing children depends on the *definition* of missing children. Unlike, say, twins or low-birth-weight babies, "missing children" do not make up an objective category that can be measured precisely. Instead, as the NISMART researchers candidly explained, the number of missing children that you find depends on the definition of missing children that you choose: "The missing children's field is littered with definitional disputes. These disputes are not minor and arbitrary. . . . It is not possible to count instances of a phenomenon until the phenomenon is clearly defined. But there is no agreement on definitions."[28]

The point, of course, is that counting victims of abductions (or domestic violence, or even rape) isn't an altogether objective enterprise; instead, researchers must make decisions about what counts and what doesn't that are necessarily subjective. But by giving only one of the two sets of figures, the *Times* and the *Globe* concealed that subjectivity from their readers and made the NISMART conclusions seem far more solid, objective, and immutable than is actually the case. What we find depends upon how we've defined.

In other words, too often newspaper stories are content to tell us "how many" of something researchers have found without also telling us "of what different kinds." (This is so, as the NISMART example indicates, even when the researchers themselves make it clear that the difference between the various kinds is of crucial importance.) For this reason, statements about the frequency with which various crimes occur should always be examined skeptically, until you know what the definition is. You should never assume that all of the incidents are equally serious; instead, a good working assumption is that the worst incidents are the least common (and the least grave ones most common). Just as tomatoes can vary drastically in size, so incidents (all of which can be subsumed under the definition of one particular offense) can vary drastically in their seriousness. Someone who tries to paint all offenses with a uniform brush, glossing over the differences among them, is likely to be practicing a "bait and switch": be careful what you buy from him.

CHAPTER 4

THE PERILS OF PROXIES
Is There a There There?

The lead story on the CBS evening newscast was a bombshell: "A startling number of American children in danger of starving. Dan Rather reporting. Good evening. One out of eight American children under the age of twelve is going hungry tonight. That is the finding of a new two-year study."[1]

By contrast, a *Washington Post* front-page story conveyed encouraging news about a different (but related) social problem: "The number of Americans living in poverty dropped by 1.2 million last year."[2]

Summarizing a National Research Council (NRC) report on research in an altogether different field, a front-page *New York Times* story stated that "exposure to electric and magnetic fields" has not been found to present "a health hazard"—even though there is a "small increase in childhood leukemia in houses close to power lines."[3]

On the surface, these three news stories differ in obvious crucial respects. CBS broadcast an alarming finding taken from research undertaken by an activist group, the Food Research and Action Center (FRAC), that aims to highlight the problem of hunger and to increase government spending to fight it. Furthermore, CBS misreported the FRAC study, which claimed that one out of eight children had gone hungry at some point in the previous year—not that one out of eight was currently hungry.

The *Post* and the *Times*, on the other hand, accurately reported comparatively encouraging news derived from nonpartisan researchers with no obvious ax to grind. Census Bureau statisticians found that poverty had declined, and a panel of scientists established by the NRC concluded that electromagnetic fields (EMFs) do not pose an obvious health risk. It seems fair to say that in some sense FRAC wants to report alarming findings about hunger: if hunger were not a problem, FRAC wouldn't be needed to fight against it. The Census Bureau and the NRC, on the other hand, simply report the results of their research and have no clear stake in them.

On a deeper level, though, the three stories share an important common factor: each case illustrates how we can be misled by research that uses proxy (as opposed to direct) measurement. FRAC didn't measure hunger directly (that is, how much people actually eat) but instead relied on a proxy—what people said about hunger. The Census Bureau doesn't measure poverty directly (by seeing whether people are undernourished, poorly housed, and shabbily dressed) but instead relies on income as a proxy for poverty. And as the NRC report noted, much scientific research on EMF exposure is flawed, because it relies on an invalid proxy: it wrongly equates proximity to power lines with exposure to EMFs.

Both the social and natural sciences frequently employ proxies, often for a very good reason: occasionally researchers are unable to measure something directly, so they must rely on a proxy instead. But at the same time, there's always the risk that the proxy may be an inadequate stand-in for the thing that truly concerns us. To get a sense of different kinds of proxy problems, in this chapter we'll begin by examining the flaws in two important social-science proxies; we'll then look at the shortcomings of a natural-science proxy.

Social-science proxies can be problematic, especially if they are used to represent concepts that themselves are poorly understood. How best to measure hunger and poverty? Answering that question is complicated, because hunger and poverty may not be objective conditions that can be clearly defined and then precisely measured by proxy. In other words, researchers may think that they know what hunger and poverty are, and that proxies enable us to see how many hungry and poor people there are; but those assumptions, which are evident in almost all media coverage of research on poverty and hunger, are debatable.

The problem is that hunger and poverty can't be measured in the way that, say, births, deaths, or home sales can. Neither term refers to an objective condition that can be pinned down. Instead, hunger and poverty are defined by the subjective choices that researchers make in trying to measure them. The need for subjective choices is apparent when you consider the slipperiness of the dividing line separating poor from not poor or hungry from not hungry. In general it is clear when a birth, death, or home sale occurs. But what exactly is the dividing line between being "poor" and "just barely scraping by"? How do you decide when someone is "hungry" (as opposed, say, to being "between meals")? The answers to those questions are much more likely to be contested.

Doctors have agreed-upon diagnostic definitions and widely used medical equipment that enable them to say, "She has measles; he doesn't"; but there's nothing like a definitional consensus or a "hungerometer" or "poverty measurer" to enable a researcher (with or without an ax to grind) to look at a bunch of people and confidently say, "He's poor; she's not." Unfortunately, media reports almost invariably treat hunger and poverty as though they were just like measles. The CBS telecast and the *Post* story simply illustrate this tendency, which is virtually universal.

In part because hunger and poverty differ from measles, they are measured not directly, but by proxy. Because researchers don't know exactly what hunger and poverty are (and exactly how to measure them), they look for other things to measure that are thought to be reliable signs or indicators of those conditions. Thus hunger researchers don't generally look at how much (and what foods) people eat to determine whether they're hungry; instead they rely on survey data (responses to questions about eating habits) or look at participation rates in government food programs to assist the needy. Survey data (what people say) and program-participation data (whether they apply for aid for which they're eligible) are used as proxies for hunger. Researchers generally don't compile the most direct and obvious data by figuring out what people actually eat. In the words of Middle Tennessee State University sociologist Dan McMurry, "Hunger . . . has been virtually ignored by medical and public health professionals" and has instead become the province of activist groups;[4] empirical studies of food consumption (carried out by branches of the federal government) have been ignored in favor of activist studies that do not make use of the most relevant evidence.

Much the same story can be told about poverty, except here it is government research that relies on a proxy. The federal government calculates its official poverty rate not by looking at objective material conditions (whether people are well-fed, well-clothed, well-housed, and recipients of good medical care) to measure poverty but by calculating people's income. The emphasis is on what people earn—not on how they actually live. Again, the most direct and obvious data are ignored. As American Enterprise Institute demographer Nicholas Eberstadt has observed, "The poverty rate . . . is estimated on the basis of reported annual household *income*; material deprivation, however, can be gauged only by patterns of *consumption*. By focusing on income rather than on consumption—which is to say, expenditures and purchasing power—our antipoverty policies have been guided by a false compass for thirty years."[5]

Everything else being equal, you may say, it's presumably better to measure something directly rather than by proxy. On the other hand, measurement by proxy would be fatally flawed only if the proxy were unreliable. Because that is so, we need to see what's wrong with proxies that have been used in researching hunger, poverty, and exposure to EMFs.

What's Wrong with Hunger Proxies?

How did FRAC arrive at its claim that one in eight American children suffers from hunger?[6] It extrapolated from a survey of 2,335 American families, even though the report's executive summary conceded that "the combined samples are not statistically representative of this population [low-income families with at least one child under the age of twelve] in the entire United States." (For example, white families made up only 29 percent of the sample surveyed by FRAC, whereas 62 percent of all low-income families with children are white.)

Far worse, though, was FRAC's method of determining whether someone should be considered "hungry." The survey posed eight questions to respondents, each of which asked if there was "ever" a time "in the past 12 months" when a specific "food shortage problem" arose in the respondent's household. (For this reason, as noted above, CBS wrongly sensationalized FRAC's survey when it claimed that "one out of eight American children under the age of twelve is going hungry tonight.")

The one-in-eight figure was arrived at in this way: respondents who answered "yes" to five or more questions were said to be "hungry"; those answering "yes" to one to four were said to be "at risk of hunger." Crucially, only 33 percent of the families said to be "hungry" answered "yes" to the most pertinent question: "Did any of your children ever go to bed hungry because there was not enough money to buy food?" Far more, 98 percent, said that they had relied "on a limited number of foods to feed [their] children": such an answer may show that the children's diet was monotonous without showing that they went hungry. Far more, 73 percent, reported that their children had ever said that "they were hungry because there was not enough food in the house." But that answer says nothing about why there wasn't enough food: it makes a difference if there was a traffic jam on the way back from the supermarket—or there wasn't enough money (or food stamps) to buy food. As Mickey Kaus wrote in the *New Republic*, this question might have drawn an affirmative answer from "Donald Trump."[7] But in spite of these failings (and many, many others) the FRAC study received overwhelmingly favorable media attention. In an unpublished paper, Ted J. Smith III and Melanie Scarborough of Virginia Commonwealth University calculated that "41 of the 47 news stories [covering the report] (87%) . . . simply relayed the findings of the FRAC study to the public without negative criticism of any kind."[8]

The extent of hunger in America has also been estimated in a series of reports by the Physician Task Force on Hunger in America, headed by J. Larry Brown of the Harvard University School of Public Health. The Physician Task Force estimated that more than twenty million Americans suffered from hunger in the 1980s, a figure that was uncritically passed along in many news accounts.[9] The use of the term "physician" might lead you to believe that the twenty-million figure was arrived at by people in white coats with stethoscopes who actually examined patients to determine the incidence of hunger, but that would be wrong. (J. Larry Brown himself is a psychologist, not a nutrition expert.)

Instead, as the better news accounts explained, the figure was largely derived by counting the number of people eligible for food stamps who did not receive them. An informative *Los Angeles Times* article explained that

> the Physician Task Force's figure is based on the 20 million food stamp recipients in 1983, subtracted from the number of people in poverty that year, 35 million. That amounted to 15 million people below the poverty line not receiving food stamps. Added to that was another 5 million, an estimate based on data from sources such as the Salvation Army and local emergency food networks which often provide food to families when their food stamp allotment is insufficient.[10]

A somewhat different explanation appeared in a *Chicago Tribune* article covering an updated report from the Physician Task Force: "The authors derived their figure of 20 million hungry by reasoning that most of the 32.4 million Americans living at or below the official 'poverty level' suffer chronic inadequacy in their diets."[11]

These "research methods" (if they can be dignified by that term) leave a great deal to be desired. In fact, the Harvard techniques almost make FRAC's look good by comparison: at least FRAC undertook empirical research of a sort, administering a (flawed) questionnaire to an (unrepresentative) sample. People who are eligible for food stamps but don't use them may be hungry, as may people with incomes below the poverty line; those are both plausible hypotheses. But the point of empirical research is to test hypotheses, to see if they are confirmed by evidence, which is exactly what the Physician Task Force didn't do.

If the task force had investigated its hypotheses, what might it have found? Dan McMurry offered some suggestions in a methodological critique. In one of its reports the task force identified the 150 counties with the worst hunger problem in the United States: counties in which more than 20 percent of the population fell below the poverty line and less than one-third of the eligible poor received food stamps. He found that many of these counties were inhabited primarily by farmers and farm owners with low per capita incomes but substantial assets. The average farm in two of the counties was valued well above half a million dollars. If farmers like these, who may technically be eligible for food stamps, fail to participate in the program, you somehow doubt that they're suffering from malnutrition.[12]

The task force report on hunger counties is a classic example of the dangers of research by proxy: it turns out that many people who do not make use of food stamps are nevertheless not hungry. And why should a proxy be used to measure the incidence of hunger in the first place? As Robert

Rector of the Heritage Foundation has noted, we have data from

> scientific surveys, conducted by the Food and Nutrition Service of the Department of Agriculture and the Centers for Disease Control of the Department of Health and Human Services. These surveys, which measure actual food consumption and physiological status in the U.S. population, show little evidence of hunger or insufficient calorie and protein intake among poor children or poor adults. . . . Little difference is found between the level of nutrients consumed by poor and affluent children.[13]

But many researchers evidently prefer researching hunger by proxy, perhaps because it enables them to make the problem seem more pressing. If researchers agreed that hunger was a specific physical condition, they would presumably measure it directly (by examining representative samples of the population). But no such agreement exists. Instead, hunger is often defined loosely, to the point where assessments of what people actually eat are essentially irrelevant to the problem. Consider for example, these words of Tufts University nutritionist Jean Mayer, an influential activist in the campaign against hunger:

> For most of the people engaged in social action, hunger has a broader meaning. It is synonymous with deprivation. Deprivation of food is one aspect, but deprivation of money, of social status, of right—all these things are part of the overall picture. Malnutrition itself has a vaguer meaning: It is a lot of things that are not being done for people that ought to be done.

In other words, in Mayer's view "hunger" is really a synonym for "poverty." It may even be a synonym for "inequality," as Mayer went on to suggest: "We are going to deal with hunger and malnutrition by having poor people go to the same . . . supermarkets as everybody else to buy food of the same quality and at the same price as everybody else."[14] An understanding of hunger as broad as this actually requires investigation by proxy. If you're chiefly interested in measuring poverty and inequality, there's little point in seeing how much iron and calcium is ingested by poor kids in Bedford-Stuyvesant and the *barrio*.

Poverty by Proxy

Unfortunately, equating "hunger" with "poverty" does not solve the problems of definition and measurement; if anything, it's less clear how poverty should be defined and how it should be measured. And poverty, too, is measured not directly but by proxy.

Poverty researchers have always recognized that the definition of poverty is necessarily arbitrary. Consider the testimony of Mollie Orshansky, a government economist who during the 1960s created the formula for measuring poverty still used in official Census statistics today:

> For deciding who is poor, prayers are more relevant than calculation because poverty, like beauty, lies in the eye of the beholder. Poverty is a value judgment; it is not something one can verify or demonstrate, except by inference and suggestion, even with a measure of error. To say who is poor is to use all sorts of value judgments. . . . When it comes to defining poverty, you can only be more subjective or less so. You cannot be non-subjective.[15]

As we saw above, poverty is measured by proxy in the official statistics, which tell us nothing about the living conditions of those said to be poor but tell us instead about their income. Orshansky (a defender, not a critic, of the poverty measurement that she devised) again pointed candidly to the problem: "The index is arbitrary in that it relies only on income as the criterion of poverty, but *income statistics happen to be the only ones currently available on a regular basis*" (our emphasis). Orshansky also conceded that "the value of consumption appears to be superior to income as a measure of poverty status. Of course, income standards are chosen only because they are to be used as a proxy for consumption potential."[16]

The problem, though, is that income may be the wrong thing to measure—because it may actually tell us little about consumption and material deprivation. The real question about poverty, it can be argued, is how many people are (in Franklin D. Roosevelt's formulation) "ill-clothed, ill-housed, and ill-fed." We use income as a proxy for material deprivation, assuming that those with little income will be materially deprived; but in many respects income may be an unreliable proxy. Why?

First, the official poverty measurement uses a misleadingly narrow definition of income, one that ignores the value of in-kind benefits received by those designated as poor: food stamps, Medicare and Medicaid, and government-subsidized housing. As Northwestern University sociologist Christopher Jencks has written, the official poverty statistics are faulty because "they do not take account of changes in families' *need* for money [resulting from the expansion of in-kind assistance to people with low incomes]. They make no adjustment for the fact that Medicare and Medicaid now provide many families with low-cost medical care, or for the fact that food stamps have reduced families' need for cash, or for the fact that more families now live in government-subsidized housing."[17]

But there's also a far more radical criticism of measuring poverty by income. It's not just that the official statistic measures income in the wrong way (a flaw that is, in any case, remedied in a number of "unofficial" poverty measurements supplied by the Census Bureau); instead it's that income may in principle be the wrong thing to measure. Although we tend to think that people with low incomes are poor, it's paradoxically the case that many people have low incomes because they are *not* poor: they have assets and savings on which they can draw to support themselves, so they do not need substantial earnings.

Thus the "income poor" includes many people who are actually quite well off: retirees who are homeowners, who may have limited income but also substantial assets on which they draw; ex-students just entering the workforce, whose low income may be supplemented by their parents; and small-business owners who suffer one bad year but have many assets and adequate cash flow. Empirical data from the Department of Labor's Consumer Expenditure Survey support this contention. The survey shows that the poor (that is, those with low incomes) consistently spend far more than they report earning. Data for 1989 show that the mean income of people in the lowest income quintile was $5,720, but their average annual expenditure came to $12,378, a figure that is more than twice as high.[18]

Some of this glaring discrepancy reflects the capacity of people with low incomes (think again of retirees) to draw on savings; some of it reflects the capacity to borrow in expectation of better times ahead (think of ex-students and small-business owners having a bad year). Finally, as David Whitman of *U.S. News & World Report* has noted, the poor (like the nonpoor) can underreport their earnings. "Often, the poorest families conceal money [that] they earn at odd jobs or receive from friends and family to ensure that they remain eligible for welfare benefits and to reduce tax liability."[19] In other words, much income earned by poor people is untaxed, "off the books" income from the "underground economy," detected by neither the Internal Revenue Service nor the Census Bureau's income tabulations.

Just as Rector argued that a direct (as opposed to proxy) measurement of hunger would reveal that hunger poses far less of a threat in contemporary America than people ordinarily assume, many poverty scholars (Rector among them) make comparable arguments about poverty. These researchers contend that if we look at the consumption of the poor (what they eat, where they are housed, how they dress, how healthy they are), we find substantially fewer poor people than the Census Bureau finds when it measures poverty through the proxy of income.[20]

We are not, however, principally concerned with showing the substantive truth about the prevalence of either poverty or hunger. Instead, it is the procedural oddity to which we call attention: the reliance on proxy measurements as opposed to more direct measurements, which is almost never observed or questioned by the media. Christopher Jencks (writing with Susan Mayer) explained the problem well, noting that we aren't measuring the right things:

> Americans are more concerned with whether their fellow citizens are getting adequate food, shelter, and medical care than with whether they have adequate incomes. . . . [Yet] the federal government collects detailed data every year on the level and distribution of family income, but no federal agency regularly tries to determine how many Americans are going to bed hungry, how many have had their gas or electricity cut off, how many have been evicted from their homes, how many live in housing that their fellow citizens judge unacceptably crowded or dilapidated, how many think they need medical care they are not getting, or how many have untreated toothaches.[21]

Measuring hunger and poverty more directly would not, of course, answer all of our questions about their severity; there would still be thorny definitional disputes about what constitutes "hunger" or "poverty." If you don't ingest enough calories one day a month, should you be considered hungry? (And in any case, how would you determine how many calories is "enough"?) If you're an illegal immigrant working as a maid, sharing a one-bedroom apartment with three other illegals, are you housed badly enough that you should be categorized as poor? (How many people can share a room—and what size room?—before their housing is judged unacceptably crowded?)

Eliminating proxy measurements wouldn't answer these questions. Hunger and poverty would still be phenomena that in some sense are created by the criteria adopted by researchers. Nevertheless, measuring food intake and living conditions more directly would at least ensure that the right questions were being posed. And posing the right questions could have practical as well as theoretical consequences. In the last thirty years we have spent immense sums in the hope of eradicating poverty and hunger; but because poverty and hunger have been measured through misleading proxies, those funds may often have been mistargeted.

Failing to Measure Electromagnetic Fields

Natural-science proxies tend to pose a somewhat different problem. Even if researchers know precisely what they want to measure, they may still be unable to measure it; they may have to resort to proxy measurements as a fallback. In one case, the use of a faulty proxy helped create a long-standing debate about the possible health hazards posed by exposure to the electromagnetic fields (EMFs) produced by power lines and electric wiring.

For more than twenty years critics have charged that exposure to EMFs poses severe health risks. For example, Paul Brodeur, a writer for the *New Yorker*, charged in 1989 that EMFs are "the most pervasive—and covered up—public health hazard Americans face,"[22] contributing in particular to an increased risk of cancer. But the case against the supposed EMF danger has also been rejected by most scientists, who note that external sources like power lines and appliances create electric fields within the human body that are far weaker than the fields that occur naturally within it. These skeptics also observe that if EMFs are an important cause of (for instance) childhood leukemia, the disease should be far more common today than a generation ago (since our exposure to EMFs is so much greater now than then); in fact, the incidence rates for childhood leukemia have been remarkably steady over time.

Hoping to resolve this controversy, the National Research Council appointed a team of scientists to review the voluminous scientific literature concerning the risk that EMFs may pose to human health. In October 1996 the committee released its report, concluding that "the current body of evidence does not show that exposure to [power-frequency electric and magnetic] fields presents a human-health hazard. Specifically, no conclusive and consistent evidence shows that exposures to residential electric and magnetic fields produce cancer, adverse neuro-behavioral effects, or reproductive and development effects."[23]

If EMFs pose any health risk at all, it would seem to be the heightened incidence of childhood leukemia cases. Summarizing the epidemiological evidence, the NRC report observed that "wire codes are associated with an approximate 1.5-fold excess of childhood leukemia, which is statistically significant."[24] But what are wire codes, and what do they have to do with the strength of EMFs?

In much research "wire codes," which measure the strength of power lines near residences, have been used as a proxy for exposure to EMFs. At first glance it might seem surprising that a proxy would be needed. To assess the relation between EMFs and leukemia, you might assume that scientists would simply measure the strength of the EMFs in some homes in which children developed leukemia and then compare the findings about EMF strength in other homes in which children did not develop leukemia. Higher EMF levels in the homes with stricken children would provide at least suggestive if not conclusive evidence that EMFs pose a risk.

Unfortunately, things aren't so simple. In the report's words, "In only a small number of studies, actual electric-field or magnetic-field measurements were made of an individual's exposure. But even then, the measurements were made of present-day field strengths rather than the strengths to which individuals were exposed when they developed health problems or, for cancer, over the years when the cancer might have been induced."[25] In other words, researchers could not actually measure what they ideally would have liked to measure. Instead, they've had to rely on proxies: differing wire codes "were expected to correlate approximately with electric- and magnetic-field measurements."[26]

The problem is that the rationale for using the wire code proxy turns out to be empirically false. It may seem reasonable to assume that "larger power lines with thicker wires, which serve more residences and other consumers of electricity, carry more current and therefore provide a measure of exposure in the past and over a prolonged period"; but in fact "the reliability of the wire codes as a quantitative measure of exposure to ... magnetic fields is very limited."[27] Wire codes account for only 18 percent of the variance in residential background fields and residential personal exposure.[28]

So even though scientists believe that differences in wire codes are associated with an increased risk of leukemia, they don't think that different levels of exposure to EMFs explain that risk. Wire codes are consequently an unreliable proxy.

If EMFs are not to blame, what explains the association between wire codes and the increased leukemia risk? That's not clear, but some scientists suspect that the wire codes may be serving as a proxy for some other—as yet unidentified—cause. Thus it's conceivable that wire codes may serve as a proxy for poverty: poorer people may be more likely to live on the wrong side of the electromagnetic track (that is, closer to strong power lines), and poorer people generally face a higher cancer risk. Other possibilities (all of which may again correlate with poverty) include proximity to high traffic density, poor air quality, and construction features of older homes.[29]

The crucial point, though, is that scientists have had to rely on a proxy measurement, and the chosen proxy is misleading. As University of Maryland physicist Robert Park has noted (citing an Office of Technology Assessment estimate), the EMF "controversy has cost the public between $1 billion and $3 billion per year in litigation, lost property values, higher utility bills and relocated power lines." And those costs have resulted in large part from flawed research, which did not "actually measur[e] the [electromagnetic] fields inside homes, [but] . . . relied on the size and location of external power lines" as a proxy.[30]

A Pox on All Your Proxies

Often researchers measure the wrong thing. They can do so (as in the hunger and poverty examples) because the "right thing" is an amorphous concept that's hard to pin down precisely. Or they can do so (as in the EMF example) even when they know exactly what the right thing is, but they cannot measure it directly.

In either case, research results can't be comprehended unless we realize what is being measured and why. In reports of research on hunger and poverty, too often the central question of exactly how those terms ought to be defined is ignored. Insofar as researchers don't really measure what they claim to be measuring, their findings can be less than illuminating. In fact, the conventional research paradigm can call to mind the act of a dog chasing (and, of course, failing to catch) its own tail. Researchers ostensibly concerned with hunger really treat hunger as a synonym for poverty; but researchers ostensibly concerned with poverty really regard poverty as a synonym for low income. Practically no one actually measures poverty, which might best be done by seeing how many people's lives are currently blighted by problems (like hunger!).

The result is a vicious circle that is well described by Gertrude Stein's famous dismissal of Oakland: "There's no there there." Our point is not that poverty and hunger themselves do not exist; we don't contend that "poverty" and "hunger" are conceptually meaningless, nor do we make any empirical claim that poverty and hunger no longer exist in contemporary America. In short, it's not the *object* of researchers' investigations—to determine the extent of hunger and poverty—that we question; instead, it's their *methods*. The proxy measurements that are most often employed just don't seem adequate to the task.

As we have seen, the problem with proxies in the natural sciences is somewhat different. Researchers know very well what they mean by electromagnetic fields; but for technical reasons, people's exposure to EMFs (particularly their exposure in the past) can't readily be measured. Scientists necessarily measure by proxy when they can't measure directly. To give another example, ethical constraints prevent medical researchers from administering suspected carcinogens to people in experiments. As a result, the suspect substances are administered in experiments to rodents instead, even though rodents seem to be unreliable proxies for human beings in assessing the substances' impact.[31]

It's clear that we want to know answers to certain questions. But it's also clear that it may be hard to get answers to them and that proxies do not always provide particularly meaningful or reliable answers. News accounts that gloss over this problem fail to point out the limitations—at times the unavoidable limitations—of research. We can illustrate the difficulty with an analogy: when a basketball player makes a lucky shot, an announcer will occasionally say "They don't ask how; they just ask how many." That may be true in basketball, but not when it comes to scientific research. Reporters shouldn't say "how many" (people are hungry, poor, endangered by high exposure to EMFs, etc.) unless they also say "how" (the researcher arrived at the number).

CHAPTER 5

IS THE GLASS HALF EMPTY OR HALF FULL?
A Look at Statistics from Both Sides Now

D id a Census Bureau study show (as one newspaper concluded) that the number of two-parent families was up? If so, why did a second newspaper account declare that traditional families were actually becoming less common? It turns out that both of these seemingly contradictory conclusions emerged from the exact same research.

The Centers for Disease Control and Prevention (CDC) found that the proportion of women among all patients diagnosed with AIDS was higher than ever before. Was this good news for women or bad news? You'd assume bad news, but probably it's actually good news.

Research appearing in the *Journal of the American Medical Association* (*JAMA*) concluded that infectious diseases, the fifth-highest cause of death in 1980, were now ranked third among all causes of death. Terrible news, you say? Yes, but it's actually also good news.

Did the Federal Reserve Bank of Chicago determine that mortgage applications from minorities were rejected twice as often or that they were approved eight-ninths as often? The correct answer again is "both."

In 1993 only 3.5 percent of senior executive positions at the National Institutes of Health (NIH), a federal agency located near Washington, D.C., were filled by blacks. On the other hand, blacks comprised 41.7 percent of all technical workers in the agency and more than 50 percent of the clerical workers. Do these figures show that blacks were discriminated against in hiring for the most prestigious jobs? Or are they instead consistent with the possibility that blacks were unfairly denied less-skilled positions for which they should have been hired?

These five stories, spanning research in the social and natural sciences, share a common theme. The initial assumption in all of these cases might be that the data speak fairly clearly: we know what the facts are, so we can easily conclude whether the news is bad or good (and easily assign praise or blame to the responsible parties). But a deeper probing shows that things are somewhat more complicated. Newspaper reports too seldom make apparent the often deep ambiguity of data. That's true not just in the obvious cases, when two studies will come to opposite conclusions, with Dr. X's research showing (to make up an example) that orange juice wards off cancer, while Dr. Y's research finds that drinking Minute Maid is almost as bad for you as smoking Marlboros.

The point we're making here may be less obvious. It's not that two bits of data can contradict one another; it's that the same bit of data can be read in (at least) two ways. For understandable reasons, press accounts generally provide not only the data but also the conclusion to be drawn from the data. That's fine as far as it goes. But the problem is that news stories often don't probe deeply enough, so they don't show how the data are amenable not only to one "obvious" reading, but also to a second, less apparent reading that can draw a radically different conclusion from the same data.

A classic (though probably apocryphal) example of this phenomenon is the contrasting newspaper coverage of a two-car race between Soviets and Americans during the Cold War. An American newspaper described the race this way: "American car beats out Soviet competitor." But a Russian newspaper told the exact same story somewhat differently: "Soviet car finishes second; American car is next-to-last." The Russian summary was just as accurate as the American one; the two accounts told the same story, only in ways designed to leave the reader with very different impressions.

In this chapter we'll look at some of the ways in which different stories can be told about ambiguous data. We'll illustrate our account with press stories that too often are content to indicate only that the glass is half full (or half empty)—without pausing to explain that in fact the same glass is both things at the same time.

Family Findings

A Census Bureau report, "Household and Family Characteristics," (March 1994) found that there were almost 25.1 million married couples with children, an increase of over half a million from the 1990 level and close to the 1970 peak of 25.5 million. The *USA Today* front-page story was headlined "Number of Two-Parent Families Up."[1] *USA Today* chose to emphasize the raw number of two-parent families, which was indeed up. Only in the fourth and fifth paragraphs did the story note that the number of single parents had also risen, going from 3.8 million in 1970, to 9.7 million in 1990, and to 11.4 million in 1994.

The *Washington Times* take on the Census report (again in a front-page story) was notably different.[2] The *Times* headline was "'Traditional' Families Less Common." Although the article's lead sentence began with the point made in *USA Today* ("'Traditional' families made up of two parents and their children are becoming more plentiful in number"), it then put a notably different spin on the research findings, noting that two-parent families were "still shrinking as a percentage of American households." (As the Census defines the terms, a household is a housing unit occupied by one or more persons; a family household consists of two or more persons, with one being the householder and at least one of the others a relative by birth, marriage, or adoption.)

A reader of *USA Today* could perhaps have guessed that two-parent families were still decreasing as a percentage of all households, since that paper's story also spoke of a continued increase in single-parent families. But *USA Today* did not directly address the issue of two-parent families as a percentage of all households. The *Washington Times*, by contrast, highlighted not the raw numbers but the percentages. Its article stressed that the number of households with two parents and at least one child under eighteen has continued to drop, going from 40.3 percent in 1970 to 25.8 percent in 1990. Furthermore, among family groups with children, 87.1 percent in 1970 had two parents, down to 69.2 percent in 1994; and single-parent families went from 12.8 percent in 1970 to 30.8 percent in 1994.

In short, the reported stories about two-parent families are very different, depending on whether you emphasize raw numbers or the percentage of the whole—either of all households or of all families. The crucial thing to realize is that a rise in raw numbers in one category can coincide with a drop in that category's percentage of the whole, provided that the raw numbers rise still more sharply in the other categories.

In this case the rise in raw numbers for two-parent families is somewhat misleading. Since the population is growing, and more households are forming (particularly among baby boomers who are now at an appropriate age to have kids), you might expect the absolute number of two-parent families to grow. But to get a sense of whether such families are actually becoming more common, you also should know what percentage of all households (and of all families) is made up of two-parent families. Here the *Times* story was more informative than *USA Today*'s.

Interestingly, despite their contrasting emphases, both stories shared a flaw common to many news stories on many subjects: they made too much of a limited sample of data. Both papers ignored the Census report's caution "not to place too much emphasis on changes that occur over any one-year period."[3] Newspapers, of course, like to stress the importance of the news they report, not to qualify or minimize its possible significance.

But the disparity between the two contrasting accounts nicely exemplifies how the same data can be read in almost diametrically different ways. *USA Today* pointed to the continued rise in single-parent families, and the *Washington Times* began by acknowledging the numerical rise in two-parent families. You draw one conclusion if you emphasize the raw data and a substantially different conclusion if you emphasize the percentages. In cases like these, the most informative news stories will therefore give you both sorts of data, enabling you to draw the appropriate conclusions yourself.

AIDS among Women

A similar discrepancy between raw data and percentages is at work in the CDC's discussion of women diagnosed with AIDS. Consider, for example, a *Chicago Tribune* article reporting that "women accounted for 19 percent of all AIDS cases among adults and adolescents [in 1995], their highest proportion yet."[4]

This report (courtesy of the Associated Press) accurately summarized the CDC's own take on its findings. In its 1995 year-end *HIV/AIDS*

Surveillance Report, the CDC declared that "women accounted for 19 percent of adult/adolescent AIDS cases in 1995, the highest proportion yet reported among women."[5] Note, though, that the CDC summary provided only a percentage for women's cases—not raw data.

That omission is significant, because the raw data, provided in one of the report's tables, tell a very different story. As we saw in chapter 1, the number of AIDS cases diagnosed in 1995 fell substantially from the 1994 total, going from 78,863 to 73,380. Not surprisingly, then, the number of cases among men fell, declining from 64,975 to 59,616. Significantly, though, *the number of cases among women also dropped*, falling from 13,887 to 13,764. Women's cases increased as a percentage of all cases; however, women's cases decreased in raw numbers.[6]

In this example we see the mirror image of the two-parent–family example: here a rise in one category's percentage of the whole turns out to be consistent with a decline in raw numbers. By definition, the total of all people diagnosed with AIDS in 1995 had to equal 100 percent; and because the number of infections among males declined, the percentage of females among those infected rose. Since AIDS diagnoses among men fell still more sharply than they did among women, the small *decrease* in the actual number of women's new cases in 1995 (123 fewer than in 1994) registered as a small *increase* in the percentage of all cases (from 18 percent to 19 percent). For this reason, the focus on the percentage of all cases—which the CDC's presentation of its findings encouraged—wrongly suggested that the 1995 news was bad for women. In fact, the 1995 news, while good for women, was simply less good for them than it was for men.[7]

The CDC has been accused of underwriting a misleading public relations campaign, designed to convince Americans that AIDS is "an equal-opportunity scourge," even though "the disease was, and remains, largely the scourge of gay men, intravenous drug users, their sex partners and their newborn children."[8] Emphasizing that the *percentage* of women among those diagnosed with AIDS has risen while ignoring the fact that the *absolute number* of women diagnosed with AIDS has fallen would seem to be consistent with the strategy to create a false AIDS universalism, suggesting that all are equally at risk.

Our more general point, though, is once again that a statistic is amenable to very different interpretations. A rise in the percentage of women among people diagnosed with AIDS seems much more ominous if you don't realize that the total number of women diagnosed with AIDS actually fell. Again, it's a good idea to be skeptical of a news story that cites only percentages, or only raw numbers; stories that cite both are more likely to enable you to realize whether the glass is half empty or half full.

Dying of Infectious Diseases

An article appearing in the *JAMA*, which captured much media attention early in 1996, pointed to a disturbing rise in mortality from infectious diseases. Media coverage of the article was overwhelmingly bleak in tone, as it recorded the apparent failure of American medicine to put an end to the scourge of infectious diseases. One particular finding mentioned in the *JAMA* article was that infectious diseases, which had been the fifth leading cause of death in 1980, had surged to become the third leading killer in 1992.[9] This fact was reported in the *Los Angeles Times*[10] and on *ABC World News Tonight*.[11]

The problem is that this finding is not terribly informative all by itself. It is true that deaths from accidents and strokes exceeded deaths from infectious diseases in 1980 and that deaths from infectious diseases exceeded deaths from accidents and strokes in 1992. But what conclusions can we draw from this shift?

In the absence of additional information, very little. The shift could mean that deaths from infectious diseases had increased during the twelve-year time span (which would be bad news), but it could also mean that deaths from accidents and strokes had decreased (which would be good news). The mere fact that A has become more common than B tells you only about the relationship between A and B; it tells you nothing about whether either A or B is now more (or less) common than it used to be.

What really did happen in the mortality statistics between 1980 and 1992? In fact, the news was both good and bad. The good news— ignored in the coverage of death increases from infectious diseases—was that deaths from accidents and strokes had significantly declined, going from 42.3 to 29.4 per 100,000 people (for accidents) and from 40.8 to 26.2 per 100,000 (for strokes).[12]

According to the *JAMA* article, there were 41.1 deaths from infectious diseases per 100,000 people in 1980, which means that even if the rate had remained steady at 41.1 (or fallen more than 25 percent to 30 deaths per 100,000), it would still have exceeded the death rates for accidents and strokes in 1992. It is true that the death rate from infectious diseases rose significantly between 1980 and 1992, to 65.1 deaths per 100,000 people. This increase, however, chiefly reflected the onset of AIDS and the failure to adjust the data for the aging of the American population, hence the increased likelihood of deaths, from 1980 to 1992. In other words, more deaths would be expected for 1992 than for 1980, simply because there were more elderly people in the latter year; but the presence of more of the elderly, of course, is a sign of medical success rather than failure.

In any case, the switch in positions between infectious diseases and accidents and strokes must be understood both as bad news about infectious diseases and good news about accidents and strokes. In other words, while infectious-disease deaths increased, it's also important to realize that deaths from the other causes decreased; paradoxically, what appears as the increased likelihood of death from infectious diseases should also be considered good news about the decreased likelihood of other causes of death. If people who in the past might have died of strokes now succumb later on to an infectious disease, that is not unambiguously good news—but it is not unambiguously bad news either.

Thus the surge of infectious diseases to the number-three position on the mortality tables needed to be, and lamentably was not, put in perspective. In this context, an observation by the noted economist John Maynard Keynes is particularly relevant: in the long run, we are all dead. If a cure is found for a particular mortal disease, eventually more people must necessarily die of other causes. (The converse is equally true. For example, deaths from AIDS are presumably reducing the toll of deaths from lung cancer; if AIDS did not exist, some of its victims would certainly have lived long enough to come down with—and die of—lung cancer.) Thus, when you examine a population over a long enough period of time, it is mathematically certain that all causes of death cannot decline simultaneously. As people age, they unfortunately must die of something; and if they do not die of cancer or heart disease, they are likely to die of infectious diseases like pneumonia.

The more general point is that reports of unalloyed bad news (and, for that matter, good news) should generally be viewed skeptically, because phenomena tend to interact. More of one bad thing may mean less of a contrasting good thing, but it will often mean less of some other bad thing as well. To give another example, unemployment resulting from technological innovation is generally balanced out (though not immediately, and not for the exact same pool of workers) by increased job opportunities resulting from the same technological innovation that eliminated jobs. Properly understood, statistics often bear out some familiar bromides: clouds do have silver linings, and even an ill wind will blow somebody good. Even news that is bad, when put into perspective, can often be shown to have its good side as well.

Mortgages for Minorities

The Federal Reserve Bank of Chicago published a study comparing the treatment of white and minority mortgage applicants with bad credit histories. The study found that blacks and Hispanics with bad credit received their loans 81.19 percent of the time, whereas whites with similar histories received loans 89.62 percent of the time.

A number of questions can be raised about how to explain that discrepancy. Most obviously, we would want to know whether it is explained by racial discrimination. Drawing that conclusion, however, might be complicated, because one can wonder whether people with bad credit histories comprise a useful category. Some people in the group presumably have much worse credit histories than others, so it may not be meaningful or fair to lump all of them into the same category.

Our concern here, though, is more technical. We aren't as interested in how to interpret the finding as how to report it. The question is whether to focus on the percentages of people who received loans (as we did above) or the percentages of those denied them. Focusing on denials makes the disparity between whites and minorities seem much larger.

Thus the *New York Times* story on the Chicago study began with this lead sentence: "White mortgage applicants with bad credit histories were only half as likely to be rejected for loans as black or Hispanic applicants with similar credit records."[13] Why only half as likely? Because the percentage of rejected whites (100 percent minus the 89.62 percent who were approved, or 10.38 percent) is indeed close to half the percentage of rejected minori ties (100 percent minus the 81.19 percent who were approved, or 18.81 percent). So a focus on loan recipients (minorities received loans roughly eight-ninths as often as whites) yields a very different impression than a focus on rejects (minorities were rejected almost twice as often).

Which is the more valid comparison? As we argued above (concerning percentages and raw numbers), the best reporting should probably alert readers to both of the comparisons, to enable them to make the judgment themselves. The *Times* account, however, focused only on the rejection data: "Only 9 percent of the white applicants were disapproved, compared with 18 percent of the black and Hispanic applicants."[14] And as John Leo has noted, comparing only the races' rejection rates exaggerates the statistical disparity: "If 99 percent of whites and 98 percent of minorities were successful . . . whites would still be rejected half as often."[15]

The broader statistical issue is usefully treated in a discussion by sociologists Susan E. Mayer and Christopher Jencks.[16] Mayer and Jencks take a hypothetical example—comparing the percentage of the poor with complete kitchens to the percentage of the rich—and note the difficulty that we have already observed: "Since there is no obvious way of deciding whether to focus on the proportion of people with or without kitchens, this general approach soon leads to total confusion." Their proposed answer to the dilemma is to measure "the arithmetic difference between the proportions of rich and poor [in our example, whites and minorities] with each advantage that interests us." In our example, then, the disparity between whites and minorities would be 9 percentage points: the difference between the acceptance rates (or rejection rates) between whites and minorities. "This measure of inequality," they note, "yields the same answer regardless of whether we measure the presence or absence of kitchens" or, in our example, the rejection or acceptance of loan applications. Treating the percentage of rejected minority applicants as a multiple of the percentage of rejected white applicants unfairly exaggerates the statistical disparity.

Employment Disparities

In this section we again look at different outcomes for whites and minorities, this time regarding employment. Here, however, our emphasis is not so much on how to report the size of the difference as on how to interpret the difference.

A *Washington Post* story reported that black employees at the NIH perceived themselves to be victims of employment discrimination. The *Post* provided data that showed disparities in the treatment of blacks and whites in the NIH workforce: "The average salary for white employees at NIH is $44,615; for black males $34,191; and for black females, $29,502." The article went on to note that only eight of the 225 senior executives at the NIH were black, whereas "blacks represent 41.7 percent of all technical workers at the agency, compared with about 26 percent in the nation's clerical work force. Blacks make up more than 50 percent of NIH workers in clerical jobs, NIH figures show."[17]

Is the disparity between blacks' employment in senior executive positions and their employment in technical and clerical jobs evidence of discrimination? Perhaps, but not necessarily.[18] There is no reason to expect that minorities and whites (or, for that matter, women and men) will be equally distributed in all levels of a government agency's workforce.[19] Senior executives are drawn from a different labor pool than are technical and clerical workers, and blacks and whites are unlikely to be equally represented in both pools.

For this reason, a disparity in black representation in the two sorts of jobs could actually be anticipated at NIH or other federal agencies located in or near Washington, D.C. Senior executives would tend to be hired from a national pool of individuals with advanced degrees and administrative and scientific experience; that labor pool includes comparatively few blacks. But the technical jobs (and especially the clerical ones) would tend to be filled chiefly from the area labor pool, which includes a notably high percentage of black workers. Thus, considering the relevant labor pools, we should expect blacks to be better represented among NIH technical and clerical workers than they are in the nation's civilian workforce as a whole and to be worse represented among senior executives.

In short, the disparity between the small percentage of black senior executives and the large percentage of black technical and clerical workers does not prove that blacks were discriminated against in hiring at the senior executive level; evidence for discrimination would at the least require a comparison of the percentage of blacks among those eligible for senior executive positions with the percentage of blacks among those hired. Without such data, we cannot say that blacks were underrepresented among NIH senior executives any more than we can say that whites were underrepresented among NIH technical and clerical personnel.

In fact, the disparity between the small number of black senior executives and the large number of black technical and clerical employees is even consistent with the possibility of employment discrimination against blacks in hiring for technical and clerical positions. If such a disparity is itself seen as evidence of discrimination, it could be lessened in one of two ways: either the percentage of black senior executives could be increased or the percentage of black technical and clerical workers could be decreased. If the fact of heavy minority representation in less prestigious (but often still quite good) positions is thought by itself to show that minorities are discriminated against for the most prestigious positions, an employer might conceivably decide to hire fewer minorities for the former positions. To avoid the appearance of discriminating against blacks for the best jobs, in other words, an employer might end up discriminating against black applicants for other jobs.[20]

The Equal Employment Opportunity Commission tends to examine disparities between the average civil service job ranking of blacks and whites as evidence of whether a federal agency treats minority employees fairly—exactly the sort of data emphasized in the *Post* article. But the difficulty with this approach has been well stated by James P. Scanlan: "That average, however, is . . . often more a reflection of the high minority . . . representation in the lower-grade jobs—which is a good thing—than an indication of the exclusion of minorities . . . from higher-grade jobs. Thus, each year the National Gallery of Art is rated last among federal agencies in relative pay grades for black and white employees, solely because it gives several hundred black residents of greater Washington jobs as security guards."[21]

In short, statistical disparities of the sort we have looked at do not by themselves prove that blacks are discriminated against in hiring for the best jobs; remarkably, they also do not rule out the possibility that blacks are discriminated against in hiring for the less-prestigious jobs in which they appear to be overrepresented. It may seem "obvious" that a disparity demonstrates discrimination; but on closer examination, the discrimination may turn out to be exactly where you didn't expect to find it.

Throughout this chapter we have shown that the "obvious" meaning of a statistic can turn out to be false—or if not false, at least partial and hence misleading. In examining statistics, it's always a good idea to heed singer Joni Mitchell's advice and look at them from "both sides now." Newspaper accounts will often state (or at least imply) that a statistic points in only one direction. Often that is indeed the case; but it frequently happens that the statistic itself will be ambiguous (or that its interpretation can lead one in radically unexpected directions). We hope that these examples will encourage you to see for yourself how often a research finding can be "spun" in two diametrically opposite ways: the same statistical glass often is both half empty and half full.

CHAPTER 6

POLLS APART
The Gertrude Stein Approach to
Making Sense of Contradictory Surveys

We're all aware that different surveys asking questions about the same set of issues can result in startlingly different responses. Here are a few examples.

Does the public support school choice programs that would make it easier for parents to send their children to private schools? The Phi Delta Kappa poll found that 60 percent of respondents oppose school choice. According to a second poll, commissioned by the Center for Education Reform, 73 percent of Americans support it.

Should federal funding for public television be cut back or eliminated? The Public Broadcasting Service (PBS)—not exactly a disinterested party—released the results of a survey showing that over 80 percent of respondents are opposed to cuts. But a *Reader's Digest* poll found that 52 percent of respondents support cuts in federal funding.

What percentage of American teenagers have faced a serious threat of being shot at? If you believe a recent Louis Harris survey, it's 13 percent; but if you believe the federal government's National Crime Victimization Survey (NCVS), it's less than 1 percent.

Do over a third of Americans believe that the Nazi extermination campaign against European Jews may never have happened (as one poll reported)? Or should we believe a second poll, which found that less than one-tenth were unsure of its reality?

In 1991, according to the NCVS, about 130,000 rapes or attempted rapes occurred in the United States. In 1992, the survey upped that figure to over 300,000. Did that startling change point to a dramatic, sudden increase in sexual violence against women? Not according to the Bureau of Justice Statistics (BJS), the agency responsible for the survey. The BJS believes that the change simply resulted from a different way of asking respondents about rape.

A group of researchers conducted two surveys of child abuse, in 1975 and 1985. Their second survey found that reports of child abuse had dropped by almost 50 percent. In 1975, though, respondents were interviewed in their homes whereas 1985 respondents were interviewed on the phone. Could this change in interviewing technique have contributed to the decrease? Or would the change have made an increase in reports more likely?

As all of these examples suggest, the answers that pollsters receive (and newspapers report) greatly depend on precisely what the pollsters ask and how they ask it. For this reason, the most important problem with survey data was outlined in a conversation having nothing to do with polling that took place at the deathbed of the modernist writer Gertrude Stein. Alice B. Toklas, Stein's companion, hoping for a final illumination from her brilliant friend, is reported to have asked this question: "Gertrude, Gertrude, what is the answer?" But Stein offered no blinding insight, instead parrying Toklas's question with one of her own: "Alice, Alice, what is the question?"

The single greatest problem with newspaper coverage of survey results is illustrated in that exchange. Understandably, newspapers are interested in telling us the *answers*, the findings of polls and the conclusions (whether offered by the pollster, the group commissioning the poll, or the newspaper itself) that interpret those findings. But the answers are sometimes determined (and always influenced) by the *questions*—the exact wording of the questions posed by the interviewers, the order in which the questions are asked, and in some cases even the way in which they are asked (in person or via the telephone). For this reason, the answers are seldom very meaningful unless you also know about the questions that elicited them.

Unfortunately, newspapers often fail to provide readers with the questions—in some cases, to be sure, because pollsters do not share them with reporters. On the other hand, newspapers have become increasingly conscientious about providing data concerning a survey's sample. Stories routinely mention the size of a sample (how many people were interviewed in the survey) and the size of the poll's margin of error. For example, candidate A leads candidate B by 52 percent to 38 percent, with a margin of error of plus or minus 3 percent. The real gap between the candidates might be anywhere between 20 points (55 minus 35) and 8 (49 minus 41). But newspaper stories generally pay much less attention to the wording and ordering of questions, which are likely to skew a poll's results much more dramatically. In the words of pollster Burns W. Roper: "The major source of survey error stems from question wording. The smallest error comes from the most often cited source of error, sampling error."[1]

In this chapter we will look at conflicting surveys on six subjects and some of the newspaper stories that they generated to illustrate how questions yield answers. We will begin by looking at some polls in which questions seem to have been worded tendentiously, so as to produce the answers desired by the sponsoring organizations: polls that measured opinion on school choice and federal funding for public broadcasting and a poll that measured the incidence of gun violence among American youths. As we will see, if you ask a tendentious question, you can get a predictable and desired answer.

We then will look at a poll on the Holocaust, where the problem was not tendentiousness but sloppiness: a poorly worded question yielded a shocking answer that turned out to have little validity. If you ask a stupid question (or rather, if you ask a question stupidly), you can get a misleading answer. Next we will look at the revision of the NCVS survey to determine the incidence of sexual violence: the two versions of the survey show that if you ask a question elliptically, you get a different answer than if you ask it directly. Finally, we look at two surveys on child abuse to see the possible impact of asking questions in person and on the telephone.

Choosing among School Choice Polls

According to a front-page story in the [Minneapolis] *Star Tribune*, a poll conducted by Gallup for the Phi Delta Kappa teachers' society found that about 60 percent of the respondents "said students should not be able to attend a private school at public expense."[2] A second front-page story, in the *Christian Science Monitor*, referred to another poll, sponsored by the teachers' union, the National Education Association (NEA): "A recent NEA commissioned poll of Republican voters, a key [school] reform constituency, showed that 61 percent say tax dollars should be spent to improve public schools rather than to assist parents who send their children to private or parochial schools. Nearly 57 percent said they would be less likely to vote for a member of Congress who supports vouchers," that is, giving parents public money to help them defray the costs of sending their children to private schools.[3]

The *Christian Science Monitor* story, which was primarily about the NEA's ambivalence toward school reform (rather than the NEA survey), cited the poll's findings without discussing the questions that had elicited them. The *Star Tribune* article, whose chief focus was the Phi Delta Kappa poll, mentioned that it surveyed "1,329 randomly selected adults nationwide. Its margin of error [wa]s plus or minus 3 percentage points." But the *Star Tribune* did not discuss the wording of the poll's questions, though it did include a dissent from Jeanne Allen, director of the Center for Education Reform, a pro-voucher organization. Allen spoke of "another poll," conducted by the Public Agenda Foundation, which showed that "nearly six of 10 parents with children in public schools would send them to private schools if they could afford it."

Allen later wrote a *Wall Street Journal* op-ed in which she attacked the methodology of the two polls that found opposition to school choice.[4] She claimed, not implausibly, that the polls—both commissioned by organizations of public school employees—elicited opposition to school choice by framing questions likely to evoke it. She objected that the pollsters' questions encouraged "negative responses" by using "loaded phrasing," incorporating terms like "at public expense" or "with public tax dollars." Thus she cited a question from each poll. Phi Delta Kappa: "Do you favor or oppose allowing students and parents to choose a private school to attend at public expense?" NEA: "Do you think that tax dollars should be used to assist parents who send their children to private, parochial or religious schools, or should tax dollars be spent to improve public schools?"

As Allen observed, the NEA question seems particularly tendentious, implying as it does that one can *either* improve public schools *or* introduce school choice; proponents of choice would argue that introducing choice would increase competition between public and private schools, which in turn would spur improvements in public education.

The most interesting aspect of Allen's op-ed, though, was not the critique of the two anti-choice polls, but Allen's discussion of her organization's own poll, which produced (again, not surprisingly) a pro-choice result. Allen claimed that "we crafted our questions to ensure that they were unbiased and informative enough to make clear what we were asking." But she also made this concession: "One can easily object that our group is biased too, since we favor school choice." She encouraged readers to decide for themselves, including the text of one of her poll's questions (to be compared with the other polls'): "How much do you support providing parents with the option of sending their children to the school of their choice—either public, private or parochial—rather than only to the school to which they are assigned?"

Is that question any less tendentious than the other two? Not obviously. Note first that Allen's question seems to presuppose support for school choice: it asks "How much do you support," rather than "Do you support." Furthermore, if the other two polls were tendentious in speaking of "public expense" and "tax dollars," is it not also tendentious to speak only of giving parents "the option" to send their children to private schools as opposed to financial aid, provided by the government, to help them exercise that option? Parents already have the option of sending their kids to private schools; they're not required to send them to public schools. The difficulty is that many parents lack the money to send their kids to private schools. By speaking only of an "option" (and skirting the inconvenient fact that choice proponents favor government support to make the option affordable), the Center for Educational Reform's question was as likely to yield positive responses as the other polls' questions were to yield negative ones. All three polls, in short, seem to have been designed to get the responses wished for by the polls' sponsors.

The lesson seems clear enough: don't trust a poll's answers unless you can examine the poll's questions. In particular, unless you see the poll's questions, don't trust a poll commissioned by an organization that uses the poll to support its own predetermined position, since the questions may well have been rigged to reach the organization's desired conclusion.

Polling for PBS

Leaders of the Republican Congress elected in 1994 advocated cutting if not eliminating federal funding for public broadcasting. In an evident attempt to ward off that threat, PBS commissioned a poll that showed strong popular support for continued funding. The poll was reported, altogether uncritically, in the *Washington Post*: "Nearly half of all Americans—Republicans and Democrats alike—think federal funding for public television should be increased this year, and an additional 35 percent think it should be maintained at its current level, according to a new survey commissioned by the Public Broadcasting System."[5] The article noted that "the survey of 1,005 adults 18 and older was conducted Jan. 5–8 by Opinion Research Corp. of Princeton, N.J. It has a margin of error of plus or minus 3 percent." But this ritual disclaimer about margin of error was not accompanied by a discussion of the ways in which the wording and ordering of questions might have introduced substantially greater errors.

An informative critique of the PBS poll appeared soon thereafter as an op-ed in the [Cleveland] *Plain Dealer*.[6] Ironically, the author of the critique was Richard Morin—who is director of polling for the *Washington Post*. Morin's judgment was as follows: "In critical ways, the survey questionnaire fails to pass methodological muster and seemed, at least to some reputable researchers, to be the kind of poll that gives polling a bad name."

The PBS survey consisted of nine questions, opening with several that apparently aimed to make PBS look good by pointing to the deficiencies of commercial television. In this way the survey could well have increased support for PBS by asking respondents for their assessment only after they had been cued to focus on the supposed failings of commercial television. Pollster Everett Carll Ladd has criticized this tactic, noting that "Clever sequencing [of questions] is the sophisticated manipulator's tool of choice."[7]

Morin's op-ed criticized one of the questions about commercial television, which was worded like this: "A recent study by a psychology professor at a leading university concluded that the amount of violence children see on television has an effect on their likelihood of being aggressive and committing crimes. From what you have seen or heard about this subject, do you agree strongly with that conclusion, agree somewhat, disagree somewhat or disagree strongly?" But as Morin noted, this question (with its reference to "a psychology professor at a leading university") seems designed to elicit agreement from the respondents. In the words of a pollster quoted by Morin, "It would be almost impossible for a respondent to say, 'I have a different point of view from this expert and the findings of that study.'"

Two other questions, which asked directly about PBS, were still more obviously loaded, designed to yield a desired response. In one question respondents were asked, "Which segment of the television viewing audience do you think would suffer more if federal funding for PBS was cut back sharply or eliminated—children or adults?" But asking this is like asking someone if he's stopped beating his wife: the question assumes the validity of the premise that needs to be examined. The question doesn't ask whether or not people really would suffer if federal support for PBS were reduced; it's assumed that they will suffer, and the only question is who will suffer more. PBS could just as well have asked (but for obvious reasons chose not to ask) a question like this: "If federal funding for PBS was cut back sharply or eliminated, do you think that children and/or adults would suffer (a) a great deal; (b) a little; or (c) not at all?"

In a third question, six statements about PBS were read to respondents, who were asked how apt the statements were. Did they describe PBS extremely accurately, somewhat accurately, not very accurately, or not at all accurately? The problem here, Morin argued, was that each of the statements "cast PBS in a bright, favorable light. For example: 'Noncommercial PBS has a higher standard of program quality than commercial TV or cable television' and 'PBS provides more educational and informative benefits to its viewers than most other television.'" Because respondents tend to accept repeated favorable emphases as a sign that researchers want them to express a favorable view (and then to respond accordingly), public opinion is surveyed more accurately if the researcher alternates positive statements with negative ones, inviting respondents to agree or disagree with each. Of course, that's the preferred technique if you really want to find out what people think—not to show that they think what the sponsoring organization wants them to think.

Reader's Digest commissioned a second poll about federal funding for PBS, with very different results. According to this poll, "a majority of

Americans (62 percent) say it is not the government's job to financially support television programming." And while 54 percent of the respondents said that they would be disappointed if Congress cut funding for public television, "when the issue [wa]s posed as part of an overall effort to reduce federal spending, 52 percent agree[d] that cuts *are* justified."[8]

In short, people support federal funding for PBS when they're encouraged to consider it in the context of the vast wasteland of commercial television; but they support a cut in the funding when they're encouraged to consider it in the context of the still vaster wasteland of the federal budget. Context is all. It's not sufficient to know how a question is worded to assess whether a poll's results are meaningful; ideally, you also need to know what the respondents were primed to think about before the question was asked.[9]

Teenagers as Targets

In 1993 Louis Harris conducted a poll to determine how many youths have experienced gun violence; it was commissioned by a philanthropic group (the Joyce Foundation) campaigning to prevent firearms injuries. The poll produced startling results. Among a group of students in grades 6–12, 13 percent claimed that someone had seriously threatened to shoot them in the past year; 11 percent claimed that that they actually had been shot at in the last year. Almost 4 percent claimed to have been wounded in a gunshot attack in the last year; 15 percent claimed to have carried a handgun in the previous month; and 9 percent claimed to have shot a gun at another person in their lifetime, which, given the respondents' ages, must have meant in the past six or seven years.

This survey differs from the others we have looked at in a number of ways. First, it was not a survey of opinions, but of experiences; and experiences are presumably more objective, less fleeting, than opinions. (What do I think about school choice? My opinion may be complicated, and a pollster's yes-or-no question may not elicit the true ambivalence of my view. But have I been shot at in the past year? That's an empirical question, to which I should be able unequivocally to respond "yes" or "no.") Secondly, the population surveyed consisted of adolescents, not adults. Are adolescents more suggestible than adults? Are they more prone to exaggerate or (not to put too fine a point on it) lie, so as to make themselves look cool? Either is surely possible, though by no means certain.

Finally, the questions effectively replicated some of those asked in an official government survey, the NCVS. There isn't (and shouldn't be) an authoritative governmental survey of our opinions about school choice or public broadcasting; but there is an authoritative governmental survey of people's experiences with criminal violence. Each year the Census Bureau (acting on behalf of the BJS) surveys a nationwide sample of about 120,000 persons to determine how many Americans overall have been victims of different sorts of crime. And since the NCVS breaks down its results by respondents' ages, it's not hard to derive figures for a population comparable in age (twelve to nineteen) to that surveyed by the Joyce Foundation.

Significantly, the NCVS's results are far less worrisome, across the board, than the Harris poll's. If NCVS figures are to be believed, each year 1 percent of adolescents claim that someone seriously threatens to shoot them (as opposed to 13 percent in the Harris poll). One-seventh of 1 percent claim that that they actually are shot at (as opposed to 11 percent in the Harris poll), .02 percent claim to have been wounded in a gunshot attack (as opposed to almost 4 percent in the Harris poll), and over a seven-year period perhaps 1 percent claim to have shot a gun at another person (as opposed to 9 percent in the Harris survey).[10]

What could account for the glaring discrepancies between these two sets of figures? In a critique of the Harris poll, Florida State University criminologist Gary Kleck advances a number of hypotheses.[11] First, in this case sampling error may be at issue: the students who were polled may not have comprised a truly representative sample. Harris surveyed 2,508 students in ninety-six schools; principals had to agree before their students could be surveyed. It is possible, Kleck noted, that principals of schools in high-crime areas might have been more supportive of the survey (hence more eager to have their students participate), which would have skewed the sample. Unfortunately, the report of the poll results did not say what percentage of principals agreed to the survey or whether crime rates in the areas with participating schools were typical or atypically high.

Kleck then turns to our usual source of error: the wording of the questions. Here his criticisms were less speculative. The questionnaire began by asking the students to respond to a series of unbalanced statements highlighting the problem of youth violence: the students were cued that the investigators were troubled by the prevalence of youth violence. As Kleck put it, "The authors might as well have asked if the students thought the problem of youth violence as (a) huge, (b) enormous, or (c) very large." Before the students were asked any factual questions, they had read no less than twelve items about violence, and eight others referring specifically to guns or other weapons. At least three of the items asked students to rate how serious gun violence was, or how much they felt endangered by guns. Kleck therefore hypothesizes that in the poll impressionable adolescents were "especially prone to tell the adult surveyors what they apparently wanted to hear."

It seems equally plausible that many of the respondents were not so much eager to be "good" (that is, to give the answers desired by adult authorities) as to be "bad" (that is, to demonstrate how tough they were by recounting fabricated stories about their brushes with firearm violence). But in either case, the Harris poll should not have been reported in the press without some reference to other surveys—drawn from far larger and more reliable samples—with findings that are much less worrisome. Pollster Robert Teeter provides useful advice: "Be very suspicious of any poll that claims to reveal new or startling results. If it's out of line with the other polls, it could very well be wrong."[12]

How was the Harris poll actually covered by the press? Some stories were clearly better than others. The *Los Angeles Times* coverage was poor: it simply reported the results uncritically, with no reference to the NCVS findings or reactions from disinterested parties (whether skeptical or supportive).[13] But the *Boston Globe* report was much more balanced. It included a reaction from a skeptical pollster (G. Donald Ferree Jr. of the Roper Center), who pointed to loaded wording in some of the questions and observed that some of the findings may result from the fact that "it is difficult for many adults answering polls, not to mention teenagers, to acknowledge being ignorant or 'out of the loop.'" The *Globe* also provided data from a survey by the Centers for Disease Control and Prevention (CDC) that contrasted sharply with the Harris poll's finding. According to the CDC, "5.4 percent of high school students said they had carried a gun in the previous 30 days for self-defense or because they thought they might need it"; the comparable figure in the Harris poll was 15 percent.[14]

Best of all was the coverage in the *New York Times*. The *Times* story included reactions from "several experts on guns [who] were skeptical about the results," among them Gary Kleck. It also contrasted the Harris findings with the NCVS results.[15]

The most informative coverage of surveys, in short, will include a range of reactions. The sponsoring organization's take on a poll's findings should be balanced with reactions from experts who may have different perspectives. And the results should always be compared with results from other surveys on the same subject. Again, context is everything; no poll is an island, so it should not be examined in isolation from previous polls that are relevant.

Denying the Holocaust? Or Misunderstanding a Question?

In April 1993, just as the United States Holocaust Memorial Museum opened, the American Jewish Committee (AJC) released the results of a Roper Organization survey that it commissioned, which seemed to show that more than one-third of Americans doubted the reality of the Nazi extermination campaign against European Jews. Twenty-two percent of the survey's respondents thought that the Holocaust might never have occurred; an additional 12 percent did not know.

Appropriately, this finding was the cause of much concern in the media and elsewhere. It was unclear whether a large proportion of the American population consisted of ignoramuses or anti-Semites—either way, the news was disheartening. A *New York Times* editorial understandably worried about "anti-Semitism" and "ignorance."[16] A *San Francisco Chronicle* editorial hypothesized that America was "in deep dumbo" and spoke of "pervasive skepticism," "Holocaust denial," and the "willfully stupid" respondents.[17] But the poll's frightening finding turned out to be false, an artifact, this time, not of tendentiousness but of awkward wording. The AJC and Roper did not intend to alarm the American people, but carelessness, no less than conscious duplicity, can make a survey's conclusion unreliable.

The survey question was deeply confusing, because it was worded as a double negative: "Does it seem possible, or does it seem impossible to you that the Nazi extermination of the Jews never happened?" When

Roper asked the same question more clearly in a later survey ("Does it seem possible to you that the Nazi extermination of the Jews never happened, or do you feel certain that it happened?"), only 1 percent thought that the Holocaust might never have occurred, and only 8 percent said that they did not know. Rewording the question dropped the percentage of those who thought that the Holocaust may have been a fabrication from 22 percent down to 1 percent—and those lacking knowledge from 12 percent down to 8 percent.[18] To his credit, Burns W. Roper, head of the Roper Organization, called attention to the error himself and apologized for it: "I deeply regret this entire incident, and I feel it most important to set the record straight publicly." Roper added that the poorly worded question yielded results that "served to misinform the public, to scare the Jewish community needlessly, and to give aid and comfort to the neo-Nazis who have a commitment to Holocaust denial."[19]

The problem of double negatives, of course, goes beyond this particular example. Questions with double negatives (and awkwardly worded questions in general) can confuse potential respondents, so answers to such questions need to treated with caution. Ironically, Burns W. Roper himself had pointed this out years earlier, in an article in which he compared the results of different wordings of a question about women's capacity to be good business executives. When asked the double negative variant ("Is it not true that women don't make as good executives as men do?"), 50 percent agreed, 42 percent disagreed, and 7 percent didn't know; but when asked to react to a straightforward statement ("Women make as good executives as men do"), 87 percent agreed, only 10 percent disagreed, and just 3 percent didn't know.[20] In short, even where tendentiousness is not at issue, lack of clarity may be. Again, you need to know what the question is before you can interpret its answer.

Asking Directly and Asking Obliquely

The BJS believed that the survey it had been using through 1991 to estimate criminal victimization was seriously undercounting the number of rapes and attempted rapes. Furthermore, the survey provided no information about sexual assaults other than rapes and attempted rapes. For that reason, beginning in 1992 the NCVS (the BJS survey) was altered to obtain different and presumably more reliable figures for the total number of sexual assaults. As a result, data from 1993 and onward regarding rape and sexual assault are no longer comparable to earlier data.

There are obvious difficulties in attempting to estimate the number of sexual assaults through a survey: because sexual assault is such an ugly crime, and because its victims are still often stigmatized, interviewed victims may be unwilling to discuss the experience (especially in the presence of family members, in an interview conducted by strangers). Thus any total will necessarily be uncertain. Still, the BJS believed that an altered questionnaire would produce a higher and more accurate count. Under the old questionnaire, the NCVS found that there had been about 130,000 rapes and attempted rapes per year (between 1987 and 1991). The annual estimate derived from the new questionnaire came to 170,000 rapes, 140,000 attempted rapes, and 190,000 other sexual assaults.

The BJS made it clear that this increase did not mean that sexual assaults had suddenly become much more common, but that an altered interviewing procedure was bringing to light incidents of a sort that had gone unreported in the past. Newspaper accounts of the dramatic rise in the numbers faithfully reported the BJS rationale. The *New York Times* account (taken from the Associated Press) was typical in this respect: "The Federal Government more than doubled its annual estimate today of rapes or attempted rapes—to 310,000. But officials said actual assaults were not up; rather, after years of debate, the Government's biggest crime survey finally asked a direct question about rape."[21] Faulty newspaper reporting is not at issue here. Still, it is remarkable that a different way of asking about some phenomena should double our count of them; it is worth looking briefly at the redesign of the NCVS questionnaire to see once again how different questions produce different answers.

The redesigned survey was intended in part "to produce more accurate reporting of incidents of rape and sexual assault and other crimes committed by intimates and family members. . . . Questions were added to let respondents know that the survey is interested in a broad spectrum of incidents, not just those involving weapons, severe violence, or violence perpetrated by strangers." The questionnaire used through 1992 had not asked about rape directly, asking instead (in the last of six questions about force) "Did anyone TRY to attack you in some other way?"

Thus, not only was rape not asked about directly, it was not even asked about obliquely, since the rape victim herself had to raise the issue, when asked about an attack "in some other way."[22] The new questionnaire poses a direct question about rape. It asks specifically about "any rape, attempted rape, or other type of sexual assault"[23] and also asks about being "forced or coerced to engage in unwanted sexual activity by . . . a casual acquaintance OR someone you know well."

In short, the new questionnaire was designed to uncover more sexual assaults, specifically more of them committed by acquaintances of the victims. In this way it aimed to dissuade respondents from the incorrect presumption that sexual assaults are committed only by strangers. And the redesigned survey discovered what it expected to find: over half of all sexual assaults were committed by acquaintances of the victims, and less than a fifth were perpetrated by strangers.[24] In fact, a remarkable finding, which seems to have gone altogether unnoticed, is that rapes and attempted rapes by strangers actually seem to have *declined* slightly between 1987 and 1991 (the last period covered by the old survey) and 1992 and 1993 (the first period covered by the new one), even though the new survey, designed to correct for a previous undercount, might have been expected to disclose more rapes and attempted rapes by strangers as well.[25]

The more general conclusion, though, relates not to the substance of sexual assault statistics but to the procedure of interviewing respondents: it makes a big difference if you ask elliptically or directly about a sensitive matter. A co-author of the BJS report on violence against women, statistician Ronet Bachman, put it simply: "When you ask directly, you get more information."[26] Once again, what people answer depends on how (not just what) they are asked.

Asking in Person and on the Phone

In 1975 sociologists Murray A. Straus of the University of New Hampshire and Richard J. Gelles of the University of Pennsylvania conducted the National Family Violence Survey to determine the incidence of child abuse and spousal abuse in the United States. In 1985 they conducted a second survey (the National Family Violence Re-Survey) to update their findings. Their most striking discovery was that child abuse (which they defined as kicking, biting, punching, beating, threatening with a gun or knife, or using a gun or knife) had declined by 47 percent among two-parent families with at least one child aged three to seventeen. There were thirty-six incidents of child abuse per thousand children in 1975, but only nineteen such incidents per thousand children in 1985.[27]

Straus and Gelles stressed that this encouraging finding could be interpreted in different ways: child abuse could actually have decreased over the ten years, or respondents could have been more reluctant to admit to child abuse in 1985 than in 1975. They argued that the decrease probably reflected real behavioral changes (resulting from factors such as the rise in average age for first-time parents, the decline in the number of unwanted children, an improved economy, expanded treatment programs for offenders, and a greater sense that child abuse is wrong and that abusers risk punishment). They did not, however, rule out the possibility that abusers were becoming less willing to own up to their deeds in interviews with strangers.[28] Because child abuse is stigmatized, one must always be cautious about equating what people report with what they actually did.

For our purposes, though, the possible impact of the methodological changes between the two surveys is of greatest interest. The 1975 findings on child abuse derived from hour-long in-person interviews with parents in 1,146 households; the 1985 data emerged from thirty-five-minute telephone interviews with parents in 1,428 households.[29] What was the likely impact of the methodological changes between the two surveys?

Interestingly, Straus and Gelles contended that "the differences in methodology should have led to higher, not lower, rates of reported violence." First, "the anonymity offered by the telephone [used in 1985 but not 1975] leads to more truthfulness and, therefore, increased reports of violence." In addition, 85 percent of the 1985 telephone interviews were completed, compared with only 65 percent of the 1975 in-person interviews; and it is "more likely that the violence rate is higher among those who refuse to participate." Thus "a reduction in refusals would tend to produce a higher rate of violence, whereas we found a lower rate of violence in 1985 despite the much lower number of refusals." Finally, in 1975 "never" was an option offered respondents as an answer to questions about violent acts; in 1985, by contrast, the response categories began with "once" and continued to "more than 20 times," so that respondents had to volunteer an answer of "never" themselves. Again, this shift in interviewing technique would tend to have decreased the number of denials that child abuse ever occurred.[30]

In short, the reported decline in child abuse was all the more significant because it seems to have occurred in spite of the methodological changes between the two surveys. We see yet again that survey answers are much more meaningful when they are understood in the context of the way in which the questions are asked. It is interesting to look at newspaper reports of Straus and Gelles's 1985 survey to see how the methodological issues were covered or ignored. Bear in mind that it required no effort to address the survey's methodology; Straus and Gelles did not conceal the methodological issues (as tendentious researchers will sometimes do) but instead called attention to them.

The *New York Times* reporting was exemplary. To begin with, the *Times* story was careful to note (both in the headline and in the body of the story) that the survey examined admissions of child abuse (as opposed to incidents of it): Straus and Gelles necessarily looked at what parents said they did, not what they actually did. The story also took note of the competing interpretations of the decline in reports and explored the possible impact of the switch from in-person to telephone interviews.[31] The *San Diego Union-Tribune* also noted the possible impact of interviewing by telephone;[32] but the *Chicago Tribune*[33] and *Christian Science Monitor*[34] ignored the methodological context for Straus and Gelles's substantive findings. Too often, even when researchers themselves stress the importance of methodology, reporters limit themselves to recounting substantive findings in a procedural vacuum.

Substantive Surveys or Procedural Polls?

As we've seen repeatedly, survey results can be affected dramatically by the ways in which questions are asked; that is why two polls on the same subject taken at the same time can yield very different conclusions. The differences can result from deliberately chosen tendentious wording, introduced by a group that commissions a poll to prove that the public shares its policy stance. Differences can also be produced inadvertently, when one poll's questions are worded clumsily and confuse respondents.

In surveys as in real life, you can get one answer if you ask a question directly and a different answer if you ask it elliptically. In both surveys and real life, it's important to know the context in which a question is asked: people will view, say, hot fudge sundaes one way in a context provided by the American Dairy Association, but rather differently in a context provided by the American Dental Association or the American Heart Association.

For these reasons, simply knowing the answers generated by a survey is never sufficient to understand what its findings mean. Furthermore, simply knowing the answers is completely useless if the survey's reliability is to be judged—as it obviously must. That is why the best and most informative newspaper coverage of surveys will offer considerable information about the questions as well as the answers. A survey's substantive conclusions mean little or nothing if the survey's procedures go unexamined.

Substantive answers, of course, are what interest us, because we want to know what public opinion is. The journalistic emphasis on substance as opposed to procedure is therefore altogether understandable. But a survey's answers accurately gauge public opinion only to the extent that they are responses to questions that fairly measure it rather than illicitly shaping it through loaded wording and prejudicial sequencing. Inside each of us, reporter and newspaper reader alike, is an Alice B. Toklas demanding to know the answer; but she very much needs to be balanced by a Gertrude Stein inquiring about the question.

CHAPTER 7

THE REALITY AND RHETORIC OF RISK
Telling It Like It Is—and Isn't

The media have often trumpeted—and often questioned—the claim that one out of eight American women will contract breast cancer. What does the statistic mean, and why is it so controversial?

A campaign to increase government regulation of meat safety emphasized that *E. coli* bacteria found in meat cause 20,000 illnesses and 500 deaths a year in the United States. How accurate are the numbers? How relevant are they to the debate over regulation?

A front-page *Washington Post* story called attention to a large number of deformities found in Minnesota frogs. Are humans at risk as well?

By now it's almost a commonplace that many Americans are overly afraid of risks[1]—and that their fears are often magnified by alarmist reporting.[2] Why are journalists sometimes prone to exaggerate the health and environmental risks faced by Americans? We can suggest a few preliminary answers, drawing from a substantial literature addressing this question.

First, the media primarily focus on events, for example, an oil spill or a forest fire, rather than risk per se. Reporters covering an oil spill or a forest fire are often prone to assume that the event poses a grave environmental risk or has caused serious ecological damage. What should be examined, the extent or gravity of the harm, can easily be assumed.[3] In the words of John Graham, director of the Center for Risk Analysis at the Harvard School of Public Health, "What constitutes news is not necessarily what constitutes a significant public health problem." Instead the media tend to cover "the bizarre, the mysterious, that which people have difficulty imagining happening."[4]

Because reporting about hazards "is ordinarily reporting about events rather than issues, about immediate consequences rather than long-term consideration, about harms rather than risks," stories seldom offer "precise information about risks," even when it is available.[5] In that respect, what may be most noteworthy about reporting of risks is that "very little direct information" is actually provided "about the risks associated with different types of hazards. Instead, the public is left to infer the extent of danger from the amount and prominence of the coverage a hazard receives."[6]

If the media seldom excel at quantifying risk, that is largely because doing so might get in the way of telling a good (by which we mean an exciting, not necessarily an accurate) story related to risk. It's not surprising that researchers have found that stories "involving especially dramatic news of real or potential danger" are the ones that make the deepest impression on news consumers,[7] so it's also not surprising that those stories are favored by those who report the news. In other words, an attention-grabbing rhetoric of risk—you'd better worry, because we're in danger—can sometimes trump the more prosaic reality that a risk is relatively inconsequential.

The desire to tell a good story explains the emphasis, particularly pronounced in television news, to include a vignette to accompany a story. Thus a study about, say, the risks of suffering a heart attack while exercising might be illustrated with the interview of the widow of a man who died while swimming. In such a case, of course, you can wonder "what the viewer is likely to remember: the careful account of the study itself, which concludes that the benefits of exercise outweigh its costs, or the grieving widow's dramatic account of her husband's death while exercising?"[8]

Drama, of course, is most compelling when there are heroes and villains. Thus researchers have found that "risks tend to be perceived as more serious when there is someone to blame." For example, the public is more concerned about radon that results from industrial waste disposal than radon emanating from natural deposits of radioactive rock, even though scientists believe that "natural" radon actually poses a greater risk than "man-made" radon.[9] And reporting on risk often caters to this popular predisposition, by attributing too much responsibility to individual actors such as corporations, who, unlike the blind forces of nature, can be blamed when things go wrong.[10]

Furthermore, the interest in drama means that the qualifications, caveats, and uncertainties that are the bread and butter of scientific research can instead be treated as the roughage of journalistic accounts. As we have seen repeatedly in this volume, the procedural and methodological components of scientific research—which often determine the conclusions, and always shape them decisively—tend to be downplayed if not altogether ignored in news accounts that concentrate on a study's substantive conclusions.[11] But we can't, of course, rely on research declaring that a certain chemical does (or does not) pose a risk unless we also know how the research arrives at its conclusion.

Finally, scientific researchers themselves obviously understand the media's interest in good stories and dislike for qualifications. As a result, some researchers and activists have clearly adopted a tactic candidly described by climatologist Stephen H. Schneider, a believer in the danger posed by global warming.

> On the one hand, as scientists we are ethically bound to the scientific method, in effect promising to tell the truth, the whole truth and nothing but—which means that we must include all the doubts, the caveats, the ifs, ands, and buts. On the other hand, we are not just scientists but human beings as well. And like most people we'd like to see the world a better place, which in this context translates into our working to reduce the risk of potentially disastrous climatic change. To do that we need to get some broad-based support, to capture the public's imagination. That, of course, means getting loads of media coverage. So we have to offer up scary scenarios, make simplified, dramatic statements, and make little mention of any doubts we might have.[12]

Schneider's statement nicely illustrates the tension between being a scholar (aiming to understand the world) and being an activist (aiming to make it "a better place"). Environmental activists often are only too eager to feed journalists just the sort of story—and just the sort of science—that many journalists like. Activists tell dramatic stories, with suffering innocents who are victimized by culpable forces of evil; their brand of "science" also tends to eliminate the caveats and equivocations that are the hallmark of genuine science. For that reason, media exaggeration of risk ultimately stems from activist exaggeration of risk.

Many activists excel at getting the media to act as their intermediaries by bringing the activist message to the broader public. At the same time, some reporters on the environmental beat are clearly eager to transmit that message. Thus Charles Alexander, a senior editor at *Time* magazine, freely admitted at a 1989 Smithsonian Institution conference on the environment that "on this issue we [journalists] have crossed the boundary from news reporting to advocacy."[13]

Which risks do Americans take seriously and which do they mostly ignore? We seem to worry more than we should about some things and less than we should about others, for reasons that transcend (though they may help explain) the impact of activists or the media. Psychological and cultural factors are clearly important. In the view of risk specialists Paul Slovic and Baruch Fischhoff (summarized in a *New York Times* article), "Easily tolerated risks include ones that people can choose to avoid (chain saws, skiing), that are familiar to those exposed (smoking), or that have been around a long time (fireworks). Poorly tolerated risks are involuntary (exposure to nuclear waste), have long delayed effects (pesticides), or unknown effects (genetic engineering)."[14] Slovic has also found that risk perception is influenced by race and gender: blacks tend to worry more about environmental and health risks posed by things like electromagnetic fields and global warming than do whites, and white women tend to worry more about them than white men.[15]

In any event, it is noteworthy that popular beliefs—however erroneous— rather than expert opinion largely determine our allocation of resources to lessen and eliminate risks. Thus in a 1987 report the Environmental Protection Agency (EPA) declared that "overall, [its] priorities appear more closely aligned with public opinion than with [its] estimated risks."[16] Although the media do not simply determine public opinion, it is nevertheless reasonable to suppose that they play a role in shaping it. "What the mass media report about hazards—which ones they select for emphasis and what information they present about them—becomes crucial in shaping public perceptions of hazards and their attendant risks."[17]

Having laid this theoretical groundwork, let's turn now to our case studies. In our first example (breast cancer) we'll concentrate on interpreting risk data; in the second (illnesses caused by *E. coli* bacteria in beef) we'll focus on arriving at the data and policy responses to the risk. In our third (frog deformities) we briefly explore a purported risk for which no data exist.

The Breast Cancer Debate over One in Eight

The popular perception that breast cancer poses an enormous risk to women is a sign of the remarkable success of activist groups that have moved the fight against it to the top of the national health agenda. An indication of the size of the activist movement is evident in a *New York Times Magazine* report that "women with breast cancer are turning scores of support groups into a national political advocacy movement" that incorporates "more than 180 advocacy groups . . . united under the National Breast Cancer Coalition."[18] The activists have attempted to drum up support by emphasizing—and, we will see, exaggerating—the very grave danger posed by breast cancer. Activists work tirelessly to publicize claims (derived from authoritative bodies like the American Cancer Society and the National Cancer Institute) that American women face a one-in-nine (or one-in-eight) chance of falling ill with the dreaded disease.

These efforts have borne obvious fruits, in the form of heightened media attention and increased governmental funding for breast cancer research. *Los Angeles Times* media critic David Shaw has observed that in 1993 about 46,000 American women died of breast cancer, and about 38,000 American men died of prostate cancer. Breast cancer therefore killed 22 percent more people than prostate cancer. Yet breast cancer was mentioned almost 5,800 times in major magazine and newspaper stories in 1993, compared with fewer than 1,800 mentions for prostate cancer. In other words, breast cancer received 233 percent more attention from the media. Significantly, the greater media attention given to breast cancer correlated with far more government funding for breast cancer research. In 1993 the National Cancer Institute earmarked $213 million for breast cancer research, compared with only $51 million for prostate cancer research. As Shaw pointed out, this 418 percent difference "is much closer to the relative media coverage of the diseases than to the relative number of deaths."[19]

Still, the political success of breast cancer activists comes at a price: the continual emphasis on the disease's horrors (to justify funding increases) seems also to have created a large disparity between women's perception of their risk from breast cancer and the reality of that risk. Thus Dr. Eugene Pergament of Illinois's Northwestern Memorial Hospital High Risk Breast Cancer Center claims that "the difference between [women's] actual risk and what they perceive is astounding." Pergament conducted a survey of 150 women who are at high risk for breast cancer, because family members have contracted the disease; their actual breast cancer risk was 6 percent, but their perceived risk was 36 percent, or six times greater.[20]

Summarizing May 1995 research that appeared in the *Journal of the National Cancer Institute*, Dr. David Plotkin reported an even more impressive finding. He noted that "the median estimate female Baby Boomers gave of their chance of dying of breast cancer within a decade was 10 percent. A substantial minority thought the risk was 30 percent or more. In fact, the likelihood that a woman in her forties will die of breast cancer in the next ten years of her life is on the order of 0.4 percent."[21]

The one-in-eight statistic referring to breast cancer risk is undeniably frightening—especially in contrast to the one-in-twenty risk that prevailed in 1960.[22] But what does it mean? The National Cancer Institute (NCI) currently calculates that a baby girl born today faces a 12.3 percent risk of developing breast cancer during her life, which does indeed translate into roughly one in eight. But that figure assumes, first of all, that the incidence of the disease will not change in the future, which may or may not be true. Of greater importance, 12.3 percent is a lifetime figure, which assumes that the baby girl will live to age ninety-five. But the more relevant figure for an individual woman is her risk at any specific age. In the words of Edward J. Sondik, deputy director of NCI's Division of Cancer Prevention and Control, "Lifetime risk . . . is not the same thing as the risk that a woman is exposed to at any given time in her life."[23]

Thus a forty-year-old woman has a 1.6 percent chance of getting breast cancer by the time she turns fifty, which is a one-in-sixty-three chance, not one in eight. A fifty-year-old has a 2.4 percent chance of contracting the disease by age sixty, a one-in-forty-one chance. The ten-year odds for a sixty-year-old woman rise to one in twenty-eight and those for a seventy-year-old to one in twenty-four. The risk then starts to decline, as the chances of succumbing to other diseases of old age increase: an eighty-year-old's risk is one in twenty-nine.

At no particular point in a woman's life, then, is the risk nearly as high as one in eight. Up until about age eighty, the odds of getting breast cancer increase over the short term. At the same time, though, a woman's lifetime risk actually declines as she ages, since a fifty-year-old has already weathered some of the years that are included in the lifetime calculation that there is a one-in-eight risk. (That is to say, the baby girl has a one-in-eight lifetime chance of contracting breast cancer, which includes the chance that she may contract the disease in her forties; but the fifty-year-old's lifetime chance is lower, because clearly she can no longer get breast cancer in her forties.[24])

Thus the one-in-eight statistic is something of an artifact that does not speak to the odds facing any individual woman—odds that are themselves strongly affected by factors like family history, age at menarche (that is, the age when a woman begins to menstruate), and age when a woman first gives birth.[25] For this reason, Elin Bank Greenberg, chairman of the Susan G. Komen Breast Cancer Foundation, has argued that "There's only one reason to use those numbers [like one in eight], and that is to frighten women." In reality, "among women aged 50, one in 50 will get the disease; the rate increases with age, and the true risks are being female and getting older."[26]

What causes breast cancer? Many activists, searching for someone or something to blame, have focused on the environment. In the words of Jane Alsobrook of the Los Angeles Breast Cancer Alliance, "People keep looking at the link to hormones and the diet. But it's the environment that seems suspicious to us."[27] Another activist has suggested that emphasizing risk factors like a woman's age when she first gives birth or her decision not to breastfeed amounts to "blaming the victim."[28] But if victims should not be blamed, it's also true that one's preferred villains are sometimes not guilty: the best current evidence "finds no link between breast cancer and exposure to the pesticide DDT or to the industrial chemicals known as PCBs."[29]

The search for a villain to blame for breast cancer is psychologically understandable, even if it may not be scientifically defensible. The disease certainly seems to have worsened over time. Breast cancer incidence has risen from 85 cases per 100,000 women in 1980 to 112 per 100,000 in 1987. But that increase is thought to have stemmed largely (though not entirely) from demographic change (as female products of the baby boom entered the age cohort in which diagnoses become more common) and, especially, improved diagnostic techniques (the introduction of mammography, which made possible the early detection of cancers that would previously have been discovered later or even gone undiscovered). In recent years breast cancer incidence has actually declined.

Writing in the *Atlantic Monthly*, Dr. David Plotkin has hypothesized that the residual increase in breast cancer (that is, the increase that remains after one accounts for demographic factors and improved diagnostic capability) may result from a surprising source—the hormonal factor rejected by Jane Alsobrook. "The expansion of opportunities for women, especially in the industrialized West, [has] altered not only women's lives but also their bodies, and especially their cycles of reproductive hormones—apparently making them more susceptible to certain cancers."

Plotkin notes that women today ovulate much more frequently than they did in the past, when menarche was later, pregnancies began earlier and were more frequent, and menopause was earlier. Thus women today "expos[e] their breasts to historically unprecedented numbers of estrogen-progesterone cycles." And since the female hormones estrogen and progesterone multiply cells within the breast (and cellular multiplication increases the likelihood of the genetic accidents that cause cancer), "the strong suspicion is that repeated menstruation is a precursor to cancer of the breast." Plotkin's paradoxical conclusion, then, is that the increased incidence of breast cancer "may be an unwanted accompaniment to what most Americans view as social and material progress [for women]."[30]

What role have the media played in the activist campaign to alter our understanding of breast cancer? As we saw above, David Shaw has suggested that the media may well have been instrumental in helping the activists get their questionable message across. Even today, one can occasionally find articles in which their assertions are uncritically reproduced. In particular, unbalanced stories often appear because of the media's penchant for personalizing issues. It is not at all uncommon to read glowing profiles of women who suffer from breast cancer, whose status as victims is somehow thought to make them authorities on the disease's incidence and causation.[31]

Nevertheless, our citations clearly indicate that in recent years American newspapers have published many informative analyses of breast cancer statistics. Activist contentions have repeatedly been questioned, and alternative interpretations of the statistics have been readily offered. In this notable instance, the print media have often excelled at explaining the realities of risk.

Do We Dare to Eat the Meat?

In 1995 a fierce political battle raged over whether to alter the way in which meat is inspected by the United States Department of Agriculture (USDA) to determine its safety. The USDA itself advocated putting samples of beef under a microscope. Proponents of the change included consumer organizations like Safe Tables Our Priority (STOP) and the Center for Science in the Public Interest (CSPI); they noted that the inspection system, in which inspectors look at a side of beef, poke it, and sniff it, had gone unchanged since 1906 and could not detect the presence of deadly microorganisms that might contaminate the beef. The meat industry responded, contending that the regulation would be ineffective and would place an excessive financial burden on small producers.

Much of the controversy centered upon the threat posed by *E. coli* O157:H7, a particularly virulent strain of bacteria. As our introductory analysis of media tendencies would predict, a specific outbreak was chiefly responsible for the attention to *E. coli*. In 1993, when hamburgers contaminated by *E. coli* were sold at Seattle outlets of the Jack in the Box fast-food chain, four children died and several hundred people fell ill.

Activists and journalists involved in the 1995 regulatory debate occasionally personalized it and dramatized it by recounting the stories of *E. coli* victims. Thus a column by *New York Times* op-ed writer Bob Herbert began by recounting the horrifying death of Alex Donley, a six-year-old who died in 1993 after eating a hamburger.

> He died horribly. "Nearly all of the organs in Alex's body were destroyed," said his mother, Nancy Donley. "Portions of his brain were liquefied. That's how virulent a pathogen this is. My husband and I wanted to donate his organs and have him live on in another child, but we couldn't. We were able to donate his corneas. That's all."

The import of Herbert's column was to attack opponents of the proposed new regulations, "the meat industry and its stooges in the Republican Party," who "have ganged up on the Agriculture Department (and the American consumer) to make sure the new inspection system never sees the light of day." As a result, Herbert concluded, other children would share the fate of Alex Donley, dying "in excruciating pain because the meat they ate was contaminated."[32]

Herbert excelled at telling a heartrending story, complete with innocent victim and nefarious perpetrators. He did not, however, offer much of a sense of the size of the risk posed by *E. coli*—or an explanation of how the proposed regulatory remedy would reduce it. What do we actually know about both the risk and the proposed remedy? Looking first at the risk, the most frequently cited figures in the media were that "the disease kills more than 500 and sickens 20,000 annually."[33] Those figures were also cited by STOP and the CSPI.[34] But what was their provenance? How reliable are they?

The figures are found in the *Federal Register*, in which the USDA proposed the heightened inspection standards for meat. But both numbers are high-end estimates: according to the USDA, there are somewhere between 10,000 and 20,000 illnesses caused by *E. coli* O157:H7 each year and somewhere between 200 and 500 deaths.[35] But the lower-range figures were effectively ignored by the media. The USDA also provided a second set of more relevant numbers for meat- and poultry-related illnesses and deaths, which also received no attention in the debate. Illnesses related to meat and poultry (that is, illnesses that might conceivably be prevented by improved regulation) were said to range from 6,000 to 12,000; deaths were said to range from 120 to 300.[36]

The ultimate source for the data was a journal article written by two researchers at the Centers for Disease Control (CDC).[37] The article cited three different studies estimating the incidence of diarrhea caused by *E. coli* O157:H7, all of which were conducted in the mid-1980s. According to the studies, the incidence ranges somewhere between 2.1 and 8 illnesses per 100,000 population, which would come to somewhere between 5,460 and 20,800 illnesses annually in the United States.[38]

In short, for all we know, the 20,000 figure may well be far too high: a considerably lower number is also plausible. On the other hand, it is likely that many cases go unreported (since doctors may not test for *E. coli* when they encounter patients with bloody diarrhea, and since many states do not require physicians to report *E. coli* outbreaks). Thus Dale Hancock, a Washington State University veterinarian, has argued that "the big outbreak of 1993 would never have been noticed if it had happened in Texas,"[39] because the illnesses wouldn't have been reported to a statewide authority. In any case, it's fair to say that knowledge of *E. coli* incidence was easily outstripped by people's pretensions to knowledge: the number of illnesses caused by the bacteria is very uncertain.

If the figure of 20,000 illnesses is questionable, the figure of 500 deaths is almost certainly too high. In fact, the CDC researchers' article included no estimate for number of deaths. It did, however, state that hemolytic uremic syndrome (HUS), the most serious complication that can be caused by *E. coli*, occurs in somewhere between 2 percent and 7 percent of all cases.[40] In turn, somewhere between 3 percent and 5 percent of those stricken with HUS are likely to die.[41] A high-end figure— derived from 20,800 illnesses from *E. coli*, 7 percent of which involve HUS—would yield 1,456 cases of HUS annually. The high-end 5 percent death rate would result in some seventy-three *E. coli*–related deaths annually. A low-end figure—assuming 5,460 illnesses from *E. coli*, 2 percent of which result in HUS, with 3 percent of HUS victims dying— yields only three deaths.

This range of figures is also somewhat speculative, of course, in part because *E. coli* can cause deaths even among those who do not develop HUS.[42] Nevertheless, because HUS is a particularly severe complication, it is likely that the widely and uncritically reported figure of 500 deaths a year is significantly overstated. In any case, it is apparent that the most commonly cited numbers were probably too high and definitely imprecise. How big a threat does *E. coli* pose? Because of the unacknowledged limitations of the data, no one can say for sure.

Still, no one would argue that poisonous hamburgers are a good thing, no matter how few of them there are. For that reason, the really important question was how best to keep poison out of our hamburgers—the focus of the debate over increased regulation of the meat industry. What explained the push for stepped-up governmental regulation? In the words of a National Academy of Sciences (NAS) study, the premise was that "the public expects the government to ensure zero risk of meat-borne disease through inspection." Unfortunately, the NAS study then went on to say that this public expectation is unreasonable: "Some bacterial contamination of raw meat is inevitable."[43]

In other words, the regulatory response could not satisfactorily address the threat posed by *E. coli*: microbial inspection of meat could not result in the destruction of the deadly bacteria. Remarkably, proponents of the stricter regulatory approach conceded as much themselves. Thus USDA official Michael R. Taylor admitted that inspecting samples of beef "is not by itself likely to detect a significant number of contaminated [raw beef] lots and will not by itself significantly reduce the likelihood of future outbreaks of food-borne illnesses attributed to O157:H7."[44]

The difficulty is that an inspector could not look at a sample of beef with any confidence that it was representative of the whole. Bacteria are not evenly distributed throughout a carcass, so the absence of bacteria in the sampled portion does not prove their absence anywhere else. Nor, for that matter, would the presence of bacteria in a sampled portion prove their presence anywhere else. Thus, even if an inspector were to come upon a contaminated sample of beef, it's unclear what should be done with the unsampled portion.

Thus the controversy centered on a proposed regulation that was not an appropriate means of reducing the risk. In the words of Russell Cross, director of the Institute of Food Service and Engineering at Texas A & M University, "The idea of testing is easy to sell to consumers because it makes it look like the government is doing something."[45] In other words, although increased regulation may have political appeal, it would not really ensure safety.

Elizabeth M. Whelan Jr., president of the American Council on Science and Health, nicely articulated the problem in an op-ed.

> Many in search of a risk-free society are now demanding that the burden of destroying bacteria be lifted from the food preparer and transferred to industry and the Department of Agriculture by requiring the increased inspection and microbial testing of meat before it goes to market. Such action, however, will only add to the cost of meat without promoting public health, because no matter what the level of federal expenditure might be, we will not be able to eliminate naturally occurring pathogens through inspection.[46]

Ironically, encouraging consumers to believe that the government can ensure meat safety could well create added risk: if people imagine that governmental action can guarantee safety, they may take fewer pains to handle food safely themselves, thus actually increasing the danger.

How could the dangers posed by *E. coli* be lessened? Two suggestions have been offered. Both of them, ironically, have met with resistance from the activists who worry about the *E. coli* threat. First, consumers themselves (and restaurants) can eliminate *E. coli* bacteria, simply by cooking beef thoroughly: a temperature of 160° Fahrenheit is recommended. But this recommendation has been rejected by STOP, which regards it as a way of "blaming the victim." Thus a STOP press release took the American Meat Institute to task, arguing that the institute is guilty of "holding victims of *E. coli* disease responsible when a loved one dies because they didn't cook their meat properly."[47]

For their part, the would-be regulators also were eager to absolve the consumer of any responsibility. In proposing its heightened regulation, the USDA asserted that "consumers fail to make a connection between their food handling behavior and safe food," adding that "food habits are the most difficult of all forms of human behavior to change."[48] In other words, consumers can't be expected to realize (or to act on the realization) that they can increase their safety by turning up the heat on their stoves. But the USDA's claims seem counterintuitive. Furthermore, they are contested by a consensus statement of the American Gastroenterological Association: "Public education should include a general food safety program directed toward all consumers. . . . Observations in the United States and other countries have shown that the incidence of foodborne illness can dramatically decline as a result of active public education and effective media coverage."[49]

There is also a more technologically advanced method of increasing meat safety: irradiating it, which would eliminate life-threatening bacteria like *E. coli*. Thus Elizabeth Whelan has pointed out that the "irradiation process does not make the food radioactive or change its taste or quality in any way—it just kills the germs that cause disease." For that reason, irradiation has also been advocated by the American Gastroenterological Association, which contends that it would "substantially reduce pathogenic bacteria, including *E. coli* O157:H7."[50]

Significantly, though, the irradiation solution has also been resisted by STOP. Donna Rosenbaum, STOP's executive director, is a staunch opponent. She worries about leakage from irradiating plants, fears that irradiation would kill useful as well as harmful bacteria, and suggests that irradiation might make slaughterhouses less sanitary than they are now.[51] Rosenbaum is prepared to accept an increased risk of meat contaminated by bacteria in order to avert what she regards as the unacceptable risk posed by irradiation. In short, even those whom Whelan regards as proponents of a risk-free society find some risks more acceptable than others. But as this example suggests, the risk-free society is an impossibility: all we can do is to choose—one hopes intelligently—among the variety of possible risks that confront us.

Fearing Frog Deformities

In September 1996 the *Washington Post* published a front-page story about the appearance of hundreds of deformed frogs in Minnesota—frogs with missing legs, withered legs, extra legs, paralyzed legs, missing eyes (and even a frog with an "eye growing inside its throat").[52] The story perfectly illustrates John Graham's point about the media's tendency to cover "the bizarre, the mysterious, that which people have difficulty imagining happening." Deformed frogs are, of course, more unusual than ordinary frogs: you wouldn't expect to see a story about the perfect health of a community of frogs (and if there were such a story, you wouldn't want to read it). But a deformed frog is like a man biting a dog—it's unusual, so it's newsworthy. That much is clear.

But why were the deformed frogs on the *Post*'s front page? Because the article implied (without ever quite saying it directly) that whatever was harming the frogs—perhaps chemical pollutants—could soon be wreaking havoc on a human being near (and like) you. Thus the article spoke of a teacher who discovered some of the frogs, whose students "immediately started asking me what the cancer rate was in the area."

Do researchers actually know what's harming the frogs? No. Do they know that human beings are also at risk? By no means. In fact, one scientist named David Hoppe (a wonderful name for a researcher who studies frogs) "concede[d] that nobody knows what to tell people in Minnesota who want to know what all this might mean for them."

In principle, of course, it's not altogether unreasonable to suppose that frogs might offer some sort of leading health indicator foretelling human health problems to come. But in fact, one of the theories explaining the deformities, which ascribes them to "naturally occurring parasites," suggests that humans are not at any risk. On the other hand, the article also

pointed to possible causes that might harm human health. Thus it indicated that many scientists believe that "some kind of chemical pollutant"
is to blame for the deformities. Other possible causes include "viral or
bacterial disease, the presence of various heavy metals known to cause
birth defects, acidification of the water, and even increasing ultraviolet
radiation as the Earth's ozone layer is depleted."

Perhaps pollutants are to blame, and perhaps they do pose a risk to
people as well as frogs. Still, it's important to realize that frogs live their
entire lives in the lakes that may (or may not) be polluted with chemicals
that cause the deformities; human contact with the same conceivable pollutants is less frequent by far, and that makes an enormous difference. It's
also important to realize, as one scientist put it, that "you occasionally
find abnormal frogs wherever you find frogs." In other words, we need to
know what the baseline is for frog deformities before we can assess the
degree to which the current wave of deformities departs from the baseline. But the article did not provide that information.

In general, the article didn't stress any of the manifold uncertainties
about what's happening to the frogs (and, in particular, how relevant or
irrelevant it might be to what will happen to people). Instead, in the
absence of published scientific research about the frog deformities, the
article seemed designed to whip up concern about human health being
put at risk by chemical pollutants. Thus the article quoted a scientist who
mentioned that "we might just be dealing with an animal Love Canal." As
the article explained, "chemical contamination drove more than 800 families from the Niagara Falls, N.Y. neighborhood [in which waste chemicals had been disposed] in the 1980s." On the other hand, somehow the
article failed to mention that the neighborhood has now been resettled—
and more to the point, that "no illness, not even a cold, can properly be
attributed to living next to Love Canal."[53]

The Blame Game

In a way, the Minnesota frogs make a perfectly good subject for a newspaper story. The deformities are weird and unexplained, and people like
to read about what's weird and unexplained. Still, it's important to
remember John Graham's distinction between significant public health

problems and what is newsworthy. The frog story would have been perfectly appropriate had it not been transformed (at least by innuendo) into a caution about a looming public health problem. The story could and should simply have said the following: scientists really aren't sure what's going on and are particularly unsure of whether human beings are at any risk whatsoever. But that story, we strongly suspect, wouldn't have made it onto page one.

Instead we believe that the frog story, like the *E. coli* story, may have achieved prominence because it fit into a master narrative—a narrative of villains and victims, in which the innocent (whether children or frogs) are endangered by callous and greedy humans who pollute and endanger our health and the environment's safety. Many journalists enjoy telling that story, perhaps for ideological reasons, perhaps merely because it's riveting. As we have seen, important uncertainties about the gravity of a risk and the best means of reducing it can easily be glossed over, given the desire to tell a dramatic story.

By contrast, it is striking how much breast cancer coverage is now devoted to analyzing the risk data in a hardheaded and informative way. To be sure, one still finds plenty of human-interest stories about victims (though not many with villains, since the tie between breast cancer and pollution is understood to be so dubious). But a great many newspaper stories now question the narrative about breast cancer propounded by activists, concerning both the size of the problem and its cause. Nevertheless, despite the spate of thoughtful journalistic analyses of breast cancer data, we've also seen that women's perception of their risk is substantially higher than their actual risk. Could there be a time lag, so that journalistic critiques alter popular perceptions only later? That's certainly possible. But there is also a more discouraging possibility.

It's conceivable that dramatic coverage designed to heighten fear is simply better remembered than more analytic coverage that might lower it. After all, drama is, well, more dramatic than cold-blooded analysis. A noted playwright once said that "satire is what closes on Saturday night." By the same token, analysis might be what's forgotten after Sunday morning.

If so, part of the problem may lie with the workings of the human brain, insofar as they determine what we remember and what we forget. But part of it may also lie with the media, which often feature scare stories far more prominently than their subsequent refutations. This tendency was nicely lampooned in the "Bloom County" comic strip for November 21, 1987, which poked fun at the press's role in promoting the hysteria about children who were abducted by strangers. In the strip, a reporter informs his editor that "the great child-stealing epidemic" promoted in "all our sensational panic-causing stories" never really existed; his boss responds by ordering a correction, to be run "below the tide schedules on page 109."[54]

In any event, it's useful to be aware of the tendency—common to much of humanity, and by no means unique to journalists—to construct a story that fits a predetermined narrative theme about victims and villains. In some cases this narrative may more or less accurately represent reality, just as some individuals' lives are more or less accurately summed up by the fairy-tale formula "and they lived happily ever after." Still, it's wise to be somewhat skeptical, both about fairy tales and about risk narratives. It's always important to know what we do (and don't) know about the extent of the risk, the cause of the risk, and the ways in which the risk can most prudently and expeditiously be reduced if not eliminated. Good reporting about risk addresses those issues; too often, bad reporting only encourages us to live fearfully ever after.

CHAPTER 8

DISTINGUISHING "REPORTS" FROM REALITY
Confusing the Map with the Territory

In 1990 the FBI reported that violent crime rose significantly. The obvious explanation—favored by a *Washington Post* news account—was that more crimes were committed. In fact, the increase may only have meant that more violent crimes were being reported by the police to the FBI.

Secretary of Health and Human Services Donna Shalala recently declared that "between 1986 and 1993, the number of children who were physically abused nearly doubled."[1] She based this claim on an increased number of reports of child abuse. But do more reports clearly show that conditions are worsening? Could they also indicate that even though behavior has not worsened, the standards by which it is judged have become more strict?

A study in the *Journal of the American Medical Association* (*JAMA*) found that women with breast implants face a 24 percent greater risk of suffering from connective-tissue diseases than women without implants. It seems clear, then, that the implants pose a small health risk. But the study cautioned that the findings might be unreliable, because they derived from women's self-reports rather than their medical records. Why might the reliance on self-reports bias the study?

Statistical information about social indicators always reflects a compilation of reports. When newspapers tell us that "crime is up," "illegitimate births have held steady," or "deaths from AIDS are down," those statements are always written in a sort of shorthand that can be (but is not always) misleading. The longhand truth of the matter is that "reports of crime are up," "reports of illegitimate births held steady," and "reports of deaths from AIDS are down."

In other words, statistical information is inevitably one level removed from reality. We don't learn directly about the subject of interest; instead we receive indirect information concerning reports about that subject. We are naturally inclined to assume a direct relation between the reports and the underlying reality that they are supposed to reflect. If reports of illegitimate births have declined, we tend to suppose that the actual number of illegitimate births (which is what we really want to know about) must also have declined.

In many cases, of course, reports do accurately mirror real changes. But in others, the supposed changes seem actually to be confined to the reporting mechanism. Reports of a phenomenon can go up (or down), not because the phenomenon has suddenly become more (or less) common, but because the method of compiling the reports has suddenly become more (or less) accurate. In those cases, the underlying reality may not have changed at all; the only change may be in the methods used by statisticians to compile information.

The 1996 concern about arson directed against black churches in the South offers a good example of the way in which changes in reporting can be confused with changes in reality. The media played an important part in a campaign that convinced people that the number of church fires had risen drastically; for example, *USA Today* featured a story that spoke of "a sharp rise in black church arsons [that] started in 1994 and continues."[2] But in fact, Michael Fumento has noted, "*USA Today*'s own chart belies this claim. It shows that two of the [Southern] states didn't start reporting data until 1993 and a third one didn't until 1995. Naturally, when they did, the numbers went up."[3] Writing in the *New Yorker*, Michael Kelly also contended that the increase in fires at black churches since 1995 was partly attributable to "an upsurge in the reporting of arsons" rather than an upsurge in arson itself.[4]

Changes in reports are sometimes mistaken for changes in reality; and when they are, our understanding of what is really going on naturally suffers. Thus, in looking at numerical rises in statistical reports, it is not always right to draw straightforward conclusions like these: "Crime is up"; "child abuse is becoming more common"; "women with breast implants tend more often to have connective-tissue diseases."

Instead, an increase in reports may reflect only a change in what has been said (as opposed to what has actually been done). In distinguishing between reports and reality, we question whether change has actually occurred, drawing conclusions like these: "Reports of crime by the police to the FBI may be up, but that does not necessarily mean that more crime is now occurring"; "social-service professionals now report more cases of child abuse, but perhaps that is because their standards have come to be more exacting—not because parental behavior has gotten worse"; "slightly more women with breast implants report having connective-tissue diseases, but some of those self-reports may be erroneous, colored by the publicity given to the health dangers posed by the implants."

It should, of course, be clear that these sorts of explanations do not altogether exclude one another. Part of an increase (in crime, child abuse, cases of connective-tissue diseases, or anything else) may be real; part of it may reflect changed reports rather than a changed reality. Still, it is important to be aware of the possible discrepancy between reports and reality; as the following case studies show, changes in what is reported can mislead when they are confused with changes in what's really been done.

Reported versus Committed Crime

In April 1991 a story in the *Washington Post* informed readers that "violent crimes—murder, rape, robbery and aggravated assault—increased by 10 percent in the United States last year, the largest annual increase since 1986."[5] But this shorthand summary was somewhat misleading. In fact, we don't really know how many crimes are committed in the United States. All we have are varying counts of how many crimes are reported. Perhaps the finding conveyed by the article showed that crime had really worsened, but perhaps it showed only that reporting of crime had improved.

It was not until the seventh paragraph (out of eleven) that the article referred to reports of crime (as opposed to actual crimes), noting that "the FBI figures . . . reflect only crimes reported to the police." But the article did not pause to consider whether the rise might mean merely that more crimes were now being reported by the police to the FBI rather than actually being committed. The article also did not mention that the FBI's annual survey of crimes reported to the police is only one of two governmental surveys measuring the number of crimes committed each year, the other being the National Crime Victimization Survey (NCVS) conducted by the Department of Justice's Bureau of Justice Statistics (BJS).

In the NCVS survey (also discussed in chapter 6) of a large and representative sample of Americans, respondents are asked whether they have been victims of a wide assortment of crimes in the past six months. Respondents who claim that they have been crime victims are also asked if they reported the crimes to the police. The NCVS produces an estimate of the total number of crimes committed, an estimate of the total reported to the police, and hence the proportion of those committed reported to the police. In 1987–88, for example, victims said that they had reported 57 percent of all aggravated assaults and robberies to the police.[6] In principle the NCVS should therefore provide a more comprehensive and accurate picture of America's crime problem, because it tells us about both crimes known to the police and those of which the police are unaware.[7]

The *Post* story did not point out that NCVS data told a very different story about the violent crime rate for 1990. Instead of a significant increase, it found a modest decrease (from 29.8 crimes of violence per 1,000 persons in 1989 to 29.6 in 1990).[8] Only a month earlier, in fact, the *Post* had run a story covering the release of NCVS data, showing that "the nationwide crime rate fell by about 3 percent last year."[9]

In choosing between the FBI figures and those of the BJS, it should be clear that we are choosing between two different measures of reported crimes as opposed to actual crimes: the only way to measure actual crimes would be to have videotape machines rolling twenty-four hours a day in every room in every house (and on every street and in every park, etc.) all over the United States. The question, then, is how to reconcile a drop in crime discovered by analyzing the self-reports of self-described victims with a rise in crime discovered by analyzing reports to and then by the police. Specifically, is there some reason other than an actual increase in crimes that might explain an increased number of reports of crime by the police to the FBI?

Northwestern University sociologist Christopher Jencks has addressed that question. Jencks observed that the NCVS was introduced in 1973, precisely because it was assumed that many unreported crimes are committed. The NCVS confirmed that assumption; as a result, the Department of Justice began to work with local police departments to improve their record-keeping, in part by computerizing records. These administrative measures did not change the proportion of crimes reported by victims to the police, but they did significantly increase the proportion of complaints to the police that were recorded by the police and later reported to the FBI.[10]

Jencks concluded that "the most likely explanation for the increase in robberies and aggravated assaults reported to the FBI is, therefore, that the police are recording more of the violence that citizens report to them."[11] Thus it's not so much that crime was rising in 1990 as that more of the crimes known to the police were reported by them to the FBI. Jencks supported this contention by comparing figures from the NCVS and from the FBI's Uniform Crime Reports. In 1973, according to the NCVS, 861,000 aggravated assaults were reported to the police; but according to the FBI, only 421,000 such assaults were recorded by the police. By 1988, however, the picture changed. The number of assaults reported to the police increased modestly (according to the NCVS), rising from 861,000 to 940,000; but the number recorded by the police and transmitted to the FBI more than doubled—going from 421,000 to 910,000. It therefore seems that the real rise was not in crimes committed but in crimes that the FBI learned about from local police forces.

The *Post*'s article about the FBI data would have been more informative, then, if it had also referred to the NCVS findings. Since our real concern is with crime (not with what the FBI says about crime), news coverage of research findings is more insightful if it provides a context of other relevant findings. But even considering the FBI data by themselves, coverage would have been improved if it had examined alternative explanations for the reported crime increase. If crimes reported by the police have gone up, that may mean that more crimes have been committed; it may also mean only that more were being recorded by the police. Again, the rival explanations are not in principle exclusive: some of the rise may have been genuine, the rest a result of administrative improvements in reporting crime. The important point, though, is to be aware of both possibilities.

Stricter Standards for Child Abuse

The National Incidence Study of Child Abuse and Neglect was released in September 1996, following up on previous studies conducted in 1980 and 1986. The study found that child abuse and neglect were seriously worsening. Between 1986 and 1993 the number of cases doubled, going from 1.4 million to 2.8 million; and the number of cases involving serious injuries nearly quadrupled, rising from 143,000 to almost 570,000.

Commendably, newspaper accounts (presumably following a lead raised by the study itself) alerted readers to the possible divergence between reports of child abuse and the reality of child abuse. The *Chicago Tribune*, for example, described the increase as "a 'true rise' in the severity of the problem rather than one based solely on heightened awareness."[12] There is certainly reason to suppose that the number of cases of actual abuse might be rising, since child abuse could be expected to rise when drug and alcohol abuse were increasing and when broken homes were becoming more common.

Nevertheless, despite the study's assurance to the contrary, there is also good reason to suppose that much of the increase reflects heightened awareness rather than worse behavior. American Enterprise Institute researcher Douglas J. Besharov (writing with research assistant Jacob W. Dembosky) advanced this argument in an article in the on-line journal *Slate*.[13] Besharov and Dembosky noted that child abuse fatalities (for which there is, of course, objective evidence that cannot easily be hidden) have risen only modestly, going from 1,104 in 1986 to 1,216 in 1993. If serious abuse has in fact quadrupled, one would expect to see a comparably enormous increase for the most deadly abuse of all.

Why might the study's alarming findings indicate heightened awareness rather than a true rise in awful behavior? Besharov and Dembosky observed that the study's conclusions emerge from a survey of a representative sample of 5,600 child-welfare professionals. Of the 1.4 million additional cases counted in 1993, almost 80 percent consisted of cases that do not involve physical or sexual abuse. (Note that the survey examined child neglect as well as abuse, although Secretary Shalala's written comments in releasing its findings referred only to abuse.[14]) Fully 55 percent of the additional cases involved endangered children: those who are not actually harmed by parental abuse or neglect, but are simply "in danger of being harmed according to the views of community professionals or child-protective service agencies." Cases of emotional abuse and neglect made up an additional 15 percent of the cases; and educational neglect, the frequent failure to send a child to school, accounted for another 8 percent.

A similar pattern emerges regarding the serious cases that were said to have quadrupled. Of the 427,000 additional cases of serious abuse found in 1993, emotional maltreatment was at issue in half. Furthermore, cases were characterized as serious physical abuse even if they were restricted to mental or emotional injury. Finally, in three categories (sexual abuse, physical neglect, and emotional neglect), the increase in serious cases was accompanied by a decline in moderate ones—which might suggest that the increases resulted in some measure from upgraded standards, whereby behavior once thought only moderately bad has now come to be considered seriously harmful.

In short, the child abuse study appears to be a perfect example of what we have elsewhere discussed as the tactic of "bait and switch": the increase does not appear to stem from many more cases of real physical abuse (as Shalala's remarks and the *Tribune* article, which nowhere discussed the study's definition of "abuse and neglect," implied). Instead, what is mostly at issue is a heightened awareness and sensitivity among child-welfare professionals, who now report more behavior as abusive and neglectful than they would have earlier.[15] It seems likely that more stringent standards, rather than a greater amount of adult depravity, is what chiefly explains the rise reported in the child abuse study.

Are Self-Reports Unreliable?

In February 1996 the *JAMA* published a study investigating whether women with breast implants were at increased risk of suffering from connective-tissue diseases.[16] Charles H. Hennekens and his colleagues designed a questionnaire that was mailed to 1.75 million female health professionals between September 1992 and May 1995, asking for information about their medical histories. They received over 425,000 responses, of which almost 400,000 were usable for purposes of their study.

The responses indicated that 10,830 women reported having received breast implants between 1962 and 1991; 11,805 reported having contracted a connective-tissue disease in that same period. (The study began with 1962 because silicone breast implants first became available that year; it ended in 1991 because breast implants received widespread publicity as a possible health hazard in the following year, and the researchers feared that this publicity might bias the respondents' self-reports.) The study found "reassuring evidence against a large hazard of breast implants on connective-tissue diseases"; but it also showed that women with implants faced a 24 percent greater risk of contracting a connective-tissue disease, which was described as "a small but significant increased risk."[17]

A 24 percent increase may seem substantial. But because of the likely impact of confounding factors (hidden variables, not under investigation, that may be the true cause of a finding of increased risk), biases (incorrect information supplied by the individuals being studied), and simple measurement error, most epidemiologists believe that only increased risks of 300 percent or more should be taken seriously.[18] In this instance it was the bias possibly introduced by the women's self-reports that the study's authors found most worrisome. They noted that women's self-reports as to whether they had implants were likely to be reliable; but they added that other studies have shown that self-reports of connective-tissue diseases are likely to significantly overstate their true incidence (when compared with medical records), in some cases by 500 percent or more.[19]

The real question is whether overreporting would be more likely for women with implants than for those without them. As the researchers noted, even though the study was restricted to diagnoses of connective-tissue diseases that occurred in 1991 or earlier (before the media began widely publicizing the possible dangers of breast implants), it is still the case that

these questionnaires were completed between 1992 and 1995, when publicity regarding the potential adverse health effects of breast implants already had surfaced. This might have led to overreporting of connective-tissue diseases among women with implants. It is also possible that heightened awareness among clinicians and among women with breast implants who reported symptoms compatible with connective-tissue disease might have contributed to overreporting. All these factors could have potentially led to observed increased risks associated with breast implants that are due to bias.[20]

Thus the study concluded with the researchers promising to "attempt to validate the self-reported diagnoses of connective-tissue diseases by independent medical record review."[21]

The *New York Times* report on the study perceptively observed that "the researchers devoted more words to explaining why the apparent slight increase in risk might be illusory—because of biases in the sample[22] and in the reporting of diseases—[than] they did to explaining what the study had found."[23] *USA Today* also excelled in pointing to the possible discrepancy between reports of connective-tissue disease and its actual incidence: its article noted that "any study flaw, such as a larger number of incorrect reports from women with implants, could easily have biased the outcome."[24] On the other hand, the *Washington Post*, while noting that the increased risk was a small one, ignored the contrast between self-reports and medical records that Hennekens and his colleagues had stressed in their article.[25]

Once again, then, we see that reports of a phenomenon can differ from actual occurrences of it. The researchers made that distinction abundantly clear in their study; but some news accounts did better than others in conveying it to their readers.

Better Accounting? Or Worsened Reality?

These examples point to different ways in which changed reporting can help account for what can easily be misconstrued as changed reality. Of the three examples, the breast implant study is in a way the most obvious. We generally believe that people should not be judges in their own cases, so there is at least some reason to be skeptical of self-reports that are not confirmed by more objective and disinterested observers.

For that reason, the other two examples may be more illuminating, precisely because they point to ways in which data compiled by objective and disinterested observers can also be misleading. Paradoxically, in these cases it was misleading not because the observers were doing their work badly; instead, the problem arose because they arguably began to do it better. Changes resulting from increased conscientiousness on the part of professionals concerned with crime and child welfare were mistakenly thought to stem from an apparent increase in the bad behavior that the professionals seek to check.

Different sorts of conscientiousness are at issue in these examples. With regard to crime, reporting simply seems to have become better, in the sense of being more accurate and comprehensive. It's not that some crimes were suddenly being classified as, say, aggravated assaults that would previously have been regarded more leniently; it's just that local police forces were passing along more information to the FBI about aggravated assaults than they did earlier.

The child abuse example, by contrast, shows how figures can be inflated when standards become more stringent. There will probably be more cases of child abuse now than there were a decade ago if behavior that would not have been classified as child abuse then is so classified today. In principle, of course, there is nothing wrong with making standards stricter, for judging child abuse or anything else; it's certainly possible that prior standards were too lax (and not that the new, toughened standards are unreasonably exacting). But in either case, the problem is that we won't properly understand the trendline unless we realize that our measuring instrument has been altered so that it catches examples of abuse that would have gone unrecognized in the past.

Ironically, then, the increased conscientiousness of public servants can be mistaken for increased social depravity. If the people who keep count of various pathologies get better at their jobs, it is easy to reach the possibly false conclusion that pathology is on the upswing. In other words, an actual decline in pathology is altogether consistent with an increased number of reports of pathology (and increased societal focus upon it). As new and higher standards arise, behavior that had once seemed acceptable comes to be thought heinous, so it is reported where once it had been ignored; what that can mean, though, is not that behavior has gotten worse, but that the standards judging it have risen.

That point has been nicely argued (with specific respect to child abuse) by sociologists Murray A. Straus and Richard J. Gelles.

> Those concerned with America's children might be pleased that each year's "official statistics" on child abuse tops the previous year's figures. This is because the figures might indicate something quite different from a real increase in the rate of child abuse. The true incidence of child abuse may actually be *declining*, even though the number of cases is increasing. . . . New standards are evolving in respect to how much violence parents can use in childrearing. . . . This can create the misleading impression of an epidemic of child abuse.[26]

In sum, being aware of the occasional disparity between reports and reality can be helpful, in that it can remind us of likely disparities between subjective self-reports and objective reality. But it may be still more helpful if we learn not to confuse objective observers' improvements in tabulating pathologies with actual increases in the pathologies themselves.

PART III

THE AMBIGUITY OF EXPLANATION

CHAPTER 9

BLAMING THE MESSENGER, IGNORING THE MESSAGE
Do Motives Matter?

A group of researchers finds that women who have had abortions face a slightly greater risk for breast cancer. One of the researchers is pro-life. Reporting on the study, the *Philadelphia Inquirer* suggests that it is suspect because of the convictions of the pro-life researcher.

A study finds that women with breast implants face at most only a small additional risk of contracting a connective-tissue disease. The study is funded by an implant maker, Dow Corning, which exercises no control over the investigators' procedures or findings. The CBS news coverage of the finding mentions Dow's financial support for the research—but not the investigators' autonomy.

According to an economist's study, states that permit their residents to carry concealed weapons have lower crime rates than those that don't, because the weapons deter crime. A gun control advocate attacks the research, wrongly proclaiming that it was funded by the Olin Corporation, the owner of a firearms manufacturer.

An environmentalist organization recommends dismissing the work of climatologists who doubt that global warming poses a serious threat, because their research is funded in part by the oil and coal industries.

The *San Diego Union-Tribune* publishes a front-page story highlighting a promising advance in gene therapy to combat brain tumors. It fails

to mention that some of the researchers own stock in the company manufacturing the vaccine that they developed. (The company's stock rose
67 percent the day after the finding was announced.)

All of these stories raise an obvious question: Do researchers'
motives—financial or ideological—invalidate or at least call into question
their findings? More broadly: On what basis can good research be distinguished from bad? These are obviously important questions for the
consumer of news who wants to know which studies to take seriously.

A familiar answer to the second question is that good research is published in what are known as peer-reviewed journals, that is, reliable
research is evaluated prior to publication by scientists who are familiar
with the subject. To give an example, the Food Nutrition Science
Alliance, representing 100,000 nutritionists and doctors, has issued ten
"red flag" warning signs to alert consumers to "research" findings that are
likely to be phony. The alliance urges us to be suspicious of (among other
things) "claims that sound too good to be true, headlines that promise a
quick fix, dire warning[s] of danger about a single product or regimen,
simplistic conclusions drawn from a complex study," and "advice based
on studies published without peer review."[1]

Peer Review in Theory and Practice

There is much truth to the claim that peer-reviewed research is legitimate
research. As we will see, the presence or absence of peer review proves
important for evaluating the quality of the research in all five of the cases
that we introduced above. Why is peer review often thought to indicate if
not guarantee reliability? In science as in law, the argument goes, people
shouldn't be judges in their own cases; it's important for claims to be
assessed by someone who is both knowledgeable and impartial. Thus
one danger is that researchers might knowingly deceive, falsifying data to
achieve a desired result; but scientific peer reviewers on the lookout for
deception presumably deter a lot of it (just as cops walking the beat presumably deter crime).

Human error on the part of researchers is far more common than outright deception, though. Researchers can make mistakes that render their
conclusions worthless; and even when they conduct their research prop-

erly, they are also all too likely to exaggerate its importance. A review by scientists familiar with the subject matter is likely to detect mistakes and to qualify exaggerated claims. Thus peer review is important because it helps determine whether a study's substantive conclusion follows logically from the procedures used to arrive at it and whether the conclusion makes a significant contribution to our knowledge.

Finally, science itself is the process through which scientists test one another's theories and evaluate and criticize one another's research. Science is supposed to be cumulative, to comprise a body of knowledge that is logically consistent, testable, and self-corrective. In that sense, peer review is more than a practice adopted by scientists. In a fundamental sense it *is* science, because only a researcher's peers will have the expertise needed to determine whether a research finding is scientific, in the sense that it adds to our knowledge and is consistent with what is already known.

Science, then, consists of claims to knowledge that successfully withstand criticisms from other scientists. Peer review is thought to provide an imprimatur of sorts because a scientist's claims are more likely to be valid if they've passed muster with competent scientific authorities. In science as in law, an unsupported assertion (or an assertion made by, say, a defendant in his own behalf) is rightly viewed more skeptically than an assertion buttressed by the support of eyewitnesses. In effect, peer reviewers, the judges of science, are also the witnesses who add credibility to the claims made by researchers.

That's the case for peer review in theory. Practice, unfortunately, is somewhat more complicated. In practice you should be suspicious of scientific claims that have not been peer-reviewed, but it is wrong to assume the validity of claims that have been peer-reviewed. To see why, it may be helpful to recall that O. J. Simpson was found not guilty by a jury of his peers—though it's hardly news that many observers believe that he was clearly guilty. A scientific jury of peers, like a citizen jury of peers, is only human; it can have biases of its own, and it can fail to weigh all the evidence impartially.

In principle, as we have said, scientific peer review should judge the importance of a conclusion and the reliability of the procedures that led to it. The substance of the conclusion shouldn't really matter as long as it is significant, and as long as it follows logically from the procedures used to arrive at it. In practice, though, peer reviewers often have their own substantive biases, which lead them to praise research supporting sub-stantive conclusions that they like and to condemn research that doesn't.

A social worker named William Epstein achieved a certain amount of notoriety a few years ago by attempting to demonstrate that the substantive biases of peer reviewers shape their evaluations. Epstein wrote two versions of an article summarizing fictitious research, in which social workers osten-sibly attempted to relieve the symptoms of a child suffering from asthma (which is often a psychosomatic disease) by separating him temporarily from his parents. He sent one version of the article (in which the social workers' intervention benefited the child) to seventy scholarly journals, and the other (in which the intervention failed) to another seventy.

Epstein found that 53 percent of the journals receiving the positive version of the paper accepted it, compared with only 14 percent of those that were sent the negative version. Thus he surmised that his paper's reviewers were biased by their substantive preferences. They approved of a paper confirming the efficacy of social work and disapproved of one questioning it—even though either conclusion was equally significant and the papers were otherwise methodologically identical.

It is interesting to note that Epstein's experiment to determine the effi-cacy of peer review led the National Association of Social Workers to bring ethics charges against him, for deceiving his research subjects (the editors and reviewers who assessed the manuscripts) and for studying them without getting their informed consent.[2] The anger with which Epstein's experiment was greeted suggests that many scientists view peer review as something of an icon. Iconoclasts, of course, are never popular with the devout.

The kind of substantive bias that Epstein detected is by no means unique to the "soft" or nonrigorous social sciences. (Though it's fair to point out that social work would probably rank as the Pillsbury Dough Boy in a competition to determine the "softest" social science.) Epidemiology is a much "harder" science; yet Marcia Angell, editor of the *New England Journal of Medicine*, has claimed that "Authors and investi-gators are worried that there's a bias against negative studies"—those con-cluding that a substance under investigation does not pose a health risk. As a result, Angell argued, "They'll try very hard to convert what is essen-tially a negative study into a positive study by hanging on to very, very small risks or seizing on one positive aspect of a study that is by and large negative."[3] In principle, of course, it should be just as important to establish that a food does not pose a health risk as to establish that it does.

Nor is referee bias the only problem with peer review. For one thing, referees disagree with one another much of the time, because they have different notions of what constitutes good science. Thus in 1981 three researchers (two sociologists of science and an applied mathematician) looked at peer review as practiced by the National Science Foundation (NSF) to evaluate proposals for funding. The researchers solicited a second set of peer reviews for 150 proposals in three disciplines (chemical dynamics, economics, and solid-state physics) that had already received peer review through the NSF. The researchers found that more than one-quarter of the funding decisions made by the NSF reviewers would have been reversed by the second set of reviewers and that many proposals ranked at the top by one set of reviewers were ranked at the bottom by the other. The researchers therefore concluded that luck is as important as merit in determining which applicants receive funding.[4]

In fairness, divergent responses are more likely to be encountered in the review of grant proposals than in the review of completed research submitted to journals. Reviewing a proposal is necessarily more speculative, because it requires intuiting what the researcher is likely to find when his work is completed (and how significant that finding will be).[5] The greater uncertainty surrounding review of proposals should not be forgotten; still, it is important to realize that in practice referees of journal articles often differ sharply as well.

Finally, it needs to be understood that peer review means just that and nothing more—peers review the work but do not necessarily approve of it. Writing in the *Weekly Standard*, Neal B. Freeman (a producer of television shows about science) has recently made this point about the *Journal of the American Medical Association* (*JAMA*). He notes that *JAMA* may send a manuscript out to as many as ten reviewers but that it may actually be reviewed by only three, two, or even one. Furthermore, an article may appear in print even if a majority of *JAMA*'s reviewers recommends against publication, provided that the editor decides in its favor.[6]

This is not an altogether shocking revelation, especially because Freeman acknowledges that *JAMA*'s editor at the time, George Lundberg, is "a man of distinguished background and, by all accounts, high character." Furthermore, one can argue that the editor of a scientific journal should be more than a rubber stamp. When peer reviewers disagree in their assessments (and as we have seen, they often do), the editor appropriately decides whose arguments are better and whose are worse. It is certainly conceivable that the reviewers or even the reviewer in the minority might have the more compelling case, which the editor is right to heed. Still, Freeman's larger point is valid: peer reviewers can err, and the fact that a study has been peer-reviewed hardly means that it is beyond criticism.

The real question, then, is the grounds on which peer-reviewed research is questioned. As the examples below illustrate, too often it is *researchers* who are criticized rather than their research. That is to say, research is often dismissed in media accounts on ad hominem grounds, because of the researcher's convictions or his funding source. Instead, it is the research itself that should be at issue: the focus should not be on what motivated the researcher to undertake his project, but instead on any procedural flaws in the investigation that may invalidate its conclusions. In scientific as in criminal investigations, motive by itself does not prove guilt: at most, motive should cause us to be suspicious, to be on the lookout for evidence of foul play. But the real scientific crime (if there was one) will always be apparent in a study's procedure. For this reason, the focus should be on that procedure, not on the researcher's possible motive.

Abortion, Breast Cancer, and Researcher Bias

The *Journal of Epidemiology and Community Health*, a publication of the British Medical Association, recently published a study by four researchers showing that women who have had abortions face a slightly higher risk of breast cancer than women who have not. The article had four coauthors, one of whom (Joel Brind of Baruch College of the City University of New York) is pro-life.

Brind's pro-life views were the focus of the *Philadelphia Inquirer*'s coverage of the study.[7] Significantly, the article's headline didn't report the results of the study, but the reaction to it: "Study Linking Abortion to Breast Cancer Drawing Criticism." The problem, the article went on to say, is that "the research was done by a biochemist opposed to the procedure": it noted that Brind has "spoken out on Christian radio, in antiabortion publications, and as an expert witness for an antiabortion group in federal court in Philadelphia." All of that may be true, but it is unclear why it is relevant. Should only pro-choice researchers be allowed to study the medical effects of abortion? (The *Inquirer* article did not mention that at least one of Brind's coauthors, Vernon M. Chinchilli, a biostatistician at Penn State's Hershey Medical Center, is pro-choice.) Or should having any views on the ethics of abortion disqualify a researcher?

The crucial question, of course, is how the study was conducted, not the content of Brind's personal views. The *Inquirer* addressed this question only after implying that Brind should be dismissed as a pro-life partisan who "has risked his scientific credibility" by criticizing abortion. Furthermore, it ignored the fact that Brind's study was published in a peer-reviewed journal.

The *Inquirer*'s critique emphasized that Brind's study is what is known as a meta-analysis: that is, not an original study but a compilation of the results of some twenty-three previous studies of the relation between breast cancer and abortion. The *Inquirer* suggested that Brind's meta-analysis could be rejected, because "the 23 studies show no pattern. Ten found an increased breast cancer risk, ten found no increased risk—and three actually found that abortion has a protective effect against breast cancer." But the whole point of meta-analysis is precisely to detect a "pattern" where none is obvious in a series of contradictory individual studies: if there had been a clear pattern in the individual studies, there would have been little reason to undertake a meta-analysis. Meta-analyses can, of course, be done poorly—it is obviously difficult to lump together different studies that may approach a common question in drastically different ways. Still, in principle meta-analysis is a valuable scientific tool. Brind's study ought not to have been dismissed simply because it is a meta-analysis.[8]

The *Inquirer* article did touch briefly on one potential problem with Brind's study: because of the sensitivity of the issue, some women may have falsely denied having had abortions.[9] Furthermore, the article mentioned but made little of the fact that even according to Brind's analysis abortion poses only a modest risk: a 30 percent increase is actually not particularly large.[10]

But the important point is that the *Inquirer* was wrong to focus on Brind's opinions when it should have been examining his research. In the words of Zane Berzins (described as Brind's spokesman), "His research is quite independent of whatever personal views he has on this. Besides, he's one of four authors, and Mr. Chinchilli is a pro-choice person."[11] Arguably, the *Inquirer* displayed more pro-choice bias in its ad hominem critique of Brind than Brind displayed pro-life bias in his study.[12]

Dow Corning and Dr. Hennekens's Research

In February 1996 *JAMA* published a study showing that women with breast implants face a small and perhaps illusory increased risk of contracting connective-tissue disease. We have already examined this research elsewhere in this volume, to see how studies based on medical self-reports can be biased. Here we examine a second source of potential bias, stemming from the financial sponsorship of the research.

As we saw in chapter 8, Charles Hennekens and his colleagues mailed out questionnaires to 1.75 million female health professionals, who were asked for information about their medical histories. Over 425,000 of the women responded, supplying information that enabled the researchers to study whether women with breast implants were more likely to suffer from connective-tissue disease.

The study cost $18.3 million, of which $17 million was provided by the National Institutes of Health (NIH). The balance was supplied by Dow Corning, which had manufactured implants until 1992 (when the Food and Drug Administration banned their sale in the United States). Dow Corning had also filed for bankruptcy protection in 1995, anticipating its inability to pay out over $2 billion to women with implants who had sued, alleging that the implants damaged their health. Thus some 7 percent of the costs of the study were borne by a manufacturer of implants, which had a clear financial stake in its outcome—since findings minimizing the health risks posed by the implants would presumably help it survive the blizzard of litigation directed against it. Did Dow Corning's small financial stake in the study somehow call the findings into question?

A reasonable answer would be that Dow Corning's financial sponsorship is problematic only to the extent that Dow Corning affected the conduct of the study and the release of its findings. In fact, Dow Corning simply paid for (a bit of) the piper, while having no control whatsoever over the tune. It exerted no influence over the way in which the study was designed, conducted, or analyzed; and it did not even learn of the results until just before they were published. In short, Dow Corning's role in underwriting the Hennekens study was a nonissue.

For the most part, media reports were commendably straightforward in dismissing it as a nonissue. The *Boston Globe* quoted Dr. Hennekens, who stated that "it would be really unfortunate to say the money came from Dow Corning, therefore you can't believe the results of the study."[13] The *Chicago Tribune* account, taken from the Associated Press, noted that the large majority of the funding came from the NIH, with Dow Corning paying only a bit; of greater importance, it quoted Hennekens as saying that Dow Corning "had absolutely nothing to do with the design, conduct, interpretation or outcome" of the study.[14] Finally, the *New York Times* pointed out that Dow Corning "agreed to stay at arm's length" from the researchers.[15]

One notable exception to this rule, though, was the *CBS Evening News*. Although television news often treats *JAMA* articles as though they were Holy Writ,[16] CBS's coverage of the Hennekens study, provided by Dr. Bob Arnot in a brief segment, seemed to discount the study, noting (without further elaboration) that it was "partly funded by Dow Corning." Arnot declared that "major studies from Harvard and the National Institutes of Health will try to assess the real risk"—thus seeming to suggest that Hennekens's study had not done so. Furthermore, Arnot observed that "critics claim the study could underestimate the real risk, because researchers failed to ask about the type of connective disease that is most common among women with implants." He did not, on the other hand, explain the researchers' own concern that their study might overestimate the real risk, because self-reports of disease are often biased.[17]

Nevertheless, for the most part the media reported the Hennekens study accurately. Reporters recognized that Dow Corning's role in supporting the research wasn't even a cap pistol, let alone a smoking gun.

Concealing Weapons and Uncovering Funding

In August 1996 the Cato Institute, a libertarian Washington think tank, held a press conference to publicize a scientific study questioning the advisability of gun control laws. The study was conducted by John R. Lott Jr., then a professor at the University of Chicago Law School (now at Yale University), together with David Mustard, an economics graduate student at the university. Cato publicized the study prior to its appearance in the January 1997 issue of the *Journal of Legal Studies*—a peer-reviewed journal.[18]

The study found that states permitting their residents to carry concealed weapons had significantly lower rates for violent crimes such as murder, rape, and aggravated assaults than states prohibiting concealed weapons. In short, the paradoxical finding was that restrictions on guns may spur violent crime and that relaxing such restrictions would decrease it. Predictably, the study aroused the ire of gun control advocates. But much of the criticism was not directed at what would have been the appropriate target, the study's methodology. Instead, Lott's motives were attacked; he was falsely denounced as a hireling of a gun manufacturer.

The charge was first leveled by Dan Kotowski, director of the Illinois Council against Handgun Violence. As the *Chicago Sun-Times* reported, "Kotowski said the study was biased because it was funded by the parent company of Winchester Inc., a firearms manufacturer."[19] A more refined version of the accusation was launched by New York congressman Charles E. Schumer. In a letter printed in the September 4 *Wall Street Journal* (written in response to an August 28 *Wall Street Journal* op-ed by Lott summarizing his findings), Schumer observed: "The Associated Press reports that Prof. Lott's fellowship at the University of Chicago is funded by the Olin Foundation, which is 'associated with the Olin Corporation,' one of the nation's largest gun manufacturers."

In other words, Lott's research could be disregarded, because Lott himself was a shill for the gun lobby. But in fact, there is no connection between the Olin Foundation and the Olin Corporation (Winchester's parent company). In the words of *Chicago Tribune* columnist Stephen Chapman, "To suggest that [the Olin Foundation] is merely an arm of the gun industry is like regarding the Ford Foundation as a puppet of American carmakers."[20] Furthermore, as Chapman noted, the foundation did not choose Lott as a fellow at the law school, give him money, or approve his topic; it simply made a grant to the law school's law and economics program, which then awarded Lott a fellowship to do research on a subject of his own choosing.

Our point, of course, is not that Lott's research is in any way sacrosanct. Its assumptions and methodology should obviously be scrutinized carefully. Gun control advocates have argued, for example, that laws permitting the carrying of concealed weapons are often implemented after a surge in violent crimes; thus a subsequent drop in the violent crime rate might reflect not the impact of these laws, but a predictable downward drift from an uncharacteristically high "spike" in the rate to the lower long-term average level. But the criticism should have been directed not at the researcher's motives, but at the research itself. In other words, rather than blaming the messenger, scientific critics should show what's wrong with the message.

Global Warming: If It's Not the Heat, Is It the Cupidity?

A small group of climate scientists, including researchers like Robert Balling of Arizona State University, Richard S. Lindzen of MIT, Patrick Michaels of the University of Virginia, and S. Fred Singer of the Science & Environmental Policy Project, questions the conventional view that global warming poses a significant threat. Thus the scientific skeptics reject the prediction of the Intergovernmental Panel on Climate Change, which currently sees global temperatures rising by somewhere between 0.8° and 3.5° Centigrade by the year 2100.

The skeptics note, for instance, that most of the rise in global temperatures over the last century took place before World War II—that is, before the rapid increase in emissions of greenhouse gases like carbon dioxide that are thought to cause global warming. Skeptics also note that satellite measurements (as opposed to surface measurements) of the global climate actually fail to show the warming trend. Finally, the skeptics cast doubt on the computer models used to predict future warming, since it is so hard to take account of all the different factors that contribute to global climate change.

Not surprisingly, these scientific skeptics have been criticized by advocates stressing the urgency of global warming, particularly by many environmentalists. What is troubling, once again, is that much of the criticism has been ad hominem—directed not at the skeptics' arguments, but at the sources of their funding. For example, the *Washington Post* has reported that Balling and Michaels have been criticized by Ozone Action (an environmentalist group) for undertaking research paid for by the energy industry. For obvious reasons, the oil and coal industries oppose the restrictions on energy emissions advocated by those most worried about global warming.[21]

This charge is, of course, similar to that leveled against John Lott—except in this case it happens to be correct. Balling, for instance, has been funded by the Cyprus Minerals Co., which has interests in petroleum and coal; Michaels has received funding from the Western Fuels Association, an umbrella organization. But again, the question is what is proven by disclosure of the funding source. We should obviously discount fraudulent research that is funded by the energy industry to support its interests; but why should we reject good research, just because it happens to be funded by the energy industry? In other words, the important issue is distinguishing good research from bad; there may be reason to scrutinize closely research underwritten by industry sources, but it is unfairly prejudicial to suggest that it can be rejected out of hand once one knows the funder's identity.

Thus Balling makes this argument: "Regardless of the source of the funding, [the research] is peer-reviewed by specialists and published in noted scientific journals. The system provides a good screening process for good research."[22] Perhaps the researcher himself was suborned by oil industry gold; but it strains credulity to believe that a journal's editors and peer reviewers were also bribed to ensure the publication of pro-industry propaganda. Because scientific research is critically scrutinized by peer reviewers before it is published, the question of funding is just not all that relevant. Or in Balling's more colorful formulation, "I don't think the scientific community gives a rat's butt who funded the thing."[23] Similarly, Michaels notes that it is absurd to reject his findings because his research is partially funded by industry: "In fact, we receive 70 percent of funding from public and 30 percent from private concerns. By extension that would make my research 70 percent beholden to public interests and 30 percent to private interests."[24]

Furthermore, it seems unfair to suggest that government-funded research—unlike industry-funded research—is necessarily disinterested and objective. It is wrong, Michaels argues, to imply "that only one side can ask questions and that's the tax-supported side."[25] It is particularly wrong because the government may be just as unlikely to support a researcher expressing doubts about global warming as the energy industry is to support one advocating stringent limits on energy emissions.[26] Thus Fred Singer contends that "government funding goes only to those who support global warming threats." For this reason, he asserts, many scientists are reluctant to express doubts about global warming orthodoxy: in effect they say, "We agree with you, but we can't put our names down [in support of skepticism] because we will lose our research contracts."[27]

In short, much though not all funding for research comes from sources with at least some mild preference for particular substantive findings; often that is just as true of government funding as of industry funding.[28] It is easy but unproductive to calumniate researchers because of who funds them; and that calumny can be (and has been) directed against both government-funded and industry-funded research. Once again, it makes much more sense to look at what the researcher's methodology is, not where his money comes from. The message, not the messenger, is what demands analysis.

Medical Breakthroughs and Market Profits

In April the *San Diego Union-Tribune*[29] reported a promising medical advance in the fight against brain tumors; the *Los Angeles Times*[30] and *USA Today*[31] also covered the story. Researchers at the Sidney Kimmel Cancer Center in La Jolla and at UCLA injected genetically boosted cells into twelve rats with brain tumors; the tumors then disappeared and did not return when the animals were exposed to additional tumor cells. Results of the experiment were published in the *Proceedings of the National Academy of Sciences*.

One of the researchers, UCLA microbiologist Habib Fakhrai, contended that "We have taken a big first step toward finding new approaches to gene therapy for cancer."[32] The *Union-Tribune* article noted that the researchers were awaiting FDA approval to experiment on human subjects. It also stated that use of the researchers' technique had been licensed by a biotechnology company, the Immune Response Corporation.

Media coverage of this development was sharply criticized by University of Pennsylvania bioethicist Art Caplan,[33] who claimed that the story gave false hope (by suggesting that success with rats could translate fairly easily into success with humans). Furthermore, Caplan noted that the project investigators had a financial incentive to hype their achievement: they owned stock in Immune Response Corporation, whose stock rose 67 percent after news of the tumor treatment was released.[34]

In this example, then, we finally see clear grounds for suspecting a researcher because of his financial stake. Significantly, though, even here research methodology proves to be of greater importance than the researcher's (possible) motives. First, as Caplan noted, the *Proceedings of the National Academy of Sciences*, its lofty name notwithstanding, does not employ rigorous peer review, which means that reporters should have been "a little more wary" of Fakhrai's finding than they were.[35]

Even more important, Caplan contended, was the fact that the study examined only twelve rats, obviously a very small number. Furthermore, as Caplan observed, "We are actually very good at curing rats of cancer"; the problem is that cancer treatments that work on rats may produce unacceptable side effects when applied to humans.[36] Finally, the *Union-Tribune* story was problematic in that only the researchers themselves—and no outside observers who would be better able to add a disinterested perspective—were interviewed. It is unwise for reporters to interview the researchers alone, for the same reason that it is unwise for researchers to circumvent peer review: researchers, like parents, are ordinarily not well equipped to identify the shortcomings and limits of their offspring.

In short, even when a researcher's motive gives unequivocal cause for suspicion, a study will (or will not) be persuasive because of the way in which it was conducted and subsequently assessed (or not assessed) prior to publication. Even when a motive gives rise to suspicion, it's still trumped by methodology. Simply put, methodology matters far more than motive.

Judging the Quality of Research

It would be helpful if there were ironclad rules enabling readers to distinguish research to be taken seriously from research that should be suspect. Instead, however, there are only guidelines.

As we saw above, peer review is far from infallible: the peers, themselves, after all—that is, the scientific reviewers—are only human. Because reviewers can and will make mistakes, research can appear in peer-reviewed journals (even prestigious ones) but still be of dubious quality. Furthermore, some very good research is produced by think tanks that do not use peer review. Nevertheless, for all of its flaws, what Churchill said of democracy can also be applied to peer review: it is the worst system for judging research, except for all of the alternatives that have ever been tried. Findings that have been subjected to peer review are simply more credible than those that have not.

But peer review does not exempt research from criticism. (If it did, this book would be far shorter.) The real question, then, concerns the criteria for criticism. As we have seen repeatedly, knowing a researcher's motive at most offers grounds for suspicion; it does not in and of itself prove a crime. Furthermore, all researchers are likely to have motives, so a critic who attacks a researcher's motive wields a double-edged sword: the research admired by the critic will likely also have been done by a motivated researcher. For that reason, serious and persuasive criticism must address a study's methodology: What questions did the researcher choose to ask (or not ask)? How did he attempt to answer them? What might account for the answers that are generated? These are the important issues; informative reporting will address them, while inaccurate reporting will skirt over them.

CHAPTER 10

TUNNEL VISION AND BLIND SPOTS
The Danger of Hedgehog Interpretations

The Census Bureau reported that income inequality has been growing steadily since 1968. It seems clear that changes in the economy explain much of this development. But do economic changes tell the whole story? A *New York Times* news story ignored other possible explanations—explanations offered by the Census Bureau itself.

Scientists at the National Center for Infectious Diseases calculated that deaths from infectious diseases rose by an alarming 58 percent in America between 1980 and 1992. Why this sudden rise? One obvious explanation is that the microbes are becoming more deadly, and medical science is failing to meet their challenge. But the news coverage mostly failed to consider a second interpretation of the data: the microbes are killing more people because there are more old people around to be killed—a sign of the success, not the failure, of American medicine.

The health advocacy group Citizen Action released a study of American child mortality that singled out poverty as the critical variable. Why did the study discount the possible impact of parental attitudes that poverty may not predict?

All of these stories illustrate the related problems of tunnel vision and blind spots: that is, the dangers posed by looking in only one direction for an explanation, hence ignoring alternative explanations that give a rounder, fuller picture of a subject. Often a single, seemingly obvious explanation will suggest itself (or be suggested to us by researchers and reporters). Unfortunately, it is easy to be misled once you stop looking for alternative explanations. The seemingly obvious interpretation may turn out to be one-sided, causing us to overlook other explanations that can usefully supplement (or in some cases even replace) it.

Tunnel vision and blind spots are the intellectual shortcomings that bedevil the thinkers whom the intellectual historian Isaiah Berlin called hedgehogs. In a well-known essay Berlin divided intellectuals into two categories—hedgehogs and foxes, terms used by a Greek poet who stated that "The fox knows many things, but the hedgehog knows one big thing."[1] The "one big thing" that hedgehogs emphasize may be important, but focusing on it can still blind them to many other things that are also important. A single explanation, in short, shouldn't automatically cause us to ignore alternatives.

In this chapter we'll look at some factors that are often overlooked in hedgehog attempts to make sense of social indicators: demographic shifts and personal characteristics. Too often findings are understood exclusively as products of objective forces upon the people in their grip. Objective forces are emphasized in statements like the following: "Inequality among households is growing worse, because the economy isn't generating good jobs for uneducated people"; "infectious diseases are becoming more deadly, because microbes are becoming resistant to antibiotics"; "infant mortality has remained high, because poverty is so prevalent in America."

But it is also possible to understand findings as the products of more subjective forces: people's personal characteristics, including things like their age and their marital status. Personal characteristics are emphasized in explanations like these: "Inequality among households has increased, because more people today live in single-parent families that are likely to be less prosperous"; "deaths from infectious diseases have increased, because a greater proportion of Americans is elderly now, and elderly people are more likely to die of infectious diseases"; "infant mortality continues to pose a threat, because parental attitudes and behavior put too many infants at risk."

Note that these explanations are not mutually exclusive: to focus on personal characteristics as the only relevant factor, no less than to ignore them altogether, is the act of a hedgehog who knows only one big thing. Thus our first point is not that either personal characteristics or objective forces provide the "true" explanation; instead, it's that complementary explanations are likely to be more informative than any single one. But we wish to make a second point as well, concerning the motives of hedgehog researchers and reporters. We suspect that researchers and reporters are often reluctant to focus on personal characteristics, fearing that to do so is to engage in "blaming the victim." Laudable as this motive may be, though, hedgehog interpretations are still flawed: inadequate and partial understandings of social problems don't help the victims or anyone else.

Changing Economy, Changing Households

In June 1996 the Census Bureau published a report, "A Brief Look at Postwar U.S. Income Inequality." The report showed that American income distribution came to be less equal between 1968 (when the top fifth, or quintile, of households earned 42.8 percent of all household income) and 1994 (when the top quintile's share of income increased to 49.1 percent). According to the report, the middle three quintiles' share of income declined from 53.0 percent in 1968 to 47.3 percent in 1994; and the bottom quintile's share dropped from 4.2 percent in 1968 to 3.6 percent in 1994.

The report noted that a methodological change accounted for some of the recent increase in income disparity: through 1992, the wealthiest households had been permitted to report no more than $300,000 in income, but beginning in 1993 as much as $1 million could be reported.[2] The methodological changes presumably make post-1992 data more reliable, but because the incomes reported for the wealthiest households in 1992 and earlier were artificially low, the increase since 1992 is exaggerated. But regardless of the impact of the methodological change, the report concluded that "there was nonetheless a real increase in inequality between 1992 and 1993."[3]

The report was summarized in a front-page story in the *New York Times* marked by a number of more or less serious factual errors.[4] The report discussed "household income," but the graph accompanying the article purported to illustrate the gap in family income, which is not the same thing.[5] The article misstated the share of income reported by the wealthiest fifth of households,[6] and it gave two contradictory accounts of the impact of the study's methodological shift.[7]

But the real issue is how the Census findings might have been interpreted. The Census report commendably advanced both economic and demographic explanations, speaking of "changes in the Nation's labor market and its household composition." Economic explanations included the increased premium for skilled workers, the shift from manufacturing jobs to service jobs, increased global competition, and the decline in unionization. At the same time, the report also emphasized "long-run changes in living arrangements that have taken place that tend to exacerbate differences in household incomes. For example, divorces and separations, births out of wedlock, and the increasing age at first marriage have led to a shift away from married-couple households and toward single-parent and nonfamily households, which typically have lower incomes."[8]

The *Times* story, however, took note of the economic explanations but gave short shrift to the demographic ones that capture changes in American households over time. More precisely, it discussed demographic shifts among the wealthy ("Well-educated, highly skilled women . . . [marry] . . . well-educated, highly skilled men [and] create households with very high incomes") but not among the poor. The *Times* account simply ignored the shift toward single-parent and nonfamily households stressed by the Census Bureau itself. How important was this demographic shift?

A scholarly article cited in the Census report offers a useful summary. Eighty-five percent of families headed by someone aged twenty-five to sixty-four were two-parent families in 1959; the figure dropped to 71 percent in 1989. And single-parent families went from 7 percent of the total in 1959 to 14 percent in 1989. Furthermore, only 18 percent of families in the bottom income quintile were single-parent families in 1959; but the figure rose to 36 percent in 1989. And as authors Lynn A. Karoly and Gary Burtless observed, "No trend toward this form of living arrangement was evident among persons at the top of the income distribution."[9]

Clearly, the demographic shift toward single-parent families has exacerbated American income inequality: families with one earner (or none) will tend to be poorer than families with two. Whereas 92.8 percent of families in 1993's top quintile consisted of married couples (compared with 43.3 percent in the bottom quintile), only 4.8 percent of families in the top quintile were single-parent families headed by a woman (compared with 51.7 percent of families in the bottom quintile).[10] In other words, more families in the bottom quintile are headed by unmarried women than by married couples, whereas there are more than nineteen married couples in the top income quintile for every household headed by an unmarried woman. Those two statistics go far toward explaining the size of the income gap between the top and bottom quintiles.

Commendably, the Karoly–Burtless article slighted neither demographic nor economic factors. It acknowledged that "the labor market became a much more hostile place for poorly paid men after the 1960s," but it still contended that an economic interpretation of rising income inequality cannot stand alone.

> People in the bottom fifth of the income distribution have derived smaller incomes from male earnings for reasons in addition to the shrinking hourly and weekly earnings paid to low-income men. First, changes in family composition have deprived an increasing percentage of families of the presence of a male head. By definition, these families receive no income from male heads' earnings.[11]

The *Times* account is by no means unique in discussing the rise in income inequality while abstracting from demographic changes. To pick one of many possible examples, economist Robert Kuttner, discussing the Census report in an op-ed, declared that "At bottom, the widening gap between the rich and everyone else reflects the shift to a purer market economy and the erosion of institutions that once offset market forces."[12] But that is a hedgehog explanation, only a partial truth; because it ignores demographic factors, it is nothing like an exhaustive truth.

To understand the rise in income inequality, then, it helps to consider both economics and demography. Unfortunately, analysts often tend to slight the demographic component. As Robert Samuelson has written (in discussing the effect of immigration on American poverty),

> The silent [and false] assumption is that the population is static. If poverty hasn't declined, then something must be making it harder for people to escape poverty. . . . But the population isn't static. Many people at the

bottom are immigrants, and because they arrive poor, they instantly aggravate [our poverty problem].[13]

The population changes over time, and these changes need to be taken into account when we study our social problems. Thus the proportion of single-parent households in the bottom quintile has grown notably over time and thereby depressed the average bottom-quintile income. But that lower average income would not necessarily mean that single parents are now earning less on average than they did a decade ago (or even that they are earning less relative to, say, workers in two-parent families). Instead, it might tell us only that income in the bottom quintile has gone down because the proportion of single-parent families in the quintile has increased.

For this reason, as economist Herbert Stein has observed, discussions of economic inequality should always take into account the impact of demographic changes. In Stein's words, we need to distinguish between "changes in the degree of inequality among persons of similar relevant characteristics, such as 15-year-old unmarried mothers who are high school drop-outs . . . changes in the degree of inequality between persons of different relevant characteristics, such as between 15-year-old drop-out unmarried mothers and 40-year-old male lawyers . . . [and] changes in the proportion of different kinds of people in the population."[14] Changes in the distribution of income need to be understood in part as the result of demographic changes in the society. Hedgehogs who ignore such changes miss out on an important part of the picture.

Infectious Diseases and an Aging Population

Population changes are even more important in assessing the significance of death rates. For obvious reasons, everything else being equal, an older population will experience more deaths than a younger one. That fact was for the most part ignored in media coverage of Robert W. Pinner's *Journal of the American Medical Association* (*JAMA*) article on the rise in death rates from infectious diseases.[15]

The article made headlines by pointing to a 58 percent increase in deaths from infectious diseases between 1980 and 1992. But as many newspaper accounts noted, the 58 percent figure was exaggerated, because AIDS had not been recognized as a cause of death in 1980 (but killed over 30,000 people in 1992). Thankfully, there is little reason to expect another comparably deadly disease will emerge out of nowhere and kill hundreds of thousands of people in the future, so the 58 percent rise is unlikely to be replicated in years to come. For this reason the *JAMA* article noted that if AIDS deaths are excluded, the death rate for infectious diseases rose by a more modest 22 percent. Many news accounts helpfully provided both figures for the increase in deaths—with and without AIDS deaths.[16]

But virtually no newspaper pointed out that the 58 percent figure was suspect in a far more fundamental way: it did not take into account the aging of the American population between 1980 and 1992. A comparison between two crude death rates—that is, a simple comparison of the number of deaths as a percentage of the number of living persons in two different years—is of little value. Instead, it is necessary to consider the age distribution of the population to make sense of mortality data. As medical sociologists Thomas McKeown and C. R. Lowe explain, "The crude death rate (the number of deaths per 1[00],000 total population) provides a very incomplete and, indeed, a misleading picture of the amount of serious disease in the population. For, other things being equal, the more old people there are in a population, the higher the crude death rate will be."[17] Because many more elderly Americans were alive (hence susceptible to death from an infectious disease) in 1992 than 1980, a crude-rate increase in deaths is predictable and not that informative. In fact, in another article Pinner himself declared that "the proportion of persons in the United States population older than 65 years increased from 9.8% [in 1979] to 12.5% [in 1992]," an increase of almost 28 percent.[18]

The real issue, then, is the size of the increase once one takes account of the aging of the American population over time: a statistical technique makes it possible to "adjust for age," to see what would have happened in 1992 if the age distribution then was comparable to what it had been in 1980. Pinner's article reported that "age-adjusted mortality increased 39%" between 1980 and 1992:[19] in other words, fully a third of the increase in deaths was a predictable result of the aging of America—not a sign that the microbes were suddenly becoming more difficult to defeat. Pinner also pointed out that respiratory tract infections, which caused 47 percent of all deaths from infectious diseases in 1992, "occur principally in older age groups, and aging of the population partially explains the increased crude death rates from this cause."[20]

Unfortunately, this significant qualifier for the most part disappeared in the news accounts. To its credit, the *Los Angeles Times* informed its readers that some of the increase in deaths "reflected the growing number of elderly people."[21] But even the *Times* did not provide the 39 percent figure for age-adjusted deaths. The accounts in the *Boston Globe*, *Chicago Tribune*, and [New York] *Newsday* simply ignored the impact of demographic shifts on Pinner's findings.

In short, most news outlets told only part of the story, focusing on factors like "the steady emergence of virulent new infections" (*Boston Globe*) and "the uncontrolled growth of the human population" (*Chicago Tribune*). No doubt these are important factors in explaining the rise in deaths from infectious diseases, but they are not the only factors. Nevertheless, journalists by and large displayed tunnel vision in ignoring another important factor—the aging of the American population. In some measure they were encouraged to do so by the *JAMA* article itself, which was unusual in its emphasis on crude rather than age-adjusted death rates. Still, the article did provide the percentage increase for age-adjusted rates and did explain that demographic factors accounted for as much as a third of the increase in deaths (hardly a trivial amount). But reporters who excelled at conveying one part of the explanation paid no heed to an important second part.

Poverty, Illegitimacy, and Infant Mortality

In December 1994 the health advocacy group Citizen Action released a study of childhood mortality in the United States. The study was reported in the *Washington Post*, which summarized its conclusion by quoting the reaction of Eve Brooks, president of the National Association of Child Advocates: "There is a critical link between child poverty and child mortality."[22]

The report suggested that eliminating or reducing poverty would significantly decrease the number of deaths among American children. In the words of principal study author Tom Pollak, "Reducing the level of poverty in the nation is the best means of lowering infant and child death rates."[23] As the report pointed out, the problem of child mortality is really the problem of infant mortality: "A child is more than 10 times more likely to die in his or her first year of life than in any subsequent year up to age 20. Infant deaths under age 1 comprise an overwhelming majority of deaths compared to any other age group with more than 54 percent (more than 38,000 deaths per year) of all child deaths under age 20."[24]

Infant mortality is distressingly common in the United States, especially when its figures are compared with those of other Western industrialized democracies. Thus in 1995 the U.S. infant mortality rate stood at 7.5 deaths per thousand live births—the lowest ever. Still, that rate was higher than the 1994 rates in nineteen other industrialized countries.[25] How to explain America's comparatively poor ranking? The Citizen Action report faithfully argued the conventional view that "the prevalence of poverty and a corresponding lack of adequate health care" explain our death rate.[26]

But is poverty the only or even the most important factor underlying America's comparatively high infant mortality rate? One finding in Citizen Action's own report seems to suggest that poverty is not the master variable: counties with the highest levels of black child poverty turn out to have lower death rates for infants aged twenty-eight days or less than counties with the lowest levels of black child poverty.[27] Perhaps, then, the conventional explanation is wrong, or at least insufficient. Could factors other than child poverty be more important causes of America's elevated level of infant mortality?

American Enterprise Institute demographer Nicholas Eberstadt has argued that subjective factors—parental attitudes and behavior—are important causes of infant mortality that have been overlooked as a result of the single-minded focus on material deprivation. As Eberstadt notes, the U.S. infant mortality rate is comparatively high, because proportionately more American babies, both black and white, are born with low birthweights (defined as less than 2,500 grams, or roughly five and one-half pounds). "By comparison with other Western societies enjoying especially low rates of infant mortality, U.S. babies at any given birthweight appear to have unusually good chances of surviving . . . regardless of race."[28] But the large number of low-birthweight babies, who face the highest risk, elevates America's infant mortality rate.

Eberstadt has marshaled much evidence showing that "parental attitudes and behavior" seem to affect "a child's chances of being born at low birthweight."[29] For example, babies described by their parents as "mistimed or unwanted" were far more likely to be born at low birthweights than babies born to low-income parents; low-birthweight babies were also far more likely to be born to mothers who smoked heavily during pregnancy than to low-income mothers.[30]

Eberstadt's finding about illegitimacy is even more striking. Remarkably, a 1982 survey shows that "infant mortality rates for white mothers over age twenty were higher for unmarried but college-educated women than for married high school—or even grade school—dropouts. The same pattern held true among black mothers."[31] Since the poverty rate for families headed by single mothers with at least a year of college education is strikingly similar to the rate for married-couple families headed by someone with less than a high school education, it is unlikely that poverty rather than illegitimacy is the crucial factor.[32]

Behavioral differences seem to explain the link between illegitimacy, the generation of low-birthweight babies, and the increased incidence of infant mortality. Even when one controls for poverty, married women seem much more likely to obtain adequate prenatal care than unmarried ones. Thus the National Center for Health Statistics has reported that "unmarried mothers . . . are less likely than married mothers to begin [prenatal] care early."[33]

With respect to Washington, D.C.'s elevated infant mortality rate, Eberstadt has argued that the impact of factors such as poverty and lack of education "is reduced to utter insignificance if illegitimacy is added to the equation. No other factors are so closely associated with differences in low birthweight among D.C.'s neighborhoods as their ratios of out-of-wedlock births and single-parent families."[34]

For our purposes, though, it is not crucial whether Eberstadt's explanation of American infant mortality is more persuasive than the conventional focus on poverty favored by Citizen Action. More crucial is what Eberstadt has termed

the reluctance to examine a topic [the health risks that may be faced by infants born to unwed mothers] that might help to explain the U.S. infant mortality problem and possibly help save lives[.]. . . Many researchers and policy makers [have] seemed to feel that inquiries in this area were, so to speak, illegitimate. Some scholars [have] explicitly challenged the motives of investigators who pursued the issue and raised the charge of blaming the victim.

But as Eberstadt argued, "This point of view . . . does not identify newborns exposed to heightened risk of death as the victims in the drama that it frames."[35]

In short, the deficiencies of a hedgehog insistence on one and only one explanation have practical as well as theoretical implications. Not only may we understand less if we stubbornly refuse to examine alternative explanations, we may also fail to prevent the death of innocent victims.

The Absence of Alternative Explanations

How should we understand the preference for one sort of explanation over another? We can begin by noting that in two of our three case studies, the journalistic coverage more or less accurately summarized the relevant research. To put that another way, in two of the three cases, questions that journalists might have raised about the research went unasked. Citizen Action emphasized poverty as the cause of child (and hence infant) mortality; so did the *Post*'s story. The *JAMA* article emphasized crude rather than age-adjusted death rates; so did the news summaries. However, in the case of the Census study of income inequality, the *Times* coverage oversimplified research that commendably pointed to different kinds of explanations, by focusing on only one. That observation may seem to suggest that researchers are more to blame than reporters for ignoring alternative explanations: if researchers offer only one cause, what are reporters supposed to do, other than accurately summarize their findings?

It may well be true that hedgehog researchers deserve the brunt of the blame. On the other hand, recall that even the *JAMA* article and the Citizen Action report pointed to alternative explanations. The *JAMA* article did note (though it surely failed to emphasize) that the aging of the American population was partially responsible for the increase in deaths from infectious diseases, and Citizen Action's report did include the counterintuitive finding that infant mortality was actually less common in poorer black counties than in richer ones. In other words, it would not have been that hard for reporters to raise questions about the research, even while faithfully distilling it. But the major question, regarding both researchers and reporters, is why there may be a bias favoring a focus on objective forces rather than personal characteristics. Why are impersonal social forces thought to offer better explanations?[36]

We can suggest two factors, one methodological, the other ideological. First, insofar as social science has aspired to be truly scientific, one can easily see how the focus on impersonal social forces arose. Natural science, after all, focuses on impersonal natural forces; and social scientists have certainly been tempted to ape the methods adopted by their more authoritative brethren in the harder sciences. The desire to mimic the natural sciences may help explain the preference, in that impersonal social forces are easier to quantify—think of incomes, or years of education—than are more subjective forces like personal attitudes.

The ideological factor, to which we alluded above, is the desire to avoid blaming the victim. That motive probably helps explain much of the research (and the journalistic coverage that it generates) on income inequality and infant mortality. It may even help account for the research and reporting on infectious disease mortality. Doesn't it seem somewhat callous to say (as we do), "Of course more people are dying. What do you expect? They're getting older, aren't they?" Much better (both for researchers in need of financial support and for journalists eager to tell a good and exciting scare story) to focus on deadly microbes that present an increasingly grave danger.

This reasoning has an intuitive appeal: Is it not unfair to seem to blame the unfortunate for their own plight? But on the other hand (to paraphrase the philosopher George Santayana), those who do not understand their plight may be condemned to worsen it. Even from the standpoint of the prospective victims, and certainly from the larger standpoint of society as a whole, a more comprehensive and accurate understanding is preferable to a partial and less accurate one. We simply can't fix what we don't understand.

Important social problems are likely to be complicated and to derive from various interrelated causes. It's a good idea to be suspicious of monocausal explanations. In interpreting news coverage of research findings, always remember that hedgehogs who know only one big thing—the impact of impersonal forces—are necessarily also blind to many other important things.

CONCLUSION

HARD TO TELL
Journalism, Science, and Public Policy—
An Inherent Conflict?

The news, of course, marches on in its relentless fashion. In the time that has passed since the episodes chronicled above, additional stories have occurred and recurred in the morning headlines (as they will again in the perpetual tomorrow). Yet our efforts to explain what has gone wrong with yesterday's headlines should not be treated as a simple exercise in hindsight. The attempt to stem (or at least channel) the avalanche of misapprehensions may seem like the labors of Sisyphus, the mythical Greek king condemned to forever roll a rock uphill only to see it evade him and tumble back immediately upon reaching the summit. But our exercise can lead to lasting gain if the reader has developed a reasoned skepticism regarding the claims of the daily news. Our success is measured by the degree to which readers now confront the media with new questions and new standards before their assertions are allowed to pass the gates of acceptance.

This concluding chapter has two goals. One is to examine in a focused manner what happens when research findings and news accounts directly engage with public policy decision making. In general, our concern is that the principles behind each are often set at cross-purposes. The second is to explore the underlying presuppositions that guide journalistic choices, often in an unconscious way. The objective is to sum up our investigation by examining two factors that help explain why it is "hard to tell" which media stories about science are accurate. First, from a scientific perspective it is often quite literally hard to tell what public policy response should appropriately follow from the accumulation of data that are all too often inconclusive (or at least less conclusive than is often suggested). Second, from a journalistic perspective it is often hard to tell stories accurately, not only because of complexity but also because of the temptation to turn news accounts into morality plays in which opposing scientific (and political) forces are cast as heroes and villains.

The Elusive Quest for Scientific Certainty

Let us begin by taking note of American society's widespread reliance on data—but also the frequent uncertainty that such material misleadingly masks. The journalistic fixation on data is rightly attested to by media critic James Fallows: "Most ... journalists ... share the crucial ... belief that the truth lies in things that can be measured. Because they are not confident expressing judgments about the actual merits of [a claim], they seek refuge in areas where judgments are unassailable because they can be tied to 'hard' data."[1] Policymakers share this journalistic predilection: they too are fond of data, the harder the better. Both policymakers and journalists also esteem scientists, or indeed any activity that can be termed research, in large measure because research produces a valuable commodity—the data that constitute the hard currency of policy debates. If you want to win an argument in policy circles, smart money knows where to turn for real clout—not to the lobby but the laboratory. Because of their capacity to help settle public policy disputes, researchers have never been so carefully courted or believed to be so consequential. Every side in a debate clamors for their allegiance, and their numbers are thought to be definitive.

For instance, justifying his recent decision to exhume the remains of a Vietnam veteran from the Tomb of the Unknowns, President Clinton declared in a Memorial Day speech that "It was the right course of action *because science has given us a chance* to restore his name ... and we had to seize it" [emphasis added]. When Health and Human Services Secretary

Donna Shalala defended the administration's decision to offer clean needles to intravenous drug users, she was asked whether politics had played
a part in her decision. Her answer went the president's not one but two
better—"Absolutely not; from the beginning of this effort, it has been
about *science, science, science*" [emphasis added]. Nor is this invoking of
science in any way the province of one political party. The conservative
Heritage Foundation has invested in its new Center for Data Analysis,
beefing up its potential to generate social-science statistics with the NCP
Viper 1000 supercomputer, which can perform 1.2 billion calculations
per second. That should generate some salvos in the policy wars. It would
seem that an appeal to science is, for political parties, somehow preferable
to a resort to mere politics—never mind the realization that claiming the
scientific high ground is itself a political act.

Policymakers, especially when on the horns of a dilemma, are often
gratified by newspaper headlines on the order of "Science Has Spoken"
or "Research Has Concluded." Often, however, it is the politician who
has actually "concluded" something or other but finds that his argument
is treated with more respect if it can be offered as more than mere opinion. As H. L. Mencken once observed, much of politics is little more than
"prejudice made plausible." Surely the plausibility is more powerful if
well dressed with data. Relying on research has an additional quality that
policymakers find attractive. Since science is regarded as an objective picture of how things inexorably are in nature, data have the effect of absolv-
ing politicians of responsibility for a decision. The political arbiter may
now claim that science not only substantiates but practically compels the
decision toward which the policymaker was inclined in the first place.
When challenged, the politician can retreat behind a screen of data and
argue that science practically made him or her do it. Science has become
authoritative in settling disputes for a variety of reasons, not the least of
which is its extraordinary effectiveness in mastering the world. But there
are politically pragmatic forces at work as well. Policymakers like to
invoke science in support of their political agendas because it lends an
aura of inevitability to their proposals by implying that Nature herself
approves of their decisions. But in reality science is frequently far less
conclusive than is claimed.

In fact, if we look carefully, we see a process that is almost alchemical:
as laboratory results make it into the headlines, scientific uncertainty

mutates into journalistic conviction. A train of events like this often unfolds in the following manner. First, a scientific body like the National Academy of Sciences convenes a panel to assess the state of our knowledge in an important area. The panel will likely be divided, as it evaluates a multiplicity of claims and demonstrations of varying quality. Out of the panel will come a recommendation, often rather tepid and sometimes even formally contested by the dissenting opinion of some panelists. A statement of this sort is then issued: "While no study is itself fully convincing, a pattern of evidence suggests that so and so is not unreasonable." But in a short while the qualifiers begin to drop out of the statement, and interested parties start to declare that "a preponderance of evidence now demonstrates so and so." By the time the investigation is deployed by a policymaker to justify a decision, all tentativeness disappears, and the media are told that "a substantial body of meticulous science has proven that x does in fact mean y." All of this ratcheting-up takes place without a single aspect of the underlying research having become more clear during the intervening period. But in the policy arena data are judged less by whether they are true or false than by whether they are useful or not.

Never before has science (or its appearance) been so pervasive in public policy, as it extends its role far beyond the traditional areas of defense or energy issues. Debates over the environment, health risks, welfare reform, trade disputes, census taking, and even sexual practices are among those that are now ceded to scientific investigations. It follows that all parties in a political dispute like to proclaim the existence of scientific backing for their proposals. The production of numbers seems to justify politicians' claims, while obscuring any weakness in their arguments. Research results, epidemiological findings, and randomized control trials are cited everywhere, as everyone proffers charts, graphs, tables, and "findings" in search of the crowning status—a conclusion deemed "statistically significant."

It may therefore be necessary to differentiate between actual science—the process of discovery through the application of systematic principles of inquiry—from a spurious imitator: "SCIENCE," which is intended only to shape public policy. In "SCIENCE" the authority and image of science are borrowed (as a sort of lightning stolen from the laboratory) to charge up an otherwise lifeless political agenda. But the public is not invariably well served when policy is determined by oracles with white laboratory coats. Whenever public policy and genuine science combine to produce "SCIENCE," problems arise, because the principles of these respective arenas differ. First, policy decisions demand closure, conclusiveness, and certainty. By contrast, science is by its nature cautious, contingent, and corrigible. Evidence is rarely conclusive and indisputable, hypotheses must bend to new facts, and definitive consensus on an issue is nearly impossible to forge. As former *Nature* editor Sir John Maddox has said, "Consensus is inherently a political (and not a scientific) act."

Hence policymakers are often frustrated by science, which offers caveats, qualifications, and complexities. Recall Harry Truman's quest for a one-handed economist, who couldn't always duck issues by saying "on the other hand." A gap inevitably opens between the needs of the story deadline or the definitive courtroom decision and what science can with assurance offer. Since journalism and policy abhor a vacuum at least as much as nature, into the breach will rush other players—advocates, special pleaders, and spin-doctors—who will claim to have the certainty, confidence, and dramatic simplicity that resolves the dilemma. Frustrated by the tentativeness of genuine science, policymakers are frequently attracted to those who offer to slash all Gordian knots, often at the expense of more cautious and contingent scientific voices. Possessed of firm convictions wedded to striking simplicities, and offering the dispatch required by doers rather than thinkers, their breathless claims of certainty relieve the anxious decision maker. The press also tends to prefer this false appearance of certainty, to which it sometimes adds a savory dash of alarm and a lump of lurking suspicion that someone, somewhere is to blame.

Climatologist Dr. Richard Lindzen of the Massachusetts Institute of Technology, speaking at a recent Washington policy luncheon, captured our frailties in the following paradigm: "Everything is connected to everything. Nothing is certain. Anything may cause anything. Therefore, something must be done." This construction, which captures the naive mindset of many journalists and regulators alike, is a false guide to wisdom. Everything *is* associated with something. Sometimes, however, not very much needs to be done, at least not just yet. Even in science, as T. S. Eliot's Prufrock found, there may be "time yet for a hundred indecisions, and for a hundred visions and revisions, before the taking of a toast and tea."[2]

A second problem is that science is inductive and proceeds by an incremental interrogation of nature. When the rules of science are followed, ideally the data alone are the ultimate determiners of reality. Science, properly constructed and argued, forces an objective appraisal of all of the facts before one, considering each in turn in relation to the hypothesis being advanced. Ideally, the research community tries to disable each claim with a systematic challenge. Mounting this challenge is the expected task of the researcher and the explicit charge of the peer-review community when publication approaches. Whatever is left standing after the assault is regarded as established, however provisionally. Policy disputes, in contrast, are conducted more on the model of courtroom litigation. The parties implore one another to just "look at the evidence," but each one acts like a defense counsel or prosecutor, reading the science selectively to establish the best "case" for their respective clients. That is, they arrange the facts that help (and ignore those that contradict) into a coherent narrative of either guilt or innocence. Thus when multifaceted scientific accounts are presented before the body politic, they are judged not according to the scientific principle that assembled them but rather by a litigation mentality that seeks to capitalize upon them by "reading through" the complexity so as to extract support. Those who argue over the political consequences of evidence are not (necessarily) lying or distorting the basic scientific facts, since the evidence is often really "there." But when they ignore the complexities or contingencies, science is simplified and distorted, providing a narrative that serves primarily to justify a particular agenda. The result, however, is that the scientific process is often betrayed in the encounter with policy.

Three Cautionary Examples

To illustrate this process, let us turn now to three recent examples. When Carol Browner—then head of the Environmental Protection Agency (EPA)—proposed new regulations on air quality, she found herself in an intense political fight. The costs of the new regulations would be considerable, while the health benefits were questionable. But at a critical juncture, Ms. Browner's case was suddenly strengthened by the report of a study of air quality and infant health undertaken by EPA scientist Tracey Woodruff in the journal *Environmental Health Perspectives*.[3] The research led to some alarming headlines: "Panel Links SIDS, Air Pollution; Doctors Blame 500 Deaths a Year on Particulates," according to the *Baltimore Sun*.[4]

SIDS (sudden infant death syndrome) death rates were indeed found to be as much as 26 percent higher in areas with high air pollution than in areas with low air pollution. According to the activist Environmental Working Group, this means that over five hundred infants a year die as a result of airborne particulate matter. But how good was the science? First, the study contained a major anomaly. Low-birthweight infants, those most likely to die and most vulnerable to air pollutants, showed no statistically significant increase in risk. This is odd, because according to a definitive, case-control study of SIDS appearing in the *British Medical Journal*,[5] low birthweight was strongly correlated with death, the relative risk standing at 380 percent.

Furthermore, many other risk factors were far greater than the 26 percent increase attributed to particulates: an infant's masculinity increased his risk by 64 percent; sleeping on an old mattress increased the risk by 250 percent; being born to an unmarried mother raised it by 422 percent; being born to a mother who left school early increased it by 428 percent; being premature raised it by 450 percent; and being poor increased it by an astounding 960 percent. It is also worth noting that SIDS deaths decreased by nearly a third overall after doctors began recommending that parents should simply have infants sleep on their backs.

Finally, according to research recently published in the *New England Journal of Medicine*,[6] infants suffering from a certain congenital heart condition face an astonishing 4,100 percent increased risk of SIDS; the condition accounted for half of the SIDS deaths in the study of 34,000 infants. What these numbers mean is that the Woodruff study, treated as compelling evidence by Browner, simply failed to tell the whole story about relative risks—as did the news accounts hooked by the alarming research. By ignoring a host of confounding factors, they left the suggestion that air pollution was a critical variable in SIDS, which could then be ameliorated by regulating factories. For researchers engaged in an effort to understand and convey to policymakers the possible causes of SIDS, presenting the entire epidemiological picture would be an imperative. But if the primary focus is to substantiate a policy decision, then SIDS epidemiology becomes an available set of facts that, if read selectively, can be arranged to support the policy inclination.

A second example of a rush to judgment based on equivocal data comes from an article entitled "Condom Availability in New York City Public High Schools," which appeared in the *American Journal of Public Health*.[7] The research compared the sexual activity of two groups of high school students, in New York City and Chicago. Although both groups received sex education, the New York students were given condoms in school, while their Chicago counterparts had to acquire them elsewhere. The results showed no effective difference in the amount of sexual activity in the two groups. In New York 60.1 percent of the teenagers were sexually active, whereas the Chicago figure was 59.7 percent: the difference between the two groups is not statistically significant. But how was this research covered by the press? Peter Jennings reported the story on *ABC World News Tonight* by leading with the statement that "Giving condoms to students leads to safer sex." Jennings continued, "Researchers have now confirmed [that] . . . giving out free condoms to high school students does not make them more likely to have sex."[8] Similarly, the *New York Times* termed the results "strong evidence that making condoms available in schools does not encourage adolescent promiscuity, as critics of condom programs had feared."[9] An accompanying editorial headline further suggested that "Congress Should Support Condom Distribution." That is, the press saw no ambiguity in the research and reported that the results had uniformly confirmed the utility of condom distribution. But in actuality studies that conclusively establish or refute an association between two facts are quite rare. Most research results are ambiguous and must be interpreted. In particular, getting results that simply return us to neutral ground produce a real dilemma for accurate reporting. In testing a hypothesis, one starts with the assumption that two variables are not associated and then seeks to disconfirm this assumption with empirical findings that show an actual link. Commonly, researchers assume no difference between two groups and then seek to discover whether an actual difference can be demonstrated. In this case, both sets of students were in sex education programs, had condoms available, and were already quite sexually active populations to begin with. The only difference was that one group of students received condoms directly in school, while the other had to go off-site. The conclusion drawn was that the distribution of condoms per se did not make a difference; but then, neither did anything else, since there was no difference. In formal terms, the study failed to "disconfirm the null hypothesis": that is, the two populations were no different even though one was treated differently. The best that can be said of this result is that it returns the issue to neutral. The research did not demonstrate that condom distribution poses a risk, but neither did it show that a risk was nonexistent.[10] However, the study did clearly demonstrate one remarkable fact, which no reporter noted. Students of different ethnic backgrounds varied widely in their rates of sexual activity. Compared with other students, those of Asian descent in both New York and Chicago were less than half as likely to be sexually active—a finding completely independent of whether condoms were distributed or not. A genuine exploration of teenage sexuality might well have studied this issue more fully. But because the press was prepared to treat the research results in terms of a preordained story line, intriguing questions contained within the actual data went unaddressed, apparently because they were not as amenable to the dominant policy presumptions as were the condom claims.

A third example of "policy first, science later" emerged in the debate over the federal government's Needle Exchange Programs (NEPs) as a means of combating AIDS. In this dispute over the advisability of providing clean needles to drug addicts, the mantle of science was donned early on by the administration's AIDS czar, Sandra Thurman: "We need to let science drive the issue of needle exchange."[11] This call for objective and cautious investigation was soon followed by claims that science had spoken definitively, as the administration pushed to lift the ban on federal funding of NEPs. As Health and Human Services Secretary Donna Shalala announced, "A meticulous scientific review has now proven that needle-exchange programs can reduce transmission of HIV and save lives without losing ground in the battle against illegal drugs."[12]

Even though efforts to lift the ban on federal funding were defeated in Congress, statements of scientific certitude regarding the effectiveness of

NEPs continue to abound. Thus the editors of the journal *Science* wrote that "AIDS prevention is only the latest example of scientifically compelling evidence ignored in favor of political expediency. . . . Study after study has shown that needle-exchange programs will reduce the incidence of AIDS, a fact acknowledged by the Clinton administration."[13] But in fact scientific consensus on the effectiveness of NEPs is a much more complicated story. A 1995 report from the National Academy of Sciences' Institute of Medicine (IOM),[14] while cautiously supporting such exchanges, noted several concerns about the weakness of the evidence. Moreover, since the date of the IOM report more sophisticated studies have become available that undermine our confidence in the exchanges. Early studies suffered from serious methodological limitations such as high attrition rates and reliance on the self-reports of drug addicts about their own behavior. More recent studies in Montreal and Vancouver reveal that, in general, the better the study design, the less convincing the evidence that distributing clean needles protects against HIV. The Montreal study found that drug users who participate in an NEP have a substantially *higher* risk of HIV infection than those who do not participate, even when researchers controlled for confounding variables. This study modestly concluded that "caution is warranted before accepting NEPs as uniformly beneficial in any setting." Furthermore, within the Clinton administration, General Barry McCaffrey's Office of National Drug Control Policy emphatically declares that "the science [on the effects of needle exchanges] is uncertain," because of "gaping holes in the data."

That is, the data taken together actually show mixed results. A 1995 New Haven study by Yale professor Edward H. Kaplan[15] claimed that "incidence of HIV infection among needle exchange participants was estimated to have decreased by 33% as a result of the needle exchange program." But in 1997 Julie Bruneau et al. reported in the *American Journal of Epidemiology* that the "adjusted odds-ratio for HIV seroprevalence in injection drug users reporting recent NEP (needle exchange) use was 2.2."[16] In other words, intravenous drug addicts who took part in the NEP were more than twice as likely to acquire HIV as those who did not. Taken together, these results offer contradictory evaluations. The debate took a decided turn with the publication in September 2000 of a series of reports on needle exchange science in the

American Journal of Public Health (*AJPH*). As Dr. A. R. Moss of the Department of Biostatistics and Epidemiology of San Francisco General Hospital put it, "it becomes very uncomfortable to point out that the data [supporting exchanges] are not as good as you thought they were." In Dr. Moss's summary, "an accelerating campaign to legitimate needle exchanges . . . has collided with some recent research studies. . . . The Canadian studies in particular did not show [exchange efficacy]."[17] Notwithstanding early and repeated claims that, in the words of HHS Secretary Shalala, "a meticulous scientific review . . . has now proven" that needle exchanges reduce HIV infection, later and more carefully constructed research not only failed to offer support but led to the suggestion that needle exchanges may actually harm participants. In sum, we simply don't yet know the whole story on NEPS. The need of policymakers for closure is understandable, yet it is sobering to realize that had the early and tentative scientific results been allowed to dictate national policy, we could today be facing a public health crisis in which that policy itself could have been a contributing factor. Had they forced premature closure on a developing scientific picture, and cloaked that decision with the aura of indisputable conviction, policymakers in their enthusiasm would have risked abetting a public health tragedy.

In each of these three cases we see the same pattern: a scientific report is seized upon, sometimes prematurely, to support a policy agenda. Then a selective reading of the evidence supplies what we have already called the Johnny Mercer method ("accentuate the positive, eliminate the negative") until the research can appear to justify a firm recommendation. Finally, a public relations effort is undertaken, sometimes at the researchers' behest, to place the conclusions before the public through the proclamations of the media. Politicians take heed of the public clamor for action, and suddenly "science" has supposedly endorsed a program to transform policy.

Hard to Tell: The Culture of News Stories

Science (or the appearance thereof) increasingly drives public policy. But rarely does it do so directly. Unlike, say, a Roman emperor who can watch immediately the action in the gladiatorial arena before him, today's modern policymaker (or regulator or judge) cannot see directly into the arena of the research laboratory. Further, the action often proceeds in a technical and quantitative language that the policymaker does not command. Hence, the policymaker must depend upon mediators for guidance before his thumb is to be cast up or down. Ideally, such mediators would be technical science advisors. More likely, however, our modern policy emperor, just as his predecessor did, listens for the clamor of the crowd—that is, rather than being driven solely by research results, he steers to the sound of applause (or to the shouts of horror). All too often the technical advisor is displaced by a new mediator, one who can assess the pulse of the populace. That is, the emperor depends upon the reports of the press. In this scenario, the emperor's most trusted mediators become even more powerful in that the media, unlike the science advisors, are able to not only report on but even manufacture the commodity of public opinion. They do this by reporting (and thus germinating) a clamor for action, often buttressed by poll results seeming to confirm the public's demands. This realization, however, is not a counsel of despair.

Science may indeed be elbowed aside in this scuffle, but it is not completely displaced. Scientific results per se still matter in modern governance, but are not of themselves determinative. That is, while good science may be necessary for sound governance, it will never be sufficient to produce good decision making. Hence, the message for the scientific community: Other players will shape and construe the results and carry them to the public in partial form. Moreover, all findings will be apprehended in terms of cultural understandings that the media bring to bear on any individual story. It follows that developing a more sophisticated appreciation of the media's interaction with public policy should be a high priority for scientists.

In many regards, the media are bearers of modern culture through the stories that they tell, and cultural presuppositions are central to the outcome of political and scientific arguments. When cultural forms are activated by a story, the settings deployed are deeper set, less conscious, and more atavistic than are dry scientific analyses. Moreover, cultural motifs are imbued with emotional valence. While harder to evict by logic and evidence, they are easier to activate and direct than are the "lessons" of data-driven efforts to educate the public through dry, propositional presentations of fact. Cultural frameworks serve as motivational triggers and once set in action are rarely countered by logic alone.

Journalists are often motivated by the rhetorical trope of "unmasking." The act of revealing the seamy underbelly of the world is seen as a high calling, and many a career has been advanced by uncovering the ulterior motives that are presumed to lie beneath the surface of social interaction. Many journalists believe that their highest calling is to "afflict the comfortable and comfort the afflicted." It follows that journalists are drawn, as we have seen, to ad hominem forms of argument, in particular ones that assume all claims of disinterestedness are at best a stance, at worst, an effort to deceive. In this mode of inquiry, irony prevails over direct motives, interestedness and desire are seen as ineluctable features of human affairs, and the struggle for power is presumed to lie beneath all protestations. Since science is a realm of activity that explicitly anchors its authority in ideals of disinterested, objective, and dispassionate observation—a world where ad hominems are an irrelevance—the encounter with a culture dedicated to a contrary set of assumptions is bound to be fraught with misunderstanding.

The larger lesson to be drawn here is the need to question our commonplace assumption that the news functions as a window on the world, transmitting images from reality into headlines. As we have argued, the news is not a purely translucent medium that passes events through to the reader. We have seen it operate more as a combination of filter and prism. Some selection always operates in news coverage, so that certain events in the world are picked out while others are ignored. Furthermore, the ones selected for transmittal are always subject to some sort of alteration, the events being cut and shaped by a variety of considerations until they literally and figuratively "fit." Thus, reporting the news is an active process of construction, as well as a passive medium of transport. While we may naively expect the news to be "newsworthy," that is, the presentation of something novel, we should recognize that novelty is only one dimension of what makes news worthy of "selection" and transmission.

There are other aspects having much in common with what is called in anthropology a *mythos*—that is, a steady reiteration and validation that the world is exactly as we expect it to be. "News" is not just "what happens" on a daily basis; it is also the reaffirming evidence that the world works today just as we always knew it should. In this respect, today's news is most satisfying when it confirms our most deep-seated beliefs about the way things really are. Many media analysts have in mind journalism's controlling *mythos* when they use terms like cultural template, scenario, or controlling narrative to explain a story's development. In a sense, we understand our world in terms of deeply embedded narratives, perennial tales with recognizable plotlines and characters that come attached to valued commitments. We are primed to expect "a moral to the story" somewhat in the fashion of Aesop. News incorporates certain modes of explanation while rejecting others. For many journalists, a primary mode of explanation is "motives." The notion that acts have agents, agents have intentions, and intentions therefore explain the acts seems to constitute the most compelling psychological template for many journalists. Unfortunately, this same logic is often applied not just to human actions but to events of the natural world as well. Thus, when something inexplicable happens in the world, be it a technological disaster or a natural catastrophe, journalists often seek the "ulterior" forces that caused the event, their inquiry coming to rest upon a likely villain who had suspect intentions. A related convention is that reporters may ascribe motives on their own authority, but if they have recourse to "causes" they must find "experts" to explain them. But these experts must in turn be interrogated as to their motives.

Journalism, we have argued, operates with several preordained underlying narratives into which current stories are often arranged in a Procrustean fashion. One of the most common is that of the villain, the victim, and the hero. If a story can be arranged in this format, it will get media attention, often without a great deal of scrutiny as to who, exactly, the respective players are and by what criteria they were assigned their roles. Nevertheless, journalists are ready to assign both black and white hats in order to render a morally satisfying narrative.

A moral stage filled with heroes and villains, dangers and triumphs, greed versus disinterested sacrifice, alarms and escapes, dastardly cover-ups by the powerful, heroic unmaskings, and plucky underdogs successfully fighting city hall is embedded in the American psyche. Journalists, often shaped by their humanities training in college, are primed to see the world in terms provided by Arthur Miller's stalwart in *The Crucible*, or by historical examples such as Galileo's confrontation with the Catholic Church, rather than by a more strictly scientific mentality. It follows that news that alerts us to dangers, thereby demanding our attention, and that can be shaped so as to confirm the moral world, thereby commanding our affirmation, is a surefire hit. Ben Bradlee, the *Washington Post's* legendary publisher, reportedly asserted that to right society's wrongs is the journalist's calling. This is surely an appealing sentiment, but it must not displace the duty to report the news. Nevertheless, science stories that can be constructed in response to this charge become enduring and appealing. They enable us to hold a moral referendum on a variety of seemingly unrelated issues by virtue of the stance that we take on scientific questions. In this respect reporters can be seen to work with broad cultural themes: for example, a controlling narrative that often catches reporters' interest is one involving lackeys in the pay of selfish interests who are confronted by white knights of the public interest. Because of this focus on moral purity, too often it is not the cogency of one's argument, or the number and importance of one's publications, that are the most highly valued chits in the battle to determine scientific legitimacy. Instead it is the contestants' motives, most often calculated by the degree to which they are perceived as disinterested parties seeking no more than the public good, that become the criteria of legitimacy. The late Carl Sagan, weighing in on the global climate debate, advised all journalists to ask, "In whose interest is it to minimize these concerns? The answer is there is an industry that would be severely affected." Following this advice, an article in the *Arizona Republic* concluded that climate change critics like Arizona State University professor Robert Balling "should continue to be heard, but they should not counterbalance the overwhelming consensus of scientific opinion."[18] But why should we assume that Dr. Balling's arguments are not legitimately part of "scientific opinion" simply because he adopts a scientific position that comforts industry? What if, in actuality, there isn't an overwhelming consensus of opinion, even among those who pass the "disinterestedness" muster? Moreover, reporters, confronted with a bewildering formal argument, often practice what is termed "rational ignorance." That is, they learn to treat signs of asserted public interest as useful indicators of motive, freeing them from the burdensome task of delving into arcane science.[19] The effect is to set up a chase where parties to a debate try to don the mantle of disinterested service while reporters simultaneously probe the appearances with steadfast suspicion. When the suspicion is applied across the board, reporters' skepticism can be a powerful corrective to public naiveté. Danger lurks, however, if the suspicion is applied selectively, holding different parties to a debate by different standards of what counts as "interestedness."

Challenges for the Future: Global Warming

To complete our picture of the problems inherent in the media's (and policymakers') engagement with science, we should turn more carefully to the story of global climate change, which exemplifies in abundance the conflicting claims and counterclaims that journalists face. Coverage of the climate debate illustrates particularly well how some science stories are treated differently by the mainstream press than others. It would appear that media discussions of research involving such topics as pollution, endocrine disruptors, mad-cow disease, AIDS, silicone gel breast implants, deformed frogs, or food safety are simply not comparable to media discussions of research concerning, for example, astronomical findings involving the moons of Jupiter. Though both depend upon scientific analysis, the first sort of research receives special treatment in part because of its more immediate policy implications. It is natural that we should attend to potential health threats more than to remote galactic discoveries. A more subtle factor, however, is that coverage of certain research produces stories that acquire symbolic value over and above their scientific substance. One's stance with respect to a particular subject—whether one professes certainty or skepticism, is eager or hesitant to act—can be treated as a symbolic expression of one's position in a larger moral and political landscape. To accept or resist a particular science claim (such as the extent of AIDS in Africa or the urgency of global climate change), once it has become laden with this additional meaning, is to cast one's lot in a virtual cultural referendum in a way in which a debate on undersea thermal vents rarely allows. Accepting or rejecting a particular scientific conclusion can be read as a signal concerning what kind of person you are, whether your motives are pure or interested, your politics progressive or reactionary. In this sense, a debate about silicone implants has meaning that a debate about silicon chips is unlikely to generate.

The effect of this additional symbolic attachment may well play out in shaping what kind of stories media are comfortable with, and this symbolic undertow appears to have affected global warming stories. On June 11, 1997, the *Washington Post*'s Fred Hiatt wrote a column (entitled "No Credible Goal for Global Warming") asserting that "Human industrial activity—particularly the burning of oil, gas, and coal—is slowly but steadily warming the earth."[20] No hedging there; Hiatt expressed the certainty of a journalist. But is such certainty justified? Our argument here is not that climate change is illusory. The bottom line is that humanity's activities are contributing to some climate change, which is a serious issue that will take decades of hard scientific research to resolve.[21] However, anyone who follows the scientific literature knows that there is more complexity and doubt in this story than the general public encounters.

For instance, greenhouse skeptics are well aware of an article in *Science* by respected journalist Richard Kerr on the uncertainties in climate modeling, in which he concluded that "most modelers now agree that the climate models will not be able to link greenhouse warming unambiguously to human actions for a decade or more."[22] That is, computer models, the basis for evaluating climate change, are far from adequate to task according to the people who design them. This means that determining the human contribution to the changes is a murkier undertaking than the *Post*'s Hiatt acknowledged. As K. Hasselmann of the Max-Planck Institut für Meterologie declared in *Science* on May 9, 1997, "the question of whether the observed gradual increase in global mean temperature . . . is indeed caused by human activities . . . remains a controversial issue."[23] In *Science* a week later NASA's David Rind added the following: "The more you learn, the more you understand that you don't understand very much."[24] Confirming experts' understanding of the uncertainty inherent in computer climate modeling, Benjamin Santer of the Lawrence Livermore National Laboratory expressed chagrin that "many people read the media hype before they read the [actual scientific reports]."[25] The most striking fact is that these cautious, reserved statements concerning the limits of climate models simply never made the news. The public policy stakes in climate science are enormous. Caught as we are between industry pressure and advocates' alarms, the gap between scientific uncertainty and media conviction is increasingly noteworthy. Yet one suspects that journalists who are aware of the caveats and demurrals in the scientific literature are shy about publishing them, for fear that they, too, will be seen as interested parties advancing an anti-environmental agenda, or worse, as gullible naifs taken in by industry. There may be a subtle form of self-censorship among science journalists because they sense that their coverage may be construed as adopting an awkward position in the larger political referendum. In any case, science and the culture of journalism have purposes once again lying athwart each other.

Summing Up—What Goes Wrong . . . and Right?

The simple answer to the question of what goes wrong in the reporting of research is "altogether too much." Error, neglect, ideology, interested motivation, malfeasance, human frailty, and the complex demands of a competitive environment have all been invoked and allotted their proportion of blame. In the preceding chapters we have witnessed a rogue's gallery of ills for which journalists are often to blame; on occasion, though, the blame must be shared by others—the scientists and policymakers with whom journalists interact. We have examined the clamor for perhaps unreachable "certainty"; we have also seen the impact of press release journalism, in which the media rely too heavily on sketchy "executive summaries" of complex findings, often generated by policy advocates. Journalists in these cases choose the path of least resistance between the press conference and their write-ups, thereby rendering themselves vulnerable to potential "spin."

Additionally, we have witnessed the imposition on the facts, albeit most often unconsciously, of a variety of narrative templates or scenarios. These frameworks operate as filters and as prisms: they preselect relevant facts and distort the natural shape of facts as they pass through the journalistic lens, while also arranging the elements into satisfying storylines that fit preconceptions or past narratives. We have seen the corollary tendency to fit facts into a morality play festooned with stock characters from dramatic vignettes who play out their assigned roles as heroes, villains, and victims. We have called attention to the importance that journalists ascribe to motives or charges of self-serving because they subscribe to an interpretation of human affairs in which the unmasking of selfish interests is a major calling as public watchdogs. In contrast with the principles of pure science, which claim that objectivity and transcendence should insulate against the motives and personal drives of those who create knowledge, we find (not without cause, we admit) a media wariness of any such claims of Olympian distance and dispassion. Ideally, reporters would instead emphasize context as well as motive, since context supplies the wider scientific picture and its complexities, as well as the alternatives among which our policies must choose. A focus on context would suggest, for instance, that health risks must be ranked in the order of the threats that they pose. It would also remind us that avoiding certain risks may well increase others.

We have seen the dangers of measuring one thing as a proxy for another, and we have pointed to the hidden dissembling contained in careless, overly broad, or deliberately altered definitions. We have noted that journalists are sometimes wrongly indifferent to varying methods and procedures, and the important transparency of the gathering and analysis of evidence; as a result, they can accept the dubious and implausible while rejecting the likely and substantive. Often, the failure to understand how science works (or when it becomes authoritative) results in a preference for hypothetical scenarios over properly qualified claims that genuinely advance our knowledge. Finally, we have noted the tendency to sensationalism and alarm that is natural to the press: the preference for the "blame game" or for stories that seemingly confirm a "master theory" or pet assumption about society's workings. Perhaps equally troubling is journalists' occasional penchant for the negative when confronted with ambiguity, their inclination to choose suspicion and the dark cloud over the silver lining and its comforts. Despite our criticism, we nevertheless have an abiding respect for the journalists who serve us in a vital capacity. Theirs is a tough job, and an absolutely imperative one; for all of the inadequacies of scientific journalism, it can be done and sometimes is done surprisingly well. By examining journalism's reporting on research, we hope to have rendered more transparent and accessible the mechanism, culture, and challenge that constitute the "reality industry." The only policy world assuredly worse than the conflicted and contentious one that we currently inhabit, in which the revolutionary engines of science daily drive us toward an uncertain future, would be one faced without the aid of journalists. Despite all our many criticisms, journalists also ask the questions that we need answered and tell the stories that we want to hear. Often they are our indispensable watchdogs (and indeed allies) as we strive to comprehend the operation of the complex and daunting world in which we live.

We have stressed throughout this book the failings of journalism, the perversions of policy, and the weaknesses of science. It is therefore appropriate that we conclude by offering a counterweight, focusing on an episode where a reporter, by following his craft with care, avoided the pitfalls and performed a public service. In this account, we will see how, failing to bite on a tempting lure, *Newsday* reporter Earl Lane helped news consumers better understand a complicated health risk charge with implications for the nation's nuclear policy.[26] The story involved the possible relationship between nuclear radiation and the health of children. Presumably, an increase in radiation exposure might be linked to adverse outcomes for infants. Since nuclear power plants have proliferated during the last decades, health records during that period might provide some clues. According to a press conference held April 26, 2000, by the Radiation Public Health Project (RPHP) and the STAR Foundation (Standing for Truth about Radiation), there is an association between radiation and one specific feature of child well-being—rates of infant mortality. But infant mortality rates in the United States (though lamentably higher than those of several other industrial nations) have been in sharp decline over the period in question. In fact, they have fallen from 20 deaths per 1,000 in 1970 to a low of 7.3 per 1,000 in 1996.[27] (This relatively good news would be even better were it not for the impact of in vitro fertilization clinics, which lead to an increasing number of vulnerable multiple-birth infants.)

How could nuclear power be linked to a *decrease* in infant deaths? Faced with the improvement in infant health, the press conference turned the usual arguments about nuclear risk upside down. Improvements in infant health were linked to the *closing* of nuclear power plants with declines following soon after nuclear sites ceased operation. This is a difficult argument to make biologically, since the best predictor of infant mortality risk is low birthweight, a factor related to complex variables such as maternal behavior, family structure, healthcare access, and race/ethnicity. Cancers or genetic mutations, which one might expect to be linked to radiation exposure, play little role. Moreover, decades of research on nuclear plant operation have shown no clear link to health risks for community residents. In fact, a recent analysis in *Environmental Health Perspectives*[28] exonerated even the 1979 disaster at Three Mile Island by showing no relationship between the explosion and the cancer status of those living nearby. But the news conference had extra-scientific features designed to draw journalists' attention—a celebrity hook in the person of (as *Reuters* termed it), "anti-nuclear activist and super-model" Christie Brinkley, an emotional appeal from a father whose child died of a mysterious malady (not an infant mortality case), and a New York congressman seeking reelection. Such a situation presents a dilemma for a science journalist—the argument seems dubious, but if one ignores the news, other outlets may cover the material with less diligence (in fact, the television program *Inside Edition* was there to interview Brinkley). Moreover, the stakes are high; an entire industry, as well as the nation's premier nuclear laboratories, could be affected if the public receives misleading health information.

In fact, the dismaying effect of alarmist claims was recently shown when Brookhaven's prestigious National Laboratory shut down a reactor after publicity involving a tritium leak into groundwater. The radiation exposure was roughly comparable to that of standing near a movie theater exit sign. But after a high-profile visit from Christie Brinkley and fellow actor/activist Alec Baldwin, Energy Secretary Bill Richardson agreed to permanent closure of the reactor.[29] Faced with multiple challenges, journalist Lane found a solution: to cover the story, stick to the science, and make the extra phone calls that provide the reader with the proper context for evaluating the claims. As *Newsday's* headline put it, "Baby Deaths Fall after Plants Shut, but Nuke Study Flawed, Some Say." The story carried the charges in the first paragraph. But Lane then offered a quick rebuttal from the Nuclear Energy Institute in the next. There is no celebrity mentioned in the piece. Most effectively, however, Lane turned to the National Cancer Institute's (NCI) radiation epidemiology branch for an evaluation—he went the extra mile to determine the actual science behind the charges. According to the NCI, the RPHP and STAR study should be "dismissed on methodological grounds." Moreover, the study lacked "control" counties matched in terms of poverty rates, smoking incidence, and other pertinent features. "You can't just use general statistics of the United States," to establish cancer deaths near nuclear facilities, said NCI epidemiologist John Boice. For the scientific record, Boice studied more than 900,000 cancer deaths in all groups between 1950 and 1984 in counties near nuclear facilities. Not only was there no evidence of increased cancer risk, the rate of childhood leukemia, for instance, was actually found to be higher *before* the plants began operating.

As super-model Brinkley demanded at the press conference, "If closing the nuclear power plants was not responsible for the decline in infant deaths, what was?" It's a question that deserves an answer, and for starters the super-model, the congressman, and the energy secretary might turn to the scientific literature—and the valuable reporting of journalists like Earl Lane (may their number increase). And while we await that development, keep always the watchword *caveat lector*—once again, "let the reader beware."

NOTES

Prologue

1. B. MacMahon, S. Yen, D. Tricholpolous, et al., "Coffee and Cancer of the Pancreas," *New England Journal of Medicine* 304, no. 11 (March 12, 1981): pp. 630–33.

2. O. Fernandes, M. Sabharwal, T. Smiley, A. Pastuszak, G. Koren, and T. Einarson, "Moderate to Heavy Caffeine Consumption during Pregnancy and Relationship to Spontaneous Abortion and Abnormal Fetal Growth; a Meta-Analysis." *Reproductive Toxicology* 12 (1998): pp. 435–44.

3. G. W. Ross, "Association of Coffee and Caffeine Intake with the Risk of Parkinson's Disease," *Journal of the American Medical Association* 24, no. 31 (May 2000): pp. 2674–79; Lindsay Tauner, "Study: Coffee Might Prevent Parkinson's," *Dayton Daily News*, May 24, 2000.

4. Bill Hoffman, "Bug Spray Could Lead to Parkinson's: Study," *New York Post*, May 6, 2000.

5. Emma Ross, "Coffee, Rheumatoid Arthritis Linked," *AP Online*, July 25, 2000, International News.

6. "Bush Hits Hard on Another One of His Main Messages Today: Education," *CBS Evening News*, October 24, 2000.

7. Mike Bowler, "Texas Education 'Miracle' Is Called into Question; RAND Report Finds Gains Modest," *Baltimore Sun*, October 25, 2000; Jim Yardley, "The 2000 Campaign: The Education Issue; Study Casts Doubt on Texas Test Scores and Gives the Democrats Ammunition," *New York Times*, October 25, 2000.

8. Tom Vanden Brook, "Report Questions Texas' Progress in Education," *USA Today*, October 25, 2000.

9. "Analysts dispute Clinton on Crime against Women: Figures at Issue as President Inaugurates Program," *Washington Post*, March 22, 1995.

10. "Notebook," *New Republic*, April 10, 1995.

Chapter 1

1. *New York Times*, "AIDS Deaths Continue to Rise in 25–44 Age Group, U.S. Says," February 16, 1996.

2. For an elaboration of this argument about the comparative importance and reliability of various AIDS statistics, see Joel Schwartz and David Murray, "AIDS and the Media," *Public Interest* 125 (Fall 1996): pp. 65, 70–71.

3. *Washington Post*, "AIDS and the City," April 25, 1996.

4. *New York Times*, "New Jersey Daily Briefing; Jersey City's Grim AIDS Toll," April 19, 1996. According to Nexis, the article appeared in the New Jersey late edition of the *Times*; it did not appear in the April 19 edition of the *Times* sold in Washington, D.C.

5. See "AIDS and the Media." See also David R. Boldt, "Aiding AIDS: The Story of a Media Virus," *Forbes MediaCritic* 4, no. 1 (Fall 1996): pp. 48–57.

6. *Washington Post*, "Crime Rate in U.S. Falls to 10-Year Low," October 13, 1996.

7. *Chicago Tribune*, "Crime Falls Again, but Experts Still Worried," May 6, 1996.

8. In our discussion of the report–reality distinction in chapter 8 we argue that the UCR appears to have improved over time, so that a UCR finding of increased crime in the early 1990s may largely have been an artifact of improved record-keeping by police departments. But this argument would not deny the reality of a decrease in crime between 1994 and 1995; we know of no recent changes in the survey's administration that would account for it.

9. The figures appear in the Bureau of Justice Statistics Bulletin (April 1996, NCJ-158022), "Criminal Victimization 1994," table 1 ("Criminal Victimizations and Victimization Rates, 1993–94: Estimates from the redesigned National Crime Victimization Survey"), p. 2.

10. See table 1 in "Criminal Victimization 1994."

11. *Pittsburgh Post-Gazette*, "Violent Crime Rates Level 1993–1994," April 18, 1996.

12. *New York Times*, "A Second Fed Bank Study Finds Disparities in Mortgage Lending," July 13, 1995.

13. See David Andrew Price, "Indiscriminate Approval," *Forbes MediaCritic* 3, no. 4 (Summer 1996): p. 18.

14. *Wall Street Journal*, "Home Loans to Blacks, Hispanics, Soared in '94," July 19, 1995.

15. *New York Times*, "Minority Applicants Gain on Home Loans," July 19, 1995. Note that the headline's "spin" is more optimistic (and, we would say, more accurate) than the story itself.

16. Lindsey's remarks are quoted in "When Good News Is No News," part of the "Media Review" section of *Forbes MediaCritic 3*, no. 4 (Summer 1996): p. 8. We first learned of the unreported good news about loans to minorities from this source.

17. The quotation appears in [New York] *Newsday*, "Ominous Trends on Infections; Diseases Once Thought Controllable Are Now Taking Record Tolls," May 20, 1996.

18. For a discussion of media perceptions of the danger posed by infectious diseases, see David Murray and Joel Schwartz, "Alarmism Is an Infectious Disease," *Society*, May/June 1997, pp. 35–40. The *JAMA* article is Robert W. Pinner et al., "Trends in Infectious Diseases Mortality in the United States," 275 (January 17, 1996): pp. 189–93.

19. "Tuberculosis Morbidity—United States, 1995," *Morbidity and Mortality Weekly Report (MMWR)* 45, no. 18 (May 10, 1996): pp. 365–70. The *MMWR* is the official publication of the CDC. The passage quoted in the text appears on p. 365.

20. *Orange County Register*, "Health & Science Briefly," May 10, 1996.

21. The CDC report also offered another interesting angle: it turns out that people born outside the United States accounted for more than one-third of all 1995 reported tuberculosis cases. See "Tuberculosis Morbidity," p. 365. The economist Robert Samuelson has argued (in a July 10, 1996, *Washington Post* op-ed, "Importing Poverty") that the worrisome increase in social indicators like poverty over time is in part explained by the rise in immigration over the last generation. The CDC report suggests that the same argument may apply to some of our health indicators as well.

22. The data appear in *New York Times*, "U.S. Reports Drop in Rate of Births to Unwed Women," October 5, 1996.

23. "U.S. Reports Drop."

24. *Los Angeles Times*, "Birthrate for Unwed Women Shows Decline," October 5, 1996.

25. We summarize the competing analyses appearing in "U.S. Reports Drop."

26. The *Times* account explained that over a third of all Hispanic babies in the United States are born in California. Many Hispanic mothers keep their maiden names after marriage; in the past, California babies born to such mothers were erroneously assumed to be illegitimate.

27. It may seem odd that 1995 statistics should have followed so rapidly on the heels of the 1994 numbers. The explanation is that the 1994 figures were final

statistics (they were published in the "Advance Report of Final Natality Statistics, 1994"), whereas the 1995 numbers (published in "Births and Deaths: United States, 1995") were preliminary, based on up to 90 percent of all birth and death records reported to the states. Detailed birth data were available on a preliminary basis for the first time in 1995, as statisticians received birth records on-line from hospital computer databases. The methods used for computing the 1995 birth statistics are explained in *Investor's Business Daily*, "Is Clinton Cooking the Books?" November 1, 1996. In view of this headline, it's important to note that the article raises no questions about the reliability of the birth data.

28. "Bad News about Illegitimacy," *Weekly Standard*, August 5, 1996, pp. 24–26.

29. Murray's preferred statistic for charting illegitimacy is the percentage of children born out of wedlock. A different statistic—number of live births per thousand unmarried women—is emphasized in the *New York Times* article on the 1995 data. Michael Lind (a one-time conservative now turned liberal) has charged that Murray's statistic is misleading and irrelevant. Lind argues that the percentage of all children, and especially black children, born out of wedlock has increased chiefly because fewer babies are now born to married couples, not because there are notably more illegitimate babies now than in the past. Thus Lind agrees that only 23 percent of all black babies were illegitimate in 1960, compared to 62 percent at the start of the 1990s. The more relevant statistic, he asserts, shows that the birth rate for unmarried black teenagers has remained steady, at roughly 80 per thousand unmarried teenagers from 1920 through 1990. He therefore contends that a decline in fertility among married blacks—not a rise in fertility among unmarried blacks—accounts for the increase in the percentage of black children born out of wedlock. For this reason Lind concludes that *"there is no illegitimacy epidemic in the United States"* (Lind's emphasis). See Lind's *Up from Conservatism: Why the Right Is Wrong for America* (Free Press, 1996), pp. 168–69. It is true that the decline in fertility among married couples exaggerates the rise in illegitimacy, but Lind nevertheless is wrong, because the rise is still all too distressingly real. Thus the supposedly more accurate statistic touted by Lind (births per thousand unmarried women) itself refutes his contention. Regardless of what happened among married couples, there were only 24.3 births per thousand unmarried women of all races aged 15–44 in 1976, but 46.9 in 1994. (The statistic for 1976 appears in the Nexis version of "U.S. Reports Drop.") If a virtual doubling in less than twenty years does not constitute an illegitimacy epidemic, what would?

30. See, for example, *Los Angeles Times*, "Birth Rates for Teens Fall in '94, 3rd Year in Row," June 25, 1996.

31. Simon & Schuster, 1984.

32. *The Good News*, p. 147.

33. *The Good News*, pp. 112–13.

34. *The Good News*, pp. 375–76. The emphases in the text are Wattenberg's.

35. For a recent nuanced discussion of the political beliefs of journalists (and their possible impact on news coverage), see S. Robert Lichter, "Consistently Liberal: But Does It Matter?" *Forbes MediaCritic* 4, no. 1 (Fall 1996): pp. 26–39. Lichter's analysis is broadly consistent with Wattenberg's.

36. Bennett is quoted in "Aiding AIDS," p. 55. The emphasis in the quotation below appears in the article.

37. A similar view was expressed by Michael Kelly, commenting on the media's exaggeration of the rash of burnings of black churches in the South: "Reporters love familiarity. Struggling on deadline to make sense of the chaos that is the daily world, they operate on a set of conventions, by fitting the confusing and often conflicting facts before them into certain well-established paradigms." See Kelly's "Letter from Washington: Playing with Fire. Who Is Burning the Churches, and Who Is Exploiting Them?" *New Yorker*, July 15, 1996, p. 30.

38. We take our account from "Legitimate News," a brief study of the noncoverage of the illegitimacy data. "Legitimate News" appears in the "Media Review" section of *Forbes MediaCritic* 4, no. 1 (Fall 1996): p. 13.

39. As we explain in our discussion of surveys in chapter 6, before 1992 the NCVS compiled data only on rapes and attempted rapes, but not on other sorts of sexual assaults.

40. "The Front Page," in *Press Watch: A Provocative Look at How Newspapers Report the News* (Macmillan, 1984), pp. 26–27.

41. "The Front Page," p. 27.

42. "The Front Page," p. 31.

43. "The Front Page," p. 32.

44. "The Front Page," p. 48.

Chapter 2

1. For an account of Pons and Fleischmann's scientific fraud, and a study of the media publicity accorded their claim, see Gary Taubes, *Bad Science: The Short Life and Weird Times of Cold Fusion* (Random House, 1993).

2. *New York Times*, "Scientists Fear Atomic Explosion of Buried Waste," March 5, 1995. See also "Theory on Nuclear Dump Peril Is Disputed," March 8, 1995; "Deadly Nuclear Waste Piles Up with No Clear Solution," March 14, 1995; and "Theory on Threat of Blast at Nuclear Waste Site Gains Support," March 23, 1995. Only one of the four articles, in other words, emphasized the critique of the explosion theory; even that story focused on criticism offered by a politician (Senator J. Bennett Johnston, a Louisiana Democrat) rather than a scientist.

3. See "Blowup at Yucca Mountain," *Science* 268 (June 30, 1995): pp. 1836–39.

4. William J. Broad, "A Mountain of Trouble," *New York Times Magazine*, November 18, 1990, pp. 36–39, 80–82. The quote about "the most dangerous nuclear facility" appears on p. 37; the quote about "a calamity of vast proportions" appears on p. 38. Note that in Szymanski's case (as in Bowman's) Broad appears to have publicized a possible danger that was subsequently discounted in a scientific review of the evidence: Szymanski's theory was later "debunked thoroughly by a 1992 National Research Council study." That statement appears in David Applegate's "Nuclear Explosions in a Geologic Repository? Peer Review Meets Politics and the Press," *Eos* [the weekly newspaper of the American Geophysical Union] 76, no. 25 (June 20, 1995): p. 252.

5. "Blowup," p. 1839.

6. See Gary Taubes, "Nuclear Waste Disposal: Yucca Blowup Theory Bombs, Says Study," *Science* 271 (March 22, 1996): p. 1664.

7. *Los Angeles Times*, "A Chemical Whirlwind on the Horizon; Health: Environmental Toxics Cause Hormonal Aberrations Such as Low Sperm Counts. Watch for Industry's Denial," January 31, 1996.

8. *U.S. News & World Report*, "Investigating the Next 'Silent Spring': Why Are Sperm Counts Falling So Precipitously?" March 11, 1996, pp. 50–52. The quotation appears on p. 50.

9. *Business Week*, "From *Silent Spring* to Barren Spring? A New Book Says Pesticides May Threaten Human Reproduction," March 18, 1996, p. 42.

10. Dutton, 1996.

11. Theo Colborn, Dianne Dumanoski, and John Peterson Myers. *Our Stolen Future* (Penguin, 1996), p. v.

12. See *Our Stolen Future*, pp. 173–74.

13. *New York Times*, "Sperm Counts: Some Experts See a Fall, Others Poor Data," March 19, 1996.

14. "From *Silent Spring*," p. 42.

15. "Investigating the Next," p. 51.

16. "Investigating the Next," p. 51.

17. *BMJ* 305 (1992): pp. 609–13.

18. "Evidence for Decreasing Quality," p. 610.

19. Geary W. Olsen et al., "Have Sperm Counts Been Reduced 50 Percent in 50 Years? A Statistical Model Revisited," *Fertility and Sterility* 63 (1995): pp. 887–93.

20. See "Importance of Empirical Evidence," *BMJ* 309: p. 22. The quotation appears in "Have Sperm Counts," p. 890.

21. The 1951 data were reported in J. MacLeod et al., "The Male Factor in Fertility and Infertility. II. Spermatozoon Counts in 1,000 Men of Known Fertility and in 1,000 Cases of Infertile Marriage," *Journal of Urology* 66 (1951): pp. 436–49. The incorporation of data through 1977 is found in J. MacLeod et al., "Male Fertility Potential in Terms of Semen Quality: A Review of the Past, a

Study of the Present," *Fertility and Sterility* 31 (1979): pp. 103–16. See "Have Sperm Counts," pp. 888 and 890.

22. See "Have Sperm Counts," p. 892.

23. See "Decreasing Quality of Sperm [letter]," *BMJ* 306 (1993): p. 461. The passage is quoted in "Have Sperm Counts," p. 891. The emphasis is ours.

24. See in particular three studies in *Fertility and Sterility* 65 (May 1996): Harry Fisch et al., "Semen Analyses in 1,283 Men from the United States over a 23-Year Period: No Decline in Quality" (pp. 1009–14); C. Alvin Paulsen et al., "Data from Men in Greater Seattle Area Reveal No Downward Trend in Semen Quality: Further Evidence That Deterioration of Semen Quality Is Not Geographically Uniform" (pp. 1015–20); and Harry Fisch and Erik T. Goluboff, "Geographic Variations in Sperm Counts: A Potential Cause of Bias in Studies of Semen Quality" (pp. 1044–46). The last study is particularly noteworthy. Fisch and Goluboff note that sperm counts seem to vary markedly from place to place: for whatever reason, sperm counts are higher in New York than in Los Angeles and higher in Western countries than in Asia and Africa. Significantly, Carlsen examined five studies of 100 men or more that were conducted between 1938 and 1970; all were studies of Americans, four of them studies of New Yorkers. By contrast, she examined fifteen studies of 100 or more men that were conducted after 1970; only three were of Americans, and four were studies of African or Asian men. Fisch and Goluboff accordingly argued (p. 1045) that "the differences in semen quality described among the different studies [discussed in Carlsen's meta-analysis] simply may reflect the clustering of significant geographic variations rather than a decline over time."

25. Thus there is reason for skepticism about the significance of the Parisian research showing a decline in sperm counts, since the study was "limited to men accepted as sperm donors and not the general fertile population." See "Semen Analyses in 1,283 Men," p. 1012.

26. See especially Daniel Pinchbeck's cleverly titled "Downward Motility," *Esquire*, January 1996, p. 80: "In a world ever more overpopulated and polluted by humans, is nature somehow trying to shut men down?"

27. *New York Times*, "Study Says Babies in Child Care Keep Secure Bonds to Mothers," April 21, 1996.

28. *Los Angeles Times*, "Child Care No Risk to Infant–Mother Ties, Study Says," April 21, 1996.

29. *Washington Post*, "Mother–Child Bond Not Hurt by Day Care, Study Concludes," April 21, 1996.

30. Other infants are classified as insecure-resistant (those who are distressed and angry but not easily comforted by their mothers) and insecure-disorganized/disoriented (those who vacillate between approach and avoidance at their mother's return). See the unpublished summary, "Infant Child Care and Attachment Security: Results of the NICHD Study of Early Child Care," p. 8.

31. Thus Alison Clarke-Stewart, one of the NICHD researchers, has argued that

> the observed difference in attachment security between children with and without child care experience could be a result of the fact that children who have experienced the multiple separations associated with child care are not especially stressed by the Strange Situation episodes designed to elicit attachment behavior. As a consequence, these children engage in less proximity seeking and more exploration during the critical reunion episodes than other children, which may be mistakenly regarded by [researchers] as avoidance. Thus, some children who are actually securely attached to their mothers and behave as independent explorers in the Strange Situation may be classified erroneously as insecure-avoidant.

This summary of Clarke-Stewart's view appears in "Infant Child Care," p. 5.

32. Note that the NICHD study examined the validity of the Strange Situation; it concluded that the test "was equally valid for children with early and extensive child care, and for those without." See "Infant Child Care," pp. 9–10.

33. Belsky is quoted in "Study Says Babies."

34. The breakdown of infants receiving the various sorts of care appears in table 6 ("Child Care Characteristics of the Sample in These Analyses") of "Infant Child Care." Note that the table provides information about the varieties of care when the infants were fourteen months old—a month before they experienced the Strange Situation.

35. See Gwen J. Broude, "The Realities of Day Care," *Public Interest* 125 (Fall 1996): pp. 95–96. Broude notes that "the audience gasped" when the NICHD study results were released, because the study seemed to represent a "dramatic turnabout in predictions about the effects of day care," and also because some of the NICHD researchers had "sounded the original alarm about the destructive effects of day care."

36. See "The Realities of Day Care," p. 97: "People who viewed the news [of research like Belsky's] about day care as a threat to working women attacked the findings and the messengers. The result: The suspected negative effects of day care were at times downplayed, even by the researchers reporting them." See also "Infant Child Care," p. 4: "In a field of inquiry where the results are controversial and politically sensitive, findings of significant differences [with children cared for by their mothers scoring better than those in day care] . . . may be relegated to the file cabinet"—that is, denied publication.

37. Camille Parmesan, "Climate and Species' Range," *Nature* 382 (August 29, 1996): pp. 765–66.

38. "Climate and Species' Range," p. 765.

39. "Climate and Species' Range," p. 766.

40. *New York Times*, "Western Butterfly Shifting North as Global Climate Warms," September 3, 1996.

41. *Atlanta Constitution*, "Butterfly Exodus: Global Warming May Be Pushing Species Northward," August 29, 1996.

42. *Baltimore Sun*, "Butterflies Flee North from Global Warming, Calif. Ecologist Finds," August 29, 1996.

43. *Los Angeles Times*, "Butterflies Head North to Beat the Rising Heat; Climate: Researchers Say They Have Found the First Biological Consequence of Global Warming as Insects Shift to Cooler Habitats," August 29, 1996.

44. *Washington Post*, "Global Warming Is Forcing Butterflies to Flee, Study Concludes," August 30, 1996. The *Post* published an abridged version of the *Los Angeles Times* article.

45. See James D. Goodridge, "Comments on 'Regional Simulations of Greenhouse Warming Including Natural Variability,'" *Bulletin of the American Meteorological Society* 77 (1996): pp. 1588–89. In Goodridge's words, "the rate of increase in temperature commonly attributed to greenhouse warming was $3.14°$ F . . . for 29 stations located in counties with over one million people and $0.04°$ F . . . for 27 stations located in counties with fewer than 0.1 million people." Thus no greenhouse warming is detected by measuring stations unaffected by urbanization.

46. The causation is actually explained more clearly in the *New York Times* summary of Parmesan's research than in her *Nature* communication. See "Western Butterfly Shifting North," which points out that "gradual climate change affects not the butterfly itself but the host plants: by changing the growing period of the plants, it interferes with the butterflies' reproduction schedule."

47. "Climate and Species' Range," p. 765.

48. Note that Parmesan is quoted in the *Los Angeles Times* to this effect: "I was interested in natural extinctions [meaning extinctions caused by warming], not extinctions caused by mankind [meaning those resulting from development]." See "Butterflies Head North."

49. In particular, the *Los Angeles Times* account included the somewhat skeptical reaction of University of California at Berkeley biologist John Harte: "Harte, however, believes that most plants and animals rely on too many local factors, from soil microbes to air quality, to simply shift northward." Harte described Parmesan's work as "exciting [and] provocative," but he also spoke of "the conventional picture . . . of how plants and animals will respond to climate change"—that is, by moving north—as "implausible." See "Butterflies Head North."

50. "Infant Child Care," p. 2.

51. Parmesan is quoted in the *New York Times* article, "Western Butterfly Shifting North."

52. For an account of Fenton's tactics, see Matt Labash, "Scaremonger," *Weekly Standard*, April 29, 1996, p. 25: "Fenton's flackmastery—along with [*Our Stolen Future*'s] publisher's six-figure publicity effort—led to breathless

coverage by all three major newsweeklies, the *New Yorker*, and *Esquire*, whose reporter even ran out to get his sperm count checked."

Chapter 3

1. *Washington Post*, "One-Third of Women in Survey Lack Preventive Health Services," July 15, 1993.

2. *New York Times*, "Science Watch: Reporting Rape," April 21, 1987.

3. *New York Times*, "Child Abductions by Parents Found to Be Far Higher than Estimates," May 6, 1990.

4. Our discussion draws from the account provided by Christina Hoff Sommers in *Who Stole Feminism? How Women Have Betrayed Women* (Simon & Schuster, 1994), pp. 196–98.

5. Straus and Gelles compare the findings from the two surveys in "Societal Change and Change in Family Violence from 1975 to 1985 as Revealed by Two National Surveys," *Journal of Marriage and the Family* 48 (1986): pp. 465–79. Straus and Gelles note that "the anonymity offered by the telephone [used in 1985 but not 1975, when respondents were interviewed in person] leads to more truthfulness and, therefore, increased reports of violence." Eighty-five percent of the 1985 telephone interviews were completed, compared with 65 percent of the 1975 in-person interviews, and Straus and Gelles "think it more likely that the violence rate is higher among those who refuse to participate." Thus "a reduction in refusals would tend to produce a higher rate of violence, whereas we found a lower rate of violence in 1985 despite the much lower number of refusals." Finally, in 1975 "never" was an option offered respondents as an answer to questions about violent acts; in 1985, by contrast, the response categories began with "once" and continued to "more than 20 times," so that respondents had to volunteer an answer of "never" themselves. Again, this shift in interviewing technique would tend to decrease the number of denials that spousal abuse ever occurred. See "Societal Change," pp. 472–73.

6. The quotation appears in Christina Hoff Sommers's *Who Stole Feminism?* p. 211; it is taken from Robin Warshaw's *I Never Called It Rape: The Ms. Report on Recognizing, Fighting, and Surviving Date and Acquaintance Rape*, which summarized Koss's study.

7. The definition is discussed in an article by Berkeley social scientist Neil Gilbert. See "Was It Rape? An Examination of Sexual Abuse Statistics," *American Enterprise*, September/October 1994, p. 73.

8. See "Was It Rape?" pp. 73–74.

9. See "Was It Rape?" p. 73. Gilbert is quoting from a scholarly article coauthored by Koss, which drew on the results of her study. See "Stranger and

Acquaintance Rape: Are There Differences in the Victims' Experience? *Psychology of Women Quarterly* 12 (1988): pp. 1–24.

10. The *Toledo Blade* published a three-part series on rape, called "The Making of an Epidemic," in October 1993. Its findings are summarized in *Who Stole Feminism?*; the quote from the *Blade* appears on p. 215.

11. See Gilbert's "Examining the Facts: Advocacy Research Overstates the Incidence of Date and Acquaintance Rape," in *Current Controversies on Family Violence*, ed. Richard J. Gelles and Donileen Loseke (Sage, 1993), p. 123:

> Applying Koss's finding . . . to the population of the University of California, Berkeley, in 1990 . . . one would expect about 2,000 women to have experienced 3,000 incidents of rape or attempted rape that year. On the Berkeley campus, 2 rapes were reported to the police in 1990, and between 40 and 80 students sought assistance from the campus rape counseling service. Although this represents a serious problem, its dimensions (3–6 cases in 1,000) are a fraction of the number . . . claimed by the Ms. study.

12. See Koss's "The Underdetection of Rape: Methodological Choices Influence Incidence Estimates," *Journal of Social Issues* 48 (1992): p. 71. See also an August 26, 1995, *New York Times* op-ed piece by NOW representative Lynn Hecht Schafran: she states forthrightly that the best survey methodology for determining the incidence of rape is one in which "no one interviewed [is] asked whether she [was] raped." "Asking about rape directly . . . is . . . inexact," Schafran contends, because many women mistakenly believe that only strangers can be rapists and that rape involves only vaginal penetration.

13. The citation is taken from *The Rape Victim* (Sage, 1991), coauthored by Mary Harvey. The passage is quoted in Neil Gilbert's "Was It Rape? An Examination of Sexual Assault Statistics" (a more scholarly version of the *American Enterprise* article cited above)—a 1995 pamphlet published by the Henry J. Kaiser Family Foundation, p. 21.

14. See the May 1990 report prepared for the U.S. Department of Justice's Office of Juvenile Justice and Delinquency Prevention (OJJDP): *Missing, Abducted, Runaway, and Thrownaway Children in America*, by David Finkelhor, Gerald Hotaling, and Andrea Sedlak, p. 182.

15. *Missing*, p. 65.

16. *Missing*, p. 66.

17. *Missing*, p. 76.

18. Note that the NISMART figure is for number of children abducted, not number of episodes: in other words, if a child was abducted twice in a year by a family member, only one abduction was counted. See *Missing*, p. 13.

19. *Missing*, p. 49.

20. *Missing*, p. 49.

21. *Missing*, p. 45.

22. Both NISMART numbers for family abductions have, in fact, been questioned. Writing with Tracy M. Thibodeau, Delaware University sociologist Joel Best found that extrapolations from reports of family abductions to eight state clearinghouses for missing children cases are far lower than either NISMART figure. Even the highest extrapolation (from family abduction cases reported to the California state clearinghouse) shows fewer than 17,000 cases nationwide. See "Measuring the Scope of Social Problems: Apparent Inconsistencies across Estimates of Family Abductions," *Justice Quarterly* (1997): p. 727. See also p. 730: Best and Thibodeau observe that the police were contacted in only 59 percent of NISMART's more serious cases and that only 53 percent of the serious cases were considered kidnappings by the respondents (as opposed to the researchers).

23. *Missing*, p. 10. Note, though, that the two definitions for nonfamily abductions do not conform to this general pattern. See *Missing*, p. 68:

> Unlike the approach we have used in all other categories, we have not distinguished between 'Broad Scope' and 'Policy Focal' cases of Non-Family Abduction. Although the media have given more attention to the Stereotypical Kidnappings, nonetheless, Legal Definition Abductions are serious crimes that engage the police, prosecutors, legislators, and the FBI. Thus, within our terminology *all* Non-Family Abductions are Policy Focal.

The emphasis is in the original.

24. "Measuring the Scope of Social Problems," p. 723.

25. *Missing*, p. 10.

26. *Missing*, pp. 65–67.

27. *Boston Globe*, "For Youths, Family More a Threat Than Strangers," May 3, 1990.

28. *Missing*, p. 8.

Chapter 4

1. *CBS Evening News*, March 26, 1991.

2. *Washington Post*, "U.S. Reports Decline in Number of Poor," October 6, 1995.

3. *New York Times*, "Panel Sees No Proof of Health Hazards from Power Lines," November 1, 1996.

4. "The Several Faces of Hunger: A Review of the Amount and Types of Information Available to the Public on Domestic Hunger," *National Journal of Sociology* 5 (1991): p. 106.

5. *The Tyranny of Numbers: Mismeasurement and Misrule* (AEI Press, 1995), p. 17. The emphases are Eberstadt's.

6. Our critique of FRAC's 1991 report draws heavily from an unpublished paper by Ted J. Smith III and Melanie Scarborough, "'A Startling Number of American Children in Danger of Starving': A Case Study of Advocacy Research."

7. "Facts for Hacks," *New Republic*, May 20, 1991.

8. "A Startling Number," p. 21.

9. See, for example, *Christian Science Monitor*, "U.S. Hunger Grows; Programs Don't Keep Up," May 20, 1986: "The best-known recent hunger study, conducted last year by the Harvard School of Public Health, concludes that up to 20 million Americans go hungry at least two days a month." The story does not explain how the twenty-million figure was arrived at. For purposes of comparison, see the *Los Angeles Times*, "Reagan Cuts in Nutrition Aid Blamed for Growing Problem: 20 Million Go Hungry in U.S. 'Epidemic,' Survey Says," February 27, 1985. In this article the shakiness of the twenty-million figure was recognized. The story's first paragraph reported that "at least 20 million Americans now suffer from varying degrees of hunger in a 'public health epidemic' that is growing because of Reagan Administration cuts in federal nutrition assistance programs, according to a yearlong, privately funded national medical survey released Tuesday." By the ninth paragraph we learn that "members of the physicians' group acknowledged that their estimates are imprecise"; in the twelfth paragraph a member of the group concedes that "Nobody, including us, knows the real number of hungry people in the United States"; and in the thirteenth and fourteenth paragraphs the twenty-million figure is disputed by the chair of a White House task force on hunger, who sensibly notes that the number "depends on how you define hunger."

10. *Los Angeles Times*, "The Hunger That Lives in America; Political Dispute Questions Whether Problem Is Growing," February 9, 1987.

11. *Chicago Tribune*, "20 Million in U.S. Hungry, Study Says," October 27, 1987.

12. See "Hunger in Rural America: Myth or Reality? A Reexamination of the Harvard Physician Task Force Report on Hunger in America Using Statistical Data and Field Observations," *Sociological Spectrum* (1991) 11:1–18. See also a commendably balanced article covering the release of the "hunger counties" report in the January 15, 1986, *New York Times*. In its second paragraph the *Times* article quoted unnamed "Government officials" who pointed out that the task force study "did not involve any field research to determine how many families actually lacked sufficient food." An assistant secretary of agriculture charged that the report "improperly equat[ed] poverty with hunger." The article gave the last word to a Missouri state official who declared that

"Trying to do an analysis of food stamps and income leads you to gibberish." Not all low-income people are eligible for food stamps, he said, because there is also an assets test. "The classic example is farmers," he said. "They may have income well below the poverty line, but they do not qualify for food stamps, because they're sitting on assets worth hundreds of thousands of dollars."

13. See "Food Fight: How Hungry Are America's Children?" *Policy Review*, Fall 1991, p. 38.

14. Mayer is quoted in George G. Graham's "Searching for Hunger in America," *Public Interest* 78 (Winter 1985): p. 5.

15. Orshansky, "How Poverty Is Measured," *Monthly Labor Review* February 1969: p. 37. See also a remark by Columbia University economist Harold Watts, as quoted in Isabel Sawhill, "Poverty in the U.S.: Why Is It So Persistent?" *Journal of Economic Literature* 26 (1988): p. 1082: "Our (official) measures are *not* grounded in some self-evident principle or expert consensus but are simply a collection of more or less arbitrary and eminently vulnerable rules. Their most remarkable feature is their widespread and persistent acceptance by the public and by those who make and criticize public policies." The emphasis is Watts's.

16. "How Poverty Is Measured," pp. 38, 40.

17. See Jencks's *Rethinking Social Policy: Race, Poverty, and the Underclass* (Harper Perennial, 1992), pp. 72–73.

18. The figures appear in Robert L. Bartley, *The Seven Fat Years and How to Do It Again* (Free Press, 1992), p. 272. As Bartley observes (p. 273), "This is not a fluke, but what the [Bureau of Labor Statistics] surveys find every year."

19. See Whitman's "The Poor Aren't Poorer," *U.S. News & World Report*, July 25, 1994, p. 36.

20. See, for example, an article by University of Texas economist Daniel T. Slesnick, "Gaining Ground: Poverty in the Postwar United States," *Journal of Political Economy* 101 (1993): pp. 1–38. For less technical presentations, see Rector's "How the Poor Really Live: Lessons for Welfare Reform," Heritage Foundation *Backgrounder* 875 (January 31, 1992); and Eberstadt's "Economic and Material Poverty in Modern America," in *The Tyranny of Numbers*, pp. 27–42. Relevant research by Jencks is summarized in David Whitman's "The Poor Aren't Poorer," cited above.

21. See Jencks and Mayer, "Poverty and the Distribution of Material

22. Brodeur is quoted in Michael Fumento, *Science under Siege: Balancing Technology and the Environment* (Morrow, 1993), p. 218.

23. National Research Council, *Possible Health Effects of Exposure to Residential Electric and Magnetic Fields* (National Academy Press, 1996), p. 1.

24. *Possible Health Effects*, p. 113.

25. *Possible Health Effects*, p. 16.

26. *Possible Health Effects*, p. 16.

27. *Possible Health Effects*, p. 37.

28. *Possible Health Effects*, p. 272.

29. We summarize the discussion of factors other than magnetic-field strength in *Possible Health Effects*, pp. 148–53.

30. See Park's op-ed piece, "Power Line Paranoia," *New York Times*, November 13, 1996.

31. See Aaron Wildavsky with Jesse Malkin, "Is DDT a Chemical of Ill Repute?" in Wildavsky's *But Is It True? A Citizen's Guide to Environmental Health and Safety Issues* (Harvard University Press, 1995), p. 60:

> There is no reason to expect that what causes cancer in mice will cause cancer in humans. Many natural substances—chemicals that most of us would not think of calling "potential human carcinogens" (such as vitamin A and salt)—have been shown to cause cancer in animals when administered experimentally at high levels. Today, scientists know that rodent carcinogens are virtually everywhere. They are present in almost all fruits and vegetables, including apples, bananas, broccoli, brussels sprouts, cabbage, mushrooms, and oranges.

Chapter 5

1. *USA Today*, "Number of Two-Parent Families Up," October 16, 1995.

2. *Washington Times*, "'Traditional' Families Less Common," October 16, 1995.

3. See U.S. Bureau of the Census, "Household and Family Characteristics," *Current Population Reports*, P20–483 (March 1994), p. vi.

4. *Chicago Tribune*, "U.S. Figures for '95 Show Drop in AIDS Cases," April 19, 1996.

5. CDC, *HIV/AIDS Surveillance Report* 7, no. 2 (December 1995): pp. 4–5.

6. *HIV/AIDS Surveillance Report*, table 3, p. 9.

7. To understand the apparent increase in AIDS cases among women, it is also necessary to realize that the CDC changed its definition of what constitutes AIDS (as opposed to HIV infection) in 1993. The broadened definition resulted in more than a doubling of reported AIDS cases that year, from 46,791 (in 1992, under the old definition) to 105,990 (in 1993, under the new definition); if the definition had not been changed, the number of AIDS cases would actually have declined in 1993. One effect of the broadened definition was to increase the proportion of women among those diagnosed with AIDS: in 1993, under the old definition, 15.1 percent of patients diagnosed with AIDS were female; but of those diagnosed under the altered 1993 definition, 16.7 percent were women. See "Update: Impact of the Expanded AIDS Surveillance Case Definition for Adolescents and Adults on Case Reporting—United States, 1993," *Morbidity and Mortality Weekly Report* (1994) 43: pp. 160–61, 167–70.

8. See in particular *Wall Street Journal*, "AIDS Fight Is Skewed by Federal Campaign Exaggerating Risks," May 1, 1996. The quotations are taken from the *Journal* article.

9. See Robert W. Pinner et al., "Trends in Infectious Diseases Mortality in the United States," *JAMA* 275 (January 17, 1996): p. 191.

10. *Los Angeles Times*, "U.S. Infectious Disease Deaths Rise Markedly," January 17, 1996.

11. *ABC World News Tonight*, June 11, 1996. The newscast did not cover the January release of the data but a proposed Clinton administration program to combat infectious diseases: the *JAMA* article's data were cited to justify the program.

12. See *Statistical Abstract of the United States 1995*, p. 91, table 124: "Age-Adjusted Death Rates, by Selected Causes: 1980 to 1992." The data for strokes are found under "cerebrovascular diseases."

13. *New York Times*, "A Second Fed Bank Study Finds Disparities in Mortgage Lending," July 13, 1995.

14. The *Times* article was in any case erroneous: the correct figures, rounded to whole percentages, should have been 10 percent for whites and 19 percent for minorities.

15. See Leo's column, "The Joys of Covering Press Releases," *U.S. News & World Report*, August 19, 1996, p. 16.

16. See Mayer and Jencks, "Recent Trends in Economic Inequality in the United States: Income versus Expenditures versus Material Well-Being," in *Poverty and Prosperity in the USA in the Late Twentieth Century*, ed. Dimitri B. Papadimitriou and Edward N. Wolff (St. Martin's, 1993), pp. 151–53.

17. *Washington Post*, "Blacks Describe How Bias Hurt Their Careers at NIH," August 10, 1993.

18. The *Post* story included statements by several black NIH employees who contended that they had been unfairly passed over for promotions. To avoid any misunderstanding, let us make it clear that we neither affirm nor deny that black employees at NIH encountered employment discrimination. Our only point is that the statistical disparity between the low percentage of blacks in senior executive positions and the high percentage of blacks in technical and clerical positions does not in and of itself suggest discrimination.

19. Our analysis draws extensively upon an essay by James P. Scanlan. See "Illusions of Job Segregation," *Public Interest* 93 (Fall 1988): pp. 54–69. The NIH story, which postdated Scanlan's article by five years, is obviously not discussed in it.

20. See an argument made by James P. Smith and Finis Welch, "Affirmative Action and Labor Markets," *Journal of Labor Economics* 2 (1984): p. 287.

Affirmative action may provide perverse incentives to firms to reduce hiring of [less skilled] minorities. In attempts to mitigate race and sex difference in existing skill distributions, the principal beneficiaries should be in more highly skilled parts of the distribution, where blacks and women have been scarce. But affirmative action may also provide an unintended incentive to firms not to overhire blacks in less skilled jobs. A firm may be labeled discriminatory not only in not hiring enough skilled blacks, but also in hiring too many unskilled blacks.

21. "Illusions of Job Segregation," p. 63.

Chapter 6

1. See Burns W. Roper, "Are Polls Accurate?" in *Polling and the Democratic Consensus, Annals of the American Academy of Political and Social Science* 472 (March 1984), ed. L. John Martin, p. 34.

2. [Minneapolis] *Star Tribune*, "Survey Finds That 60% Oppose School Vouchers, but Support Is Growing," August 28, 1996.

3. *Christian Science Monitor*, "Teachers Unions Join School Reform Effort, but Sit in Back of Class," August 30, 1996.

4. "What Americans Really Think of School Choice," *Wall Street Journal*, September 17, 1996.

5. *Washington Post*, "PBS Support Widespread, Poll Says; Both Parties' Members Found to Back Funding," January 17, 1995.

6. [Cleveland] *Plain Dealer*, "Pro-PBS Poll Full of Holes," February 6, 1995.

7. Ladd is quoted, specifically referring to the PBS poll, in Fred Barnes, "Can You Trust Those Polls?" *Reader's Digest*, July 1995, p. 51.

8. "Can You Trust Those Polls?" p. 51. The emphasis appears in the original. One can reasonably wonder whether support for cuts would have decreased if respondents had been told how little federal money goes to public broadcasting ($285.6 million in fiscal 1995, or .0003 percent of the federal budget), relative to the size of the federal deficit. On the other hand, one can reasonably wonder whether support for cuts would have increased if respondents had been told that federal funding represents only a small fraction of PBS's budget (16 percent): cutting part or all of 16 percent of the PBS budget seems less ominous than cutting part or all of 100 percent of its budget.

9. We comment here briefly on two other polls about public broadcasting. In January 1995 (just when the poll commissioned by PBS was taken) a *Los Angeles Times* poll found (in line with the *Reader's Digest* poll) that 63 percent of respondents supported cuts in public broadcasting "in order to reduce the federal deficit." (See a January 31, 1995, front-page story in the *Los Angeles Times*, "PBS: Behind the Sound and Fury"; see also "Can You Trust Those Polls?" p. 51.) Finally, also in January 1995, a *USA Today*/CNN/Gallup Poll

found that 76 percent of Americans favored "continued funding of public broadcasting at some level." (See a January 21, 1995, story in the *Washington Post*, "Independent Poll Echoes PBS Survey.") The poll consisted of one question, which the *Post* quoted in full: "As you may know, national public television and public radio—known as PBS and NPR—currently receive part of their funding from the federal government. In your view, should this federal funding be eliminated altogether, or should the funding be maintained at some level?" Note, though, that support for continued funding "at some level" is consistent with support for reduced funding: that is to say, a respondent could consistently have supported reduced funding to lower the deficit (in the *Los Angeles Times* and *Reader's Digest* polls) and opposed eliminating all funding (in the *USA Today* poll). For this reason, the *Post's* headline was inaccurate: the *USA Today* survey did not "echo" the PBS survey, because opposition to eliminating funding is not the same as support for funding at the same (or at an increased) level.

10. The figures are reported by Gary Kleck, "The Incidence of Gun Violence among Young People," *Public Perspective* 4, no. 6 (September/October 1993): pp. 3–6. Kleck drew his data from two BJS sources: *Criminal Victimization in the United States*, 1991, and (for the questions about being shot at and being wounded in a gun attack) *Handgun Crime Victims* (a compilation of statistics from 1979 through 1987).

11. See "The Incidence of Gun Violence," pp. 4–6.

12. Teeter is quoted in Michael Wheeler, *Lies, Damn Lies, and Statistics: The Manipulation of Public Opinion in America* (Liveright, 1976), p. 281.

13. *Los Angeles Times*, "59% of Schoolchildren Surveyed Say Handguns Are Easy to Get," July 20, 1993.

14. *Boston Globe*, "15 Percent of Children Said They Toted Handgun during Past 30 Days," July 20, 1993.

15. *New York Times*, "Student Poll Finds Many Using Guns," July 20, 1993.

16. *New York Times*, "The Holocaust Remembered," April 23, 1993.

17. *San Francisco Chronicle*, "Poll Shows America in Deep Dumbo," April 23, 1993.

18. See Everett Carll Ladd, "The Holocaust Poll Error: A Modern Cautionary Tale," *Public Perspective* 5, no. 5 (July/August 1994): pp. 3–5. In the article Ladd also described an experiment conducted by the Gallup Organization, which asked about the Holocaust's possible unreality in different ways. In January 1994 Gallup posed the same question asked by Roper to some of its interviewees and found that 33 percent thought that the Holocaust might not have occurred; but when it asked other interviewees two more clearly worded variants of the question, only 9 percent and 4 percent doubted the Holocaust's reality. Finally, one might argue that the differences between the Roper surveys reflect not the poor wording of Roper's original question but developments between November 1992 (when Roper asked the original ques-

tion) and March 1994 (when Roper posed its reworded question): in the interval, the American people might have been educated by the opening of the Holocaust Museum and the screening of *Schindler's List*. But Roper also asked a series of identical questions about Holocaust history in both November 1992 and March 1994 and found no significant variations in knowledge of the Holocaust. The different wordings of the question about the Holocaust's possible nonoccurrence therefore appear to explain the divergent responses.

19. Roper is quoted in *New York Times*, "Pollster Finds Error on Holocaust Doubts," May 20, 1994.

20. "Are Polls Accurate?" p. 33.

21. *New York Times*, "Survey Questioning Changed, F.B.I. Doubles Its Estimate of Rape," August 17, 1995. Note that the headline introduced an error not found in the body of the story: the survey was conducted not by the FBI (which keeps its own tally of crimes, taken from police reports), but by a different bureau, the BJS.

22. The wording of the relevant sections of the old and new NCVS questionnaires appears in the BJS's August 1995 special report, "Violence against Women: Estimates from the Redesigned Survey," p. 8.

23. According to the redesigned survey a completed rape involves "an act of vaginal, anal, or oral penetration by the offender(s), including penetration by a foreign object"; sexual assaults are "victimizations not involving completed or attempted sexual intercourse but having some form of sexual behavior forced on the victim." The definitions are supplied in "Violence against Women," p. 5.

24. See "Violence against Women," table 4, p. 3. The theme of how women (as opposed to men) tend to be victimized by acquaintances rather than strangers is picked up in the report's discussion of homicide on p. 4, which draws on the FBI's compilation of the number of homicides known to police (since victims of homicide obviously cannot discuss their experience with NCVS interviewers). The discussion nicely illustrates a statistical quirk—the unreliability of comparisons between percentages. "In 1992 approximately 28% of female victims of homicide . . . were known to have been killed by their husband, ex-husband, or boyfriend. In contrast, just over 3% of male homicide victims . . . were known to have been killed by their wife, ex-wife, or girlfriend." Someone reading this statement is tempted to conclude that almost ten times as many women as men were killed by intimates, but that conclusion is false. Because so many more men altogether are victims of homicides than women, in fact only a bit more than twice as many women as men (1,414 women, compared with 637 men) were killed by intimates.

25. Since only rapes and attempted rapes (but not other sexual assaults) were counted in both the old and new surveys, we restrict our comparison to them. Eighteen percent of 310,000 rapes and attempted rapes (or 56,000) were committed by strangers annually in 1992–93. Forty-four percent of 130,000

rapes and attempted rapes (or 57,000)—were committed by strangers annually in 1987–91. The 44 percent figure for 1987–91 is supplied by statistician Ronet Bachman of the BJS; see *Chicago Tribune*, "New Survey Finds Large Hike in Rapes; Redesigned Questions Credited for Increase," August 17, 1995.

26. Bachman is quoted in the *New York Times* article cited in note 21 above.

27. The figures appear in Murray A. Straus and Richard J. Gelles, "Societal Change and Change in Family Violence from 1975 to 1985 as Revealed by Two National Surveys," *Journal of Marriage and the Family* 48 (1986), table 1, p. 469. Both surveys included cohabiting parents who were not married.

28. See "Societal Change," pp. 473–75.

29. Gelles explained that the decision to expand the sample size for the 1985 survey meant that "it would have been extremely expensive to conduct one-hour in-person interviews," as was done in 1975; because he and Straus opted for more subjects, they "needed to choose [the] more cost-efficient data collection method [of] using [thirty-five-minute] telephone interviews." He noted that investigators of uncommon and stigmatized behavior such as child abuse "face tradeoffs of larger sample sizes and smaller amounts of data collected vs. smaller sample sizes and the ability to collect richer and more detailed information." See Gelles's "Methodological Issues in the Study of Family Violence," in *Physical Violence in American Families: Risk Factors and Adaptations to Violence in 8,145 Families*, Murray A. Straus and Richard J. Gelles (Transaction, 1990), p. 23.

30. See "Societal Change," pp. 472–73.

31. *New York Times*, "Admissions of Child Abuse Found to Drop Sharply," November 11, 1985.

32. *San Diego Union-Tribune*, "Severe Child Abuse Drops," November 12, 1985.

33. *Chicago Tribune*, "New Studies on Child Abuse Mix Hope with Concern," November 11, 1985.

34. *Christian Science Monitor*, "2 Researchers Say Family Violence Has Plunged in the Last 10 Years, but . . .," November 18, 1985.

Chapter 7

1. For early explorations of this theme, see Henry Fairlie's "Fear of Living: America's Morbid Aversion to Risk," *New Republic*, January 23, 1989, and a *New York Times* front-page story, "The American Sense of Peril: A Stifling Cost of Modern Life," May 8, 1989.

2. See, for example, a front-page *Los Angeles Times* story, "'Cry Wolf' Stories Permeate Coverage of Health Hazards; Journalism: Scientists, Others Say Alarmist Accounts Add to Fear. Facts That Mitigate a Threat Often Go Unreported," September 12, 1994.

3. See Eleanor Singer and Phyllis M. Endreny, *Reporting on Risk: How the Mass Media Portray Accidents, Diseases, Disasters, and Other Hazards* (Russell Sage Foundation, 1993), p. 7: "The media rarely report on hazards, nor, except on the financial pages, do they report on 'risks.' They report, instead, on accidents, disasters, crime, new products, new surgical techniques, a food additive scare." Summarizing a study of New Jersey newspaper coverage of environmental health risks, Aaron Wildavsky and Brendan Swedlow observed that "science did not enter into these stories in support of risk assessments because claims of harm were often not even explicitly made. Harm was simply assumed to flow from the presence of a particular chemical in a place where it was not supposed to be." See Wildavsky and Swedlow, "Reporting Environmental Science," in Wildavsky's *But Is It True? A Citizen's Guide to Environmental Health and Safety Issues* (Harvard University Press, 1995), p. 375.

4. Graham is quoted in *Los Angeles Times*, "'Cry Wolf' Stories."

5. *Reporting on Risk*, p. 163.

6. *Reporting on Risk*, p. 4.

7. *Reporting on Risk*, p. 4.

8. *Reporting on Risk*, p. 152. See also Stephen Klaidman, *Health in the Headlines: The Stories behind the Stories* (Oxford University Press, 1991), p. 16:

> In their concern to reach the public, journalists look for concrete, emotional anecdotes to make their stories accessible and compelling to an audience that is pretty close to scientifically illiterate. In television, where the emotional impact of pictures can be far more powerful than words, the availability of pictures often dictates the selection of anecdotes. This sometimes produce[s] forceful but misleading stories.

9. In the words of environmental journalist Gregg Easterbrook, it is

> a reality of human nature that many people would rather believe distant villains are to blame for any sickness they may contract. Studies constantly suggest that lifestyle choices—smoking, excessive drinking, overeating (especially of fats, strongly linked to breast and other cancers), and lack of exercise—account for 70 to 80 percent of preventable deaths in the United States. But people do not want to hear that. Once illness begins, they may prefer to view themselves as victims. For the sick to be victims, there must be a villain.

See Easterbrook's *A Moment on the Earth: The Coming Age of Environmental Optimism* (Viking, 1995), pp. 231–32.

10. *Reporting on Risk*, p. 167.

11. See *Reporting on Risk*, pp. 149–51, 157. Analyzing forty-two media treatments of scientific research assessing risk (p. 151), the book's authors found that twenty stories said nothing about research methods; fifteen did a poor job discussing methodology; and three gave erroneous accounts of methodology. Only four—less than 10 percent—gave adequate accounts of a study's methodology.

12. Schneider is quoted in *Health in the Headlines*, p. 105.

13. Alexander is quoted in "Reporting Environmental Science," p. 384. Wildavsky and Swedlow provide somewhat harder evidence to substantiate this point: they cite (p. 393) a 1993 survey showing that 22 percent of a sample of 244 journalists relied on environmental activist groups for stories, and 7 percent relied on consumer groups. By contrast, only 3 percent relied on business or industry executives and press releases, and only 1 percent relied on company or industry publications. As they put it (p. 394),

Of those sources with predictable biases—environmentalists and consumers on the one hand and business and industry on the other—the former are relied on by the media eight times more than the latter. To push the analysis a step further, this disproportionately high use of environmentalist and consumer sources occurs because reporters have their own biases. More than twice as many journalists think that "many" journalists are biased against business as think that "many" are pro-business.

14. "The American Sense of Peril."

15. See James Flynn, Paul Slovic, and C. K. Mertz, "Gender, Race, and Perception of Environmental Health Risks," *Risk Analysis* 14 (1994): pp. 1101–8. It is striking that the article abstracts from the question of whether the "white male" viewpoint is empirically right or wrong. Instead (p. 1107), the authors imply that blacks and women are somehow impervious to the sort of scientific evidence that is persuasive to white males: "Traditional attempts to make people see the world as white males do, by showing them statistics and risk assessments, are unlikely to succeed." If the world view of white males is supported by "statistics and risk assessments," it is seemingly more or less correct. Shouldn't that matter?

16. The report is quoted in *Los Angeles Times*, "'Cry Wolf' Stories." See also *Health in the Headlines*, p. 5, which quotes a former EPA official, Fred L. Smith, who stated that the EPA "finds itself selecting projects based on their political and public relations value."

17. *Reporting Risk*, p. 139.

18. Susan Ferraro, "The Anguished Politics of Breast Cancer," *New York Times Magazine*, August 15, 1993, pp. 26–27.

19. *Los Angeles Times*, "Does Rise in Breast Cancer Cases Constitute Epidemic?; Health: The Media Have Implicated Pollution. But the Facts Suggest That Early Diagnosis and a Larger Population Are behind the Increase," September 13, 1994. In fairness, Shaw's comparison between deaths from breast cancer and deaths from prostate cancer is somewhat misleading: the men who die of prostate cancer are overwhelmingly elderly, whereas the women who die of breast cancer are often in their forties and fifties. For that reason, breast cancer takes a greater toll on life expectancy than is suggested by a simple comparison of number of deaths. Still, a 418 percent disparity in funding to

research the two diseases says far more about the politics of the diseases than it does about their respective gravity.

20. Pergament is quoted in *Chicago Tribune*, "Statistics Give Confusing, Alarming View," April 10, 1994.

21. See Plotkin's "Good News and Bad News about Breast Cancer," *Atlantic Monthly*, June 1996, p. 60.

22. "Statistics Give Confusing, Alarming View."

23. Sondik is quoted in *Washington Post*, "The Misunderstood Statistics of Breast Cancer," November 8, 1995.

24. We draw this discussion from "The Misunderstood Statistics of Breast Cancer."

25. These factors are discussed in "Statistics Give Confusing, Alarming View."

26. Greenberg is quoted in "The Anguished Politics of Breast Cancer," p. 58.

27. Alsobrook is quoted in *Los Angeles Times*, "A First Step—At Last; Health: Because Causes Can Be Traced in Only 40% of Breast-Cancer Cases, Activists Say It's Time to Stop Blaming the Patient and Start Studying Environmental Factors. Now, the Government Is Listening," October 19, 1993.

28. See *Newsday*, "Finding a Voice; Breast Cancer Activists Mount Life-and-Death Campaign," October 4, 1993. When Fran Kritchek read a New York State Department of Health report that mentioned risk factors such as "being affluent or Jewish, having a first child late in life, or choosing not to breastfeed . . . [she] was mortified. Although the scientists were merely trying to identify who might develop the disease, Kritchek . . . took it personally. 'That's blaming the victim,' [she] said."

29. See *Los Angeles Times*, "Breast Cancer Study Clears DDT, PCBs; Health: New Research by Kaiser Contradicts Earlier Findings. But the Report in No Way Suggests That These Chemicals Are Safe, an Epidemiologist Warns," April 20, 1994.

30. "Good News and Bad News," p. 58.

31. See, for example, the uncritical profile of activist Sandra Steingraber in the *Chicago Tribune*'s "Womanews" section, April 24, 1994: "'We're in the middle of a cancer epidemic,' [Steingraber] says. 'Cancer rates have risen exponentially.'"

32. Bob Herbert, "In America; Let Them Eat Poison," *New York Times*, July 3, 1995.

33. See, e.g., an *Atlanta Constitution* op-ed, "Fear of Food," July 12, 1995.

34. See, for instance, a November 2, 1994, press release by Caroline Smith DeWaal, CSPI's director of food safety: "The Center [sic] for Disease Control estimates that the deadly *E. coli* bacteria causes [sic] as many as 20,000 illnesses and 500 deaths each year." The press release does not inspire confidence: it's the Centers for Disease Control, and "bacteria" is a plural noun (one bacterium, many bacteria).

35. See *Federal Register* 60, no. 23 (February 3, 1995): p. 6781, table 1, "Sources of Data for Selected Foodborne Pathogens, 1993."

36. See *Federal Register*, p. 6781, table 2, "Medical Costs and Productivity Losses Estimated for Selected Human Pathogens, 1993."

37. Patricia M. Griffin and Robert V. Tauxe, "The Epidemiology of Infections Caused by *Escherichia coli* O157:H7, Other Enterohemorrhagic *E. coli*, and the Associated Hemolytic Uremic Syndrome," *Epidemiologic Reviews* 13 (1991): pp. 60–98.

38. "The Epidemiology," p. 75.

39. *Seattle Times*, "Cleaning Up the Beef Industry—2 Years after Big E. Coli Scare, Progress Is Being Made to Reduce the Danger," February 19, 1995.

40. "The Epidemiology," p. 65.

41. "The Epidemiology," p. 66.

42. See "The Epidemiology," p. 66: "Deaths caused by *E. coli* O157:H7 occur mostly in the elderly and in persons with hemolytic uremic syndrome or thrombotic thrombocytopenic purpura. . . . Reported causes of death in the elderly have included . . . colitis, pulmonary edema, pulmonary effusions, pneumonia, myocardial infarction, congestive heart failure, and bacteremia."

43. See *Federal Register*, February 3, 1995, p. 6783, quoting the National Academy of Sciences 1990 study, *Cattle Inspection: Committee on Evaluation of USDA Streamlined Inspection System for Cattle*.

44. Taylor is quoted in Harry Hurt III, "Who's to Blame if You Get Food Poisoning?" *Self*, May 1995, p. 80.

45. Cross is quoted in "Who's to Blame," p. 82.

46. Elizabeth M. Whelan Jr., *Los Angeles Times*, "Perspective on Food Safety; Just Turn up the Heat; There's No Way That Federal Inspection Can Protect Us from Harmful Bacteria; Irradiation, However, Would Do It," February 3, 1993.

47. See STOP's November 2, 1994, press release, entitled "License to Kill."

48. *Federal Register*, February 3, 1995, p. 6783.

49. See American Gastroenterological Association, "Consensus Conference Statement: *Escherichia coli* O157:H7—An Emerging National Health Crisis, July 11–13, 1994," *Gastroenterology* 108 (1995): p. 1929.

50. "Consensus Conference Statement," p. 1928.

51. Rosenbaum's critique of irradiation is summarized in *Seattle Times*, "Fear of E. coli Virus [sic] Could Lead Public to Accept Food Irradiation," July 20, 1994. Note that Rosenbaum's final contention is analogous to our discussion of the danger that would stem from regarding federal inspection as a safety panacea. In both cases, a safety measure is criticized by hypothesizing that its adoption could lead to fewer precautions being taken elsewhere, which might then reduce the overall level of safety.

52. *Washington Post*, "In Minnesota Lakes, an Alarming Mystery," September 30, 1996.

53. See Aaron Wildavsky and Michelle Malkin, "Love Canal: Was There Evidence of Harm?" in *But Is It True?* p. 152. See also *A Moment on the Earth*, p. 604: "Health damage from anxiety, a real enough medical condition, is common among those who live near Superfund sites [such as Love Canal]. But do such people often suffer environmental harm as well? Almost from the start of the 'poisoning of America' scare, studies have shown this unlikely."

54. The comic strip is reproduced in Joel Best, *Threatened Children: Rhetoric and Concern about Child-Victims* (University of Chicago Press, 1990), p. 49.

Chapter 8

1. See Shalala's "Statement," delivered at the 11th National Conference on Child Abuse and Neglect, Washington, D.C., September 18, 1996, p. 1.

2. *USA Today*, "Flames Consume White Churches, Too. But There's No Pattern of Hatred, Investigators Say," June 28, 1996.

3. See Fumento's *Wall Street Journal* op-ed piece, "A Church Arson Epidemic? It's Smoke and Mirrors," July 8, 1996.

4. Quoted in Michael Fumento, "Politics and Church Burnings," *Commentary*, October 1996, p. 58.

5. *Washington Post*, "Violent Crimes Up 10% Last Year; FBI Finds Largest Rise Since 1986 in Murder, Rape, Robbery, Assault," April 29, 1991. The defects of this story were called to our attention by a Ben Wattenberg op-ed, "Reading beyond Media Hype Lines," that appeared in the May 22, 1991, *Washington Times*.

6. The figure is provided in Christopher Jencks's "Behind the Numbers: Is Violent Crime Increasing?" *American Prospect* 2, no. 4 (Winter 1991): p. 103.

7. As it happens, when the *Post* covered the release of the NCVS findings for 1990 (a month before the FBI released its data), it pointed out that "the National Crime Survey is sometimes used as an alternative to the FBI's Uniform Crime Reports because it estimates all crime, including incidents not reported to the police." See *Washington Post*, "3% Drop Estimated in Nation's Crime Rate," March 25, 1991.

8. The figures appear in Bureau of Justice Statistics, *Criminal Victimization in the United States: 1973–92 Trends*, table 1, p. 9.

9. See "3% Drop Estimated in Nation's Crime Rate," March 25, 1991. The article did not provide a specific rate for violent crimes, though it did note that "the rate for most major crimes either remained about the same or declined slightly," except for motor vehicle theft (which rose by 19 percent) and rape (which fell by 19 percent).

10. See "Is Violent Crime Increasing?" p. 101.

11. "Is Violent Crime Increasing?" p. 103.

12. *Chicago Tribune*, "Abuse, Neglect of Children Nearly Doubled in 7 Years, Report Says," September 19, 1996.

13. "Child Abuse: Threat or Menace? How Common Is It Really?" *Slate*, October 3, 1996.

14. Besharov and Dembosky quoted Shalala as saying that "child abuse and neglect nearly doubled in the United States between 1986 and 1993," whereas the written text quoted at the start of the chapter refers only to abuse. Since the written text of her statement includes the disclaimer that "some material may be added or omitted during presentation," it is likely that in her oral presentation—more accurate than her written text—Shalala spoke of neglect as well as abuse.

15. For a comparable argument, see an April 18, 1991 [New York] *Newsday* article, "Child Abuse, Tied to Crack, Seen Declining." The article noted that the decrease succeeded a previous increase, explained in part by the practice of "some New York City teachers [who] said they were reporting even minor bruises to the state Central Registry for fear they would miss a serious case."

16. Charles H. Hennekens et al., "Self-Reported Breast Implants and Connective-Tissue Diseases in Female Health Professionals," *JAMA* 275 (February 28, 1996): pp. 616–21.

17. "Self-Reported Breast Implants," pp. 618–19.

18. See Gary Taubes, "Epidemiology Faces Its Limits," *Science* 269 (July 14, 1995): pp. 164–69.

19. "Self-Reported Breast Implants," pp. 619–20.

20. "Self-Reported Breast Implants," p. 620.

21. "Self-Reported Breast Implants," pp. 620–21.

22. The researchers speculated that women with breast implants and connective-tissue disease might have been more likely to participate in the study (recall that only about a fourth of the women who received the questionnaire returned it), "if they suspected that we were investigating the potential health hazards of such implants." On the other hand, they might have been less likely to participate if they were involved in litigation against the manufacturers of implants. See "Self-Reported Breast Implants," p. 620.

23. *New York Times*, "Study Reports Small Risk, if Any, from Breast Implants," February 28, 1996.

24. *USA Today*, "Implant Study Shows Small Autoimmune Disease Risk," February 28, 1996.

25. *Washington Post*, "Study Cites Slight Risk from Breast Implants," February 28, 1996.

26. See Straus and Gelles, "Societal Change and Change in Family Violence from 1975 to 1985 as Revealed by Two National Surveys," *Journal of Marriage and the Family* 48 (1986): pp. 466–67. The emphasis appears in the original.

For another example of the same phenomenon, see Everett Carll Ladd, "Ethics Problems . . . and Problems in Polling on Ethics," *Public Perspective* 4, no. 6 (September/October 1993): p. 21: "The fact [that] higher proportions of the public are now professing concern about a perceived decline in ethical standards hardly constitutes proof [that] standards are actually declining." In other words, people can think that ethical standards are falling precisely because their own ethical standards are actually rising.

Chapter 9

1. The list of red flags appears in a January 31, 1996, [New York] *Daily News* food section article, "What's Fact and What's Fad? Don't Be So Quick to Swallow All These New Healthy-Eating Studies."

2. Our account of Epstein's experiment draws on a *New York Times* article: "Researcher Is Criticized for Test of Journal Bias," September 27, 1988. A subsequent *Times* article—"Charge Dropped on Bogus Work," April 4, 1989—noted that these charges were dropped but that Epstein might still be charged for discussing his case with reporters (rather than keeping his ethics case confidential).

3. Angell is quoted in Gary Taubes, "Epidemiology Faces Its Limits," *Science* 269 (July 14, 1995): p. 169. Her contention was supported by a researcher at the National Institute of Environmental Health Sciences, who added: "Investigators who find an effect get support, and investigators who don't find an effect don't get support. When times are tough it becomes extremely difficult for investigators to be objective."

4. Our account of the NSF study follows that offered in the *New York Times*, "Luck Often Decisive on Research Funds," November 13, 1981. The study, undertaken by Stephen Cole, Jonathan R. Cole, and Gary A. Simon, was summarized in "Chance and Consensus in Peer Review," an article by the researchers in the November 20, 1981 issue of *Science*.

5. Evaluating grant proposals is more difficult because it resembles evaluating promises; it's hard to know which promises will be kept and which won't. But assessing manuscripts submitted to journals is somewhat easier, because it's more like judging the worth of accomplishments. By analogy, it's easy to see today that Michael Jordan is a truly great basketball player, because his accomplishments are obvious; but it would have been much more impressive if a scout had predicted his future excellence when he was in high school, by extrapolating from current promise to future performance. Today's Michael Jordan, then, can be compared to a journal submission; but Michael Jordan in high school was only a grant application.

6. See Neal B. Freeman, "Peer Review and Its Discontents," *Weekly Standard*, August 26, 1996, pp. 29–31.

7. *Philadelphia Inquirer*, "Study Linking Abortion to Breast Cancer Drawing Criticism," October 12, 1996.

8. A similar dismissive tack was taken by Peter Jennings on ABC's *World News Tonight*, October 11, 1996: Jennings declared that Brind's study was "not original research but an analysis of 23 earlier studies." Since the "individual studies were actually inconclusive," Brind's conclusion was therefore "flawed." Again, this is to dismiss a meta-analysis for doing precisely what it is intended to do—make sense of contradictory individual studies.

9. The question of lying was addressed more extensively and satisfactorily in the exemplary coverage of Brind's study in the *Washington Post*, "Review of 23 Studies Links Abortion and Breast Cancer," October 12, 1996. In all but one of the studies, researchers asked women with and without breast cancer whether they'd ever had an abortion, and the studies showed that women who admitted to having had an abortion were at slightly greater risk for breast cancer. But the article quoted Boston University epidemiologist Lynn Rosenberg, who noted that "women grossly underreport abortion," but that "women with serious illness [like breast cancer] report more completely." In fairness it should be noted that Brind and his colleagues addressed this objection in their article, speaking of "overwhelming evidence that the association of induced abortion and breast cancer does not result from reporting bias": see "Induced Abortion as an Independent Risk Factor for Breast Cancer: A Comprehensive Review and Meta-Analysis," *Journal of Epidemiology and Community Health* 50 (1996): p. 491. Nevertheless, other epidemiologists contend that Brind's finding may be nothing but an artifact of the greater candor about abortion manifested by women with breast cancer.

10. Again, this issue was better addressed by the *Post*: "Though [30 percent] may appear to be a large increase in risk, in the world of cancer epidemiology it falls in the 'barely detectable' range. Indisputable 'risk factors' for cancer are of much higher magnitude." For example, people who smoke and drink heavily are thirty-six times more likely to contract throat cancer than nonsmoking teetotalers: that is to say, their increased risk is 3,600 percent greater, not 30 percent greater. For this reason, the *Washington Times* was wrong to declare in its headline that Brind's research showed a "strong" link between abortion and breast cancer: an increased risk of 30 percent is at most a weak link. See *Washington Times*, "Strong Abortion–Breast Cancer Link Revealed," October 12, 1996.

11. For the Berzins quotation, see *Washington Times*, "Strong Abortion–Breast Cancer Link."

12. For an illuminating critique of media coverage of Brind's study, going beyond the *Inquirer* article, see Michael Fumento's op-ed, "Breast Cancer Link Not to Their Liking," *Washington Times*, October 30, 1996. Fumento compares media coverage of Brind's study with media coverage of a 1991 study by Stanton Glantz of the dangers of secondhand tobacco smoke. He notes that Glantz's study was also a meta-analysis that also found a 30 percent increase in

risk (of heart disease, for those exposed to secondhand smoke). But Glantz's study was not dismissed because it was a meta-analysis; nor, in his case, was a 30 percent increase deemed small enough by the media to be considered insignificant. Finally, even though Glantz was an antismoking advocate of long standing, media reports at the time did not suggest that his findings could therefore be discounted.

13. *Boston Globe*, "Breast Implant Study Finds Some Risk," February 28, 1996.

14. *Chicago Tribune*, "Study on Breast Implants Finds Slight Risk of Disease," February 28, 1996.

15. *New York Times*, "Study Reports Small Risk, if Any, from Breast Implants," February 28, 1996.

16. In "Peer Review and Its Discontents," Neal Freeman speaks of the unquestioned authority accorded by journalists to *JAMA* articles: "When *JAMA* comes out with a big story, it jumps the editorial queue and appears immaculately on the evening news."

17. *CBS Evening News with Dan Rather*, February 27, 1996. CBS, it should be added, was earlier instrumental in publicizing the attacks on implants as a health risk. See Marcia Angell, *Science on Trial: The Clash of Medical Evidence and the Law in the Breast Implant Case* (Norton, 1996), pp. 53–54:

> Perhaps the most important event to bring the growing unease about breast implants to the attention of the public was Connie Chung's sensational treatment of the matter in 1990. On her TV show, *Face to Face with Connie Chung*, she conveyed the clear message that implants were dangerous devices foisted off on unsuspecting women. . . . Without questioning the presumed link between the disease and the implants, Chung implicitly blamed the FDA for permitting such risky products to be sold.

18. A gun control advocate wrongly suggested that the journal is not peer-reviewed. See the letter from Douglas Weil (research director of the Center to Prevent Handgun Violence) to the *Washington Times*, August 22, 1996: "Given that Mr. Lott has published 70 papers in peer-reviewed journals, it is curious that he has chosen a law review for his research on concealed-gun carrying laws." But as Lott noted in his letter in response (*Washington Times*, September 9, 1996), "the *Journal of Legal Studies* is the most-cited law and economics journal in the economics profession. . . . Despite the impression Mr. Weil tries to create, it is a peer-reviewed journal."

19. *Chicago Sun-Times*, "Gun Debate Flares; Study: Concealed Weapons Deter Crime," August 9, 1996.

20. Stephen Chapman, *Chicago Tribune*, "Taking Aim; A Gun Study and a Conspiracy Theory," August 15, 1996.

21. *Washington Post*, "Industry Funds Global-Warming Skeptics; Scientists Dispute Charges That Oil and Coal Money Biased Their Work," March 21, 1996.

22. Balling is quoted in "Industry Funds Global-Warming Skeptics."

23. Balling is quoted in *Houston Chronicle*, "Science on Their Side; Industry Backs Global Warming Skeptics," October 6, 1996.

24. Michaels is quoted in "Industry Funds Global-Warming Skeptics."

25. Michaels is quoted in "Science on Their Side."

26. Consider, for example, the testimony of global warming skeptic Richard S. Lindzen: "In the winter of 1989, Reginald Newell (professor of meteorology at the Massachusetts Institute of Technology) lost National Science Foundation funding for data analyses that were failing to show net warming over the past century. Reviewers suggested that these results were dangerous to humanity." See Lindzen's "Global Warming: The Origin and Nature of Alleged Scientific Consensus," in *Environmental Gore: A Constructive Response to* Earth in the Balance, ed. John A. Baden (Pacific Research Institute for Public Policy, 1994), pp. 126–27.

27. Singer is quoted in "Science on Their Side."

28. Note, for instance, that some critics of gun control reject research findings that support gun control because of their funding source. In an August 29, 1996, letter to the *Washington Times*, Val W. Finnell of the Northern Virginia Citizens Defense League rejects research "funded by the gun-prohibitionists at the [federal government's] Centers for Disease Control."

29. *San Diego Union-Tribune*, "Gene Cancer Therapy Ready for Human Test," April 2, 1996.

30. *Los Angeles Times*, "New Vaccine May Combat Brain Tumors," April 2, 1996.

31. *USA Today*, "Dismantling Cancer's Cloaking Device," April 2, 1996.

32. Fakhrai is quoted in "Gene Cancer Therapy."

33. Caplan's critique was summarized in a number of places, including a column by the *Union-Tribune*'s own media columnist, Gina Lubrano. See *San Diego Union-Tribune*, "Medical Breakthroughs That Aren't," May 20, 1996; [Minneapolis] *Star Tribune*, "Editors Need to Set Standards for Medical News," May 19, 1996; and *Toronto Star*, "Dr. Caplan Does an Autopsy," May 11, 1996.

34. For the financial impact of the announcement on Immune Response, see *San Diego Union-Tribune*, "Immune Response Stock Takes a 67% Leap," April 3, 1996. The researchers' financial stake is discussed in "Dr. Caplan Does an Autopsy."

35. Caplan is quoted in "Medical Breakthroughs That Aren't." Summarizing Caplan's views, the article noted that "the publication does not use the same standards as other scientific journals. Reviews may be done by academy members or scientists known by members, not by independent outsiders who do not know the identity of the researchers." Peer review is generally thought to be more objective when a reviewer does not know who the researchers are, so that it is the research itself that is judged—not the researcher's reputation.

36. The comparison between rats and humans appears in "Dr. Caplan Does an Autopsy."

Chapter 10

1. See Berlin's *The Hedgehog and the Fox: An Essay on Tolstoy's View of History* (Mentor, 1957), p. 7. Berlin drew the hedgehog–fox comparison from a fragment of a work ascribed to the ancient Greek poet Archilochus.

2. See the Census Bureau's *Current Population Reports*, "A Brief Look at Postwar U.S. Income Inequality," P60–191, June 1996, p. 1.

3. "A Brief Look," p. 2.

4. *New York Times*, "Income Disparity between Poorest and Richest Rises," June 20, 1996.

5. As we noted in our chapter on statistical contradictions, in the Census definition a household is a housing unit occupied by one or more persons; a family household consists of two or more persons, with one being the householder and at least one of the others a relative by birth, marriage, or adoption. Most nonfamily households consist of people—often elderly—living alone.

6. According to the *Times*, the wealthiest fifth of households received 40.5 percent of national income in 1968 and 46.9 percent in 1994: the numbers given by the Census report were 42.8 percent for 1968 and 49.1 percent for 1994.

7. In one place the article correctly stated that "the [methodological] change . . . made it look as though income disparity was widening more rapidly." Elsewhere, however, it declared that "the methodological changes made it likely that the disparities appeared smaller than they would have been." In fact, the original methodology made the disparities appear smaller than they really were through 1992; the changed methodology made them appear greater than they really were in 1993.

8. "A Brief Look," pp. 3–4.

9. Lynn A. Karoly and Gary Burtless, "Demographic Change, Rising Earnings Inequality, and the Distribution of Personal Well-Being, 1959–1989," *Demography* 32 (1995): p. 388.

10. The figures for the composition of households in 1993's top and bottom income quintiles are calculated on the basis of data provided in table 728 of the *Statistical Abstract of the United States 1995*, "Money Income of Households—Percent Distribution, by Income Quintile and Top 5 Percent: 1993," p. 472.

11. "Demographic Change," p. 401.

12. "Income Gap Widens No Matter Who Is President," *Sacramento Bee*, June 24, 1996.

13. "Importing Poverty," *Washington Post*, July 10, 1996.

14. "The Income Inequality Debate," *Wall Street Journal*, May 1, 1996.

15. See Robert W. Pinner et al., "Trends in Infectious Diseases Mortality in the United States," *Journal of the American Medical Association* 275 (January 17, 1996): pp. 189–93.

16. See, for example, *Boston Globe*, "Death Rate Is on the Rise for Infectious Diseases"; *Chicago Tribune*, "Infectious Deaths Soar as the World Overdoses on Antibiotics"; *Los Angeles Times*, "U.S. Infectious Disease Deaths Rise Markedly"; and [New York] *Newsday*, "Deadly Rise of Infections." All of these news stories appeared on January 17, 1996.

17. Thomas McKeown and C. R. Lowe, *An Introduction to Social Medicine*, second edition (Oxford University Press, 1974), p. 50. Any epidemiology text-book will make the same argument about the greater reliability of age-adjusted (as opposed to crude) mortality data. See, for example, Charles H. Hennekens and Julie E. Buring, ed. Sherry L. Mayrent, *Epidemiology in Medicine* (Little, Brown, 1987), pp. 68–73.

18. See Robert W. Pinner, "Addressing the Challenges of Emerging Infectious Diseases," *American Journal of the Medical Sciences*, January 1996, p. 5.

19. "Trends," p. 190.

20. "Trends," p. 192.

21. *Los Angeles Times*, "U.S. Infectious Disease Deaths Rise Markedly," January 17, 1996.

22. *Washington Post*, "Poverty Linked to Children's Rate of Death," December 22, 1994.

23. Pollak is quoted in Citizen Action's December 21, 1994, press release, "New Child Mortality Study Finds Deaths of 23,000 Children a Year Are Preventable: Proposed Cutbacks in Federal Social Programs Could Lead to Increase in Childhood Deaths."

24. See Citizen Action's 1994 report, *Dying before Their Time: Child Mortality in the United States*, pp. 1–2.

25. The data appear in [Cleveland] *Plain Dealer*, "New Snapshot of U.S. Vital Signs for 1995 Shows Upturn," December 11, 1996. The article summarizes National Center for Health Statistics data published in the medical journal *Pediatrics*.

26. The conventional view is characterized in Nicholas Eberstadt, *The Tyranny of Numbers: Mismeasurement and Misrule* (AEI Press, 1995), p. 44. That view is embodied in a 1990 explanation of America's infant mortality rate, offered by Congressman George Miller: "Childhood poverty, the greatest predictor of poor child health outcomes, is worse in the U.S. than in most other industrialized countries, and financial barriers are by far the most common and significant reason that women and children don't receive the health care that they need." The quote from Miller also appears on p. 44.

27. *Dying before Their Time*, pp. 25–26.

28. *Tyranny of Numbers*, p. 54.

29. *Tyranny of Numbers*, p. 56.
30. *Tyranny of Numbers*, p. 57.
31. *Tyranny of Numbers*, pp. 58–59.
32. *Tyranny of Numbers*, pp. 59–60.
33. Quoted in *Tyranny of Numbers*, p. 61.
34. Nicholas Eberstadt, "Why Babies Die in D.C.," *Public Interest* 115 (Fall, 1994): p. 12.
35. *Tyranny of Numbers*, p. 21. For a comparable argument, see Jeff Jacoby's op-ed column, "Illegitimacy—A Deadly Risk for Infants," *Boston Globe*, May 19, 1994. In it Jacoby criticized a report on infant mortality prepared by Boston's Maternal Health Commission, whose conclusion was that "the scourge we must attack is poverty." But as Jacoby noted, "What you will not read, not anywhere in the entire report, is the word 'father.' Or 'husband.' Or 'marriage.'" In Jacoby's view, the commission "lacked the honesty or the courage to say [that] what babies need to thrive is mothers and fathers living together. Preoccupied with demanding more money and programs from the state, the city, the hospitals, it never got around to demanding of young women: 'Don't have a baby if you don't have a husband. Don't get pregnant if you aren't ready to support a child.'"
36. On the limits of such forces, see Eberstadt's "Why Babies Die in D.C.," p. 15: "Impersonal 'social forces'—material deprivation, joblessness, economic insecurity—cannot explain why one of the very richest black populations in America suffers from black America's very worst infant mortality rates. This perverse situation can, however, be explained in terms of dysfunctional or even pathological behavior by parents and adults—including parents and adults who happen to be neither poor nor poorly educated."

Conclusion

1. James M. Fallows, *Breaking the News: How the Media Undermine American Democracy* (New York: Pantheon, 1996), pp. 165–66.
2. T. S. Eliot, "The Love Song of J. Alfred Prufrock," *Collected Poems 1909–1962* (New York: Harcourt Brace Jovanovich, 1963).
3. T. J. Woodruff, D. Axelrad, J. Caldwell, R. Morello-Frosch, and A. Rosenbaum, "Public Health Implications of 1990 Air Toxics Concentrations across the United States," *Environmental Health Perspectives* 106, no. 5 (May 1998): pp. 245–51.
4. *Baltimore Sun*, "Panel Links SIDS, Air Pollution, Doctors Blame 500 Deaths a Year on Particulates," July 11, 1997.
5. Hazel Brooke, Angus Gibson, David Tappin, and Helen Brown, "Case Control Study of Sudden Infant Death Syndrome in Scotland, 1992–5," *British Medical Journal* 314, no. 7093 (May 24, 1997): p. 1516.

6. Pete J. Schwartz, "Brief Report: A Molecular Link between the Sudden Infant Death Syndrome and the Long-QT Syndrome," *New England Journal of Medicine* 343, no. 4 (July 27, 2000): pp. 262–67.

7. S. Guttmacher, L. Lieberman, D. Ward, N. Freudenberg, A. Radosh, and D. Des Jarlais, "Condom Availability in New York City Public High Schools," *American Journal of Public Health* 87, no. 9 (September 1997): pp. 1427–33.

8. Peter Jennings, *ABC World News Tonight*, September 30, 1997.

9. *New York Times*, "Congress Should Support Condom Distribution," October 3, 1997.

10. Furthermore, the study lacked a proper control group of teenagers who were not in a sex-education program or without access to condoms; thus it had no baseline for the experimental group that received the condoms, since all students had already been in a sex-education program when the study began. Altogether, neither the study's method nor its results was particularly convincing. Moreover, if six out of ten high school students in either city were sexually active, it is not clear that many more students could have been affected by condom distribution one way or the other, since there are limits to the total number of students who will have sex in high school under any scenario. In other words, both sites may have come up against the "ceiling" of those who might be sexually active.

11. *Washington Post*, "AIDS Policy Director Puts Stress on Science; Activists Give New Appointee High Marks," April 22, 1997.

12. "Research Shows Needle Exchange Programs Reduce HIV Infections without Increasing Drug Use," press release, Department of Health and Human Services, April 20, 1998.

13. Floyd E. Bloom and Barbara R. Jasney, "It's Not Rocket Science—But It Can Save Lives: Concerns over Treatments of Disease Often Overshadow Efforts at Prevention," *Science* 280, no. 5369 (June 5, 1998): p. 1507.

14. "Preventing HIV Transmission: The Role of Sterile Needles and Bleach," National Research Council; Institute of Medicine (Washington, D.C.: National Academy Press, 1995).

15. Edward H. Kaplan, "Probability Models of Needle Exchange," Operations Research 43, no. 4 (July–August 1995): pp. 558–69.

16. Julie Bruneau et al., "High Rates of HIV Infection among Injection Drug Users Participating in Needle Exchange Programs in Montreal: Results of a Cohort Study," *American Journal of Epidemiology* 146, no.12 (December 15, 1997): pp. 994–1002.

17. A. R. Moss, "Epidemiology and the Politics of Needle Exchange," *American Journal of Public Health* 90, no. 9 (September 2000): pp. 1835–37.

18. *Arizona Republic*, "Can We Take the Chance Global Warming Is a Sham?" November 24, 1995: A2.

19. Journalists further act as though previous science stories offer a template or emblematic episode that helps them make sense of a new one. Sometimes this

template is treated as broadly instructive about the likely shape of new stories that are emerging. For many greenhouse skeptics, for instance, the Alar story provides a cautionary model of how a spurious alarm was driven by weak science harnessed to an effective media campaign. In the minds of many media analysts, the story of Alar is a good example of an alarm that largely dissipated after all the facts were in. Notwithstanding some dramatic Congressional hearings and the appearance of celebrity endorsements, the charge that a fungicide applied to apples in Washington state represented a serious health threat is today largely dismissed. Their experience with Alar leads them to conclude that claims about the damage to be wrought by global climate change should also be viewed skeptically, especially since they sense that political and media pressure appears to be pushing for action that may prove to be precipitous. In contrast, Time magazine journalist Eugene Linden, who is receptive to stories highlighting the danger of global warming, does not employ the Alar template. Instead, his approach to global warming is informed by his experience with issues raised by ozone depletion. Speaking at a Smithsonian Institution public forum, he drew this lesson from the ozone debate: had journalists listened to scientists such as Andrew Molina and Sherwood Rowlands of the University of California at Irvine (Nobel laureates for their work on atmospheric chemistry, which in 1974 had proposed the theoretical possibility of ozone damage), "We could have stopped ozone depletion in the late 70's, but the political climate changed and President Ronald Reagan allowed Dupont to obfuscate and delay and raise doubts and point out uncertainties." Hence Linden sees the current global-climate debate as paralleling the ozone story—that is, as a narrative involving far-sighted scientists who are hindered by industry apologists motivated by greed.

20. *Washington Post*, "No Credible Goal for Global Warming," June 11, 1997.

21. The United Nations Intergovernmental Panel on Climate Change (IPCC) made news in November 2000 when a preliminary draft of an upcoming climate report was leaked to selected reporters. The draft represented the first major update of the IPCC's 1995 climate report that had been the scientific and political benchmark for the debate. A curious aspect of the leaked summary is that it boosts the upper range of possible global-temperature increases from the 4.8 degrees Celsius that the IPCC scientific and technical review panel agreed on last March to 6 degrees Celsius. The 1995 IPCC report predicted that global-temperature increases over the next century might range from 1.8 degrees Fahrenheit to as much as 6.3 degrees Fahrenheit. The leaked report apparently raises the range from 2.7 degrees Fahrenheit to nearly 11 degrees Fahrenheit. This increase is supposed to result from reductions in sulfates released into the air by power plants and factories.

22. Richard Kerr, "Greenhouse Forecasting Still Cloudy," *Science* 276, no. 5315 (May 16, 1997): p. 1040.

23. K. Hasselmann, "Are We Seeing Global Warming?" *Science* 276, no. 5314 (May 9, 1997): p. 914.

24. Quoted in "Greenhouse Forecasting Sill Cloudy," p. 1040.

25. Quoted in "Greenhouse Forecasting Still Cloudy," p. 1040.

26. Earl Lane, "Baby Deaths Fall after Plants Shut: But Nuke Study Flawed, Some Say," *Newsday*, April 27, 2000, p. A26.

27. U.S. Bureau of the Census, *Statistical Abstract of the United States 1999*, 119th ed. (Washington, D.C.: Government Printing Office, 1999).

28. Evelyn O. Talbott, Ada O. Youk, Kathleen P. McHough, Jeffrey D. Shire, Aimin Zhang, Brian P. Murphy, and Richard A. Engberg, "Mortality among the Residents of the Three Mile Island Accident Area: 1979–1992," *Environmental Health Perspectives* 108, no. 6 (June 2000): pp. 545–52.

29. Andrew Lawler, "Brookhaven: Anti-nuke Leader Uses STAR Power in Fight to Close Reactor," *Science* 287, no. 5457 (February 25, 2000): p. 1386.

BIBLIOGRAPHY

American Gastroenterological Association. "Consensus Conference Statement: *Escherichia coli* O157:H7—An Emerging National Health Crisis, July 11–13, 1994." *Gastroenterology* 108 (1995): p. 1929.

Applegate, David. "Nuclear Explosions in a Geologic Repository? Peer Review Meets Politics and the Press." *EOS* [the weekly newspaper of the American Geophysical Union] 76, no. 25 (June 20, 1995): p. 252.

Bartley, Robert L. *The Seven Fat Years and How to Do It Again.* Free Press, 1992.

Berlin, Isaiah. *The Hedgehog and the Fox: An Essay on Tolstoy's View of History.* Mentor, 1957.

Best, Joel. *Threatened Children: Rhetoric and Concern about Child-Victims.* University of Chicago Press, 1990.

Best, Joel, and Tracy M. Thibodeau. "Measuring the Scope of Social Problems: Apparent Inconsistencies across Estimates of Family Abductions." *Justice Quarterly* (1997).

Bloom, Floyd E., and Barbara R. Jasney. "It's Not Rocket Science—But It Can Save Lives: Concerns over Treatments of Disease Often Overshadow Efforts at Prevention." *Science* 280, no. 5369 (June 5, 1998): p. 1507.

Brind, Joel, et al. "Induced Abortion as an Independent Risk Factor for Breast Cancer: A Comprehensive Review and Meta-Analysis." *Journal of Epidemiology and Community Health* 50 (1996).

Broad, William J. "A Mountain of Trouble." *New York Times Magazine,* November 18, 1990, pp. 36–39, 80–82.

Brooke, Hazel, Angus Gibson, David Tappin, and Helen Brown. "Case Control Study of Sudden Infant Death Syndrome in Scotland, 1992–5." *British Medical Journal* 314, no. 7093 (May 24, 1997): p. 1516.

Broude, Gwen J. "The Realities of Day Care." *Public Interest* 125 (Fall 1996): pp. 95–96.

Bruneau, Julie, et al. "High Rates of HIV Infection among Injection Drug Users Participating in Needle Exchange Programs in Montreal: Results of a Cohort Study." *American Journal of Epidemiology* 146, no. 12 (December 15, 1997): pp. 994–1002.

Carlsen, Elisabeth, et al. "Evidence for Decreasing Quality of Semen during Past 50 Years." *British Medical Journal* 305 (1992): pp. 609–13.

CDC. *HIV/AIDS Surveillance Report* 7, no. 2 (December 1995).

———. "Tuberculosis Morbidity—United States, 1995." *Morbidity and Mortality Weekly Report* 45, no. 18 (May 10, 1996): pp. 365–70.

———. "Update: Impact of the Expanded AIDS Surveillance Case Definition for Adolescents and Adults on Case Reporting—United States, 1993." *Morbidity and Mortality Weekly Report* 43, no. 9 (1994): 160–61, 167–70.

Cole, Stephen, Jonathan R. Cole, and Gary A. Simon. "Chance and Consensus in Peer Review." *Science* (November 20, 1981).

"Criminal Victimization 1994." Bureau of Justice Statistics Bulletin, NCJ-158022 (April 1996).

Easterbrook, Gregg. *A Moment on the Earth: The Coming Age of Environmental Optimism*. Viking, 1995.

Eberstadt, Nicholas. *The Tyranny of Numbers: Mismeasurement and Misrule*. AEI Press, 1995.

———. "Why Babies Die in D.C." *Public Interest* 115 (Spring 1994).

Fairlie, Henry. "The American Sense of Peril: A Stifling Cost of Modern Life." *New York Times*, May 8, 1989.

———. "Fear of Living: America's Morbid Aversion to Risk." *New Republic*, January 23, 1989.

Fallows, James M. *Breaking the News: How the Media Undermine American Democracy*. New York: Pantheon, 1996.

Fernandes, O., M. Sabharwal, T. Smiley, A. Pastuszak, G. Koren, and T. Einarson. "Moderate to Heavy Caffeine Consumption during Pregnancy and Relationship to Spontaneous Abortion and Abnormal Fetal Growth; a Meta-Analysis." *Reproductive Toxicology* 12 (1998): pp. 435–44.

Finkelhor, David, Gerald Hotaling, and Andrea Sedlak. *Missing, Abducted, Runaway, and Throwaway Children in America*. U.S. Department of Justice's Office of Juvenile Justice and Delinquency Prevention (OJJDP), May 1990.

Fisch, Harry, and Erik T. Goluboff. "Geographic Variations in Sperm Counts: A Potential Cause of Bias in Studies of Semen Quality." *Fertility and Sterility* 65 (May 1996): pp. 1044–46.

Fisch, Harry, et al. "Semen Analyses in 1,283 Men from the United States over a 25-Year Period: No Decline in Quality." *Fertility and Sterility* 65 (May 1996): pp. 1009–14.

Flynn, James, Paul Slovic, and C. K. Mertz. "Gender, Race, and Perception of Environmental Health Risks." *Risk Analysis* 14 (1994): pp. 1101–8.

Freeman, Neal B. "Peer Review and Its Discontents." *Weekly Standard*, August 26, 1996, pp. 29–31.

Fumento, Michael. "Politics and Church Burnings." *Commentary*, October 1996.

——. *Science under Siege: Balancing Technology and the Environment.* Morrow, 1993.

Gelles, Richard J. "Methodological Issues in the Study of Family Violence." In Murray A. Straus and Richard J. Gelles, *Physical Violence in American Families: Risk Factors and Adaptations to Violence in 8,145 Families.* Transaction, 1990.

Gilbert, Neil. "Examining the Facts: Advocacy Research Overstates the Incidence of Date and Acquaintance Rape." In Richard J. Gelles and Donileen Loseke, eds., *Current Controversies on Family Violence.* Sage, 1993.

——. "Was It Rape? An Examination of Sexual Abuse Statistics." *American Enterprise*, September/October 1994, p. 73.

——. "Was It Rape? An Examination of Sexual Assault Statistics." Pamphlet. Henry J. Kaiser Family Foundation, 1995.

——, and Mary Koss. "Stranger and Acquaintance Rape: Are There Differences in the Victims' Experience?" *Psychology of Women Quarterly* 12 (1988): pp. 1–24.

Goodridge, James D. "Comments on 'Regional Simulations of Greenhouse Warming Including Natural Variability.'" *Bulletin of the American Meteorological Society* 77 (1996): pp. 1588–89.

Graham, George G. "Searching for Hunger in America." *Public Interest* 78 (Winter 1985).

Guttmacher, S., L. Lieberman, D. Ward, N. Freudenberg, A. Radosh, and D. Des Jarlais. "Condom Availability in New York City Public High Schools." *American Journal of Public Health* 87, no. 9 (September 1997): pp. 1427–33.

Harvey, Mary. *The Rape Victim.* Sage, 1991.

Hasselmann, K. "Are We Seeing Global Warming?" *Science* 276, no. 5314 (May 9, 1997): p. 914.

Hennekens, Charles H., and Julie E. Burning. *Epidemiology in Medicine.* Edited by Sherry L. Mayrent. Little, Brown, 1987.

Hennekens, Charles H., et al. "Self-Reported Breast Implants and Connective-Tissue Diseases in Female Health Professionals." *JAMA* 275 (February 28, 1996): pp. 616–21.

Jencks, Christopher. "Behind the Numbers: Is Violent Crime Increasing?" *American Prospect* 2, no. 4 (Winter 1991): p. 103.

——. *Rethinking Social Policy: Race, Poverty, and the Underclass.* Harper Perennial, 1992.

Kaplan, Edward H. "Probability Model of Needle Exchange." *Operations Research* 43, no. 4 (July–August 1995): pp. 558–69.

Karoly, Lynn A., and Gary Burtless. "Demographic Change, Rising Earnings Inequality, and the Distribution of Personal Well-Being, 1959–1989." *Demography* 32 (1995).

Kelly, Michael. "Letter from Washington: Playing with Fire. Who Is Burning the Churches, and Who Is Exploiting Them?" *New Yorker*, July 15, 1996, p. 30.

Kerr, Richard. "Greenhouse Forecasting Still Cloudy." *Science* 276, no. 5315 (May 16, 1997): p. 1040.

Klaidman, Stephen. *Health in the Headlines: The Stories behind the Stories.* Oxford University Press, 1991.

Kleck, Gary. "The Incidence of Gun Violence among Young People." *Public Perspective* 4, no. 6 (September/October 1993): pp. 3–6.

Koss, Mary. "The Underdetection of Rape: Methodological Choices Influence Incidence Estimates." *Journal of Social Issues* 48 (1992): p. 71.

Ladd, Everett Carll. "Ethics Problems . . . and Problems in Polling on Ethics." *Public Perspective* 4, no. 6 (September/October 1993): p. 21.

Lane, Earl. "Baby Deaths Fall after Plants Shut: But Nuke Study Flawed, Some Say." *Newsday*, April 27, 2000, p. A26.

Lawler, Andrew. "Brookhaven: Anti-nuke Leader Uses STAR Power in Fight to Close Reactor." *Science* 287, no. 5457 (February 25, 2000): p. 1386.

Lichter, S. Robert. "Consistently Liberal: But Does It Matter?" *Forbes MediaCritic* 4, no. 1 (Fall 1996): pp. 26–39.

Lindzen, Richard S. "Global Warming: The Origin and Nature of Alleged Scientific Consensus." In John A. Baden, ed., *Environmental Gore: A Constructive Response to Earth in the Balance.* Pacific Research Institute for Public Policy, 1994.

McKeown, Thomas, and C. R. Lowe. *An Introduction to Social Medicine.* Second edition. Oxford University Press, 1974.

MacLeod, J., et al. "The Male Factor in Fertility and Infertility. II. Spermatozoon Counts in 1,000 Men of Known Fertility and in 1,000 Cases of Infertile Marriage." *Journal of Urology* 66 (1951): pp. 436–49.

——. "Male Fertility Potential in Terms of Semen Quality: A Review of the Past, a Study of the Present." *Fertility and Sterility* 31 (1979): pp. 103–16.

Mayer, Susan, and Christopher Jencks, "Recent Trends in Economic Inequality in the United States: Income versus Expenditures versus Material Well-Being." In Dimitri B. Papadimitriou and Edward N. Wolff, eds., *Poverty and Prosperity in the USA in the Late Twentieth Century.* St. Martin's, 1993.

"Medical Costs and Productivity Losses Estimated for Selected Human Pathogens, 1993." *Federal Register* 60, no. 23 (February 3, 1995): p. 6781, table 2.

Moss, A. R. "Epidemiology and the Politics of Needle Exchange." *American Journal of Public Health* 90, no. 9 (September 2000): pp. 1835–37.

Murray, Charles. "Bad News about Illegitimacy." *Weekly Standard*, August 5, 1996, pp. 24–26.

Murray, David, and Joel Schwartz. "Alarmism Is an Infectious Disease." *Society*, May/June 1997, pp. 35–40.

National Academy of Sciences. *Cattle Inspection: Committee on Evaluation of USDA Streamlined Inspection System for Cattle.* 1990.

National Research Council. *Possible Health Effects of Exposure to Residential Electric and Magnetic Fields.* National Academy Press, 1996.

"Notebook." *New Republic*, April 10, 1995.

Olsen, Geary W., et al. "Have Sperm Counts Been Reduced 50 Percent in 50 Years? A Statistical Model Revisited." *Fertility and Sterility* 63 (1995): pp. 887–93.

Orshansky, Mollie. "How Poverty Is Measured." *Monthly Labor Review*, February 1969, p. 37.

Parmesan, Camille. "Climate and Species' Range." *Nature* 382 (August 29, 1996): pp. 765–66.

Paulsen, C. Alvin, et al. "Data from Men in Greater Seattle Area Reveal No Downward Trend in Semen Quality: Further Evidence That Deterioration of Semen Quality Is Not Geographically Uniform." *Fertility and Sterility* 65 (May 1996): pp. 1015–20.

Pinchbeck, Daniel. "Downward Motility." *Esquire*, January 1996, p. 80.

Pinner, Robert W. "Addressing the Challenges of Emerging Infectious Diseases." *American Journal of the Medical Sciences* 311, no. 1 (January 1996): pp. 3–8.

Pinner, Robert W., et al. "Trends in Infectious Diseases Mortality in the United States." *Journal of the American Medical Association* 275 (January 17, 1996): pp.189–93.

Price, David Andrew. "Indiscriminate Approval." *Forbes MediaCritic* 3, no. 4 (Summer 1996).

Rector, Robert. "Food Fight: How Hungry Are America's Children?" *Policy Review* 58 (Fall 1991): p. 38.

——. "How the Poor Really Live: Lessons for Welfare Reform." Heritage Foundation *Backgrounder* 875 (January 31, 1992).

Ross, G. W. "Association of Coffee and Caffeine Intake with the Risk of Parkinson's Disease." *Journal of the American Medical Association* 24, no. 31 (May 2000): pp. 2674–79.

Sawhill, Isabel. "Poverty in the U.S.: Why Is It So Persistent?" *Journal of Economic Literature* 26 (1988).

Scanlan, James P. "Illusions of Job Segregation." *Public Interest* 93 (Fall 1988): pp. 54–69.

Schafran, Lynn Hecht. "Rape Is Still Underreported." *New York Times*, August 26, 1995.

Schwartz, Joel, and David Murray. "AIDS and the Media." *Public Interest* 125 (Fall 1996): pp. 57–71.

Schwartz, Pete J. "Brief Report: A Molecular Link between the Sudden Infant Death Syndrome and the Long-QT Syndrome." *New England Journal of Medicine* 343, no. 4 (July 27, 2000): pp. 262–67.

Shaw, David. "The Front Page." In David Shaw, *Press Watch: A Provocative Look at How Newspapers Report the News*. Macmillan, 1984, pp. 26–27.

Singer, Eleanor, and Phyllis M. Endreny. *Reporting on Risk: How the Mass Media Portray Accidents, Diseases, Disasters, and Other Hazards*. Russell Sage Foundation, 1993.

Slesnick, Daniel T. "Gaining Ground: Poverty in the Postwar United States." *Journal of Political Economy* 101 (1993): pp. 1–38.

Smith, James P., and Finis Welch. "Affirmative Action and Labor Markets." *Journal of Labor Economics* 2 (1984).

Smith, Ted J. III, and Melanie Scarborough. "'A Startling Number of American Children in Danger of Starving': A Case Study of Advocacy Research." Unpublished paper.

Sommers, Christina Hoff. *Who Stole Feminism? How Women Have Betrayed Women*. Simon & Schuster, 1994.

"Sources of Data for Selected Foodborne Pathogens, 1993." *Federal Register* 60, no. 23 (February 3, 1995): p. 6781, table 1.

Straus, Murray A., and Richard J. Gelles. "Societal Change and Change in Family Violence from 1975 to 1985 as Revealed by Two National Surveys." *Journal of Marriage and the Family* 48 (1986): pp. 465–79.

Talbott, Evelyn O., Ada O. York, Kathleen P. McHough, Jeffrey D. Shire, Aimin Zhang, Brian P. Murphy, and Richard A. Engberg. "Mortality among the Residents of the Three Mile Island Accident Area: 1979–1992." *Environmental Health Perspectives* 108, no. 6 (June 2000): pp. 545–53.

Taubes, Gary. *Bad Science: The Short Life and Weird Times of Cold Fusion*. Random House, 1993.

——. "Epidemiology Faces Its Limits." *Science* 269, no. 5221 (July 14, 1995): pp. 164–69.

——. "Nuclear Waste Disposal: Yucca Blowup Theory Bombs, Says Study." *Science* 271 (March 22, 1996): p. 1664.

U.S. Bureau of the Census. "A Brief Look at Postwar U.S. Income Inequality." *Current Population Reports*, P60-191 (June 1996).

——. "Household and Family Characteristics." *Current Population Reports*, P20-483 (March 1994).

——. Statistical Abstract of the United States 1999, 119th ed. Washington, D.C.: Government Printing Office, 1999.

Wattenberg, Ben. *The Good News Is the Bad News Is Wrong*. Simon & Schuster, 1984.

Wheeler, Michael. *Lies, Damn Lies, and Statistics: The Manipulation of Public Opinion in America.* Liveright, 1976.

"When Good News Is No News." *Forbes MediaCritic 3*, no 4 (Summer 1996).

Wildavsky, Aaron. *But Is It True? A Citizen's Guide to Environmental Health and Safety Issues.* Harvard University Press, 1995.

Woodruff, T. J., D. Axelrod, J. Caldwell, R. Morello-Frosch, and A. Rosenbaum. "Public Health Implications of 1990 Air Toxics Concentrations Across the United States." *Environmental Health Perspectives* 106, no. 5 (May 1998): pp. 245–51.

INDEX

ABC World News Tonight, 90, 182
abductions, 58–59, 64–68
activism, versus journalism, 117–18
adversarial tilt, 28
advocacy: media and, 117–18; and
  scientific research, 9
AIDS: incidence of, 17, 19–21;
  needle exchange programs and,
  183–85; in women, 85, 88–90
air quality regulations, 180–82
Alexander, Charles, 118
Allen, Jeanne, 100–101
Alsobrook, Jane, 120
American Gastroenterological
  Association, 127
American Jewish Committee, 107
*American Journal of
  Epidemiology,* 184
*American Journal of Public
  Health,* 182, 185
American Meat Institute, 127
Angell, Marcia, 150–51

Arizona Republic, 189
Arnot, Bob, 155
Associated Press, 88, 155
association, ix

Bachman, Ronet, 110
bait and switch statistics, 57–69
Baldwin, Alec, 195
Balling, Robert, 157–58, 189
Belsky, Jay, 47–48
Bennett, Amanda, 29–30
Berlin, Isaiah, 164
Berzins, Zane, 154
Besharov, Douglas J., 138
Best, Joel, x–xi, 66–67
BJS. *See* Bureau of Justice Statistics
black church arsons, 134
blaming: for bad news, 116–17,
  120, 129–30; messenger,
  147–61
blind spots, 163–74
Boice, John, 195

Boston Globe, 68, 106, 155, 170
Bowman, Charles D., 37–38
Bradlee, Ben, 188
breast cancer: abortion and, 147,
 152–54; risk of, 115, 119–23
breast implants, 133, 139–41,
 154–57
Brind, Joel, 152–53
Brinkley, Christie, 194–95
Broad, William J., 37–38, 52
Brodeur, Paul, 81
Brooks, Eve, 170
Browner, Carol, 180–81
Brown, J. Larry, 75
Bruneau, Julie, 184
*Bulletin of the American
 Meteorological Society,* 50
Bureau of Justice Statistics (BJS),
 22, 31, 98, 108–10, 136
Burtless, Gary, 166–67
Business Week, 41–42

Campbell, Cole, 6
Caplan, Art, 159–60
Carlsen, Elisabeth, 43
Cato Institute, 155–56
causation, viii–ix
CBS Evening News, xi–xii, 71,
 155
CDC. *See* Centers for Disease
 Control and Prevention
Census Bureau, 85, 87–88, 165–66
Center for Science in the Public
 Interest (CSPI), 123
Centers for Disease Control and
 Prevention (CDC): on AIDS,
 17, 19–21, 31, 85, 88–90; on
 meat safety, 124–25; on teen
 risk of violence, 106; on
 tuberculosis, 18, 25, 31
Chapman, Stephen, 156
Chicago Sun-Times, 156

Chicago Tribune: on AIDS in
 women, 88–89; on breast
 implants, 155; on child abuse,
 112, 138; on hunger, 76; on
 infectious diseases, 170
child abuse, 98, 110–12; reporting
 of, 133, 138–39, 141–42
child mortality, 163, 170–73;
 nuclear radiation and, 194–95
children: abducted, 58–59, 64–68;
 in day care, 35, 45–49; and
 Halloween, vii, x–xi; in poverty,
 71–74, 77–81, 163, 165–68,
 170–73
China, 29
Chinchilli, Vernon M., 153
Christian Science Monitor, 100,
 112
Citizen Action, 163, 170–73
Clinton administration, xiii–xiv,
 26, 176–77, 183–84
coffee, ix, vii, viii
Colborn, Theo, 41
cold fusion, 36
commercial negative tilt, 28
Commonwealth Fund, 57, 60
concealed weapons, 147, 155–57
connective-tissue diseases, breast
 implants and, 133, 139–41,
 154–57
copycat effect, xi
coverage, 17–34; press releases
 and, 30–32
crime rates, 21–23; concealed
 weapons and, 147, 155–57;
 reporting and, 133, 135–37. *See
 also* violent crime
Cronkite, Walter, 32
Cross, Russell, 126
CSPI. *See* Center for Science in
 the Public Interest
Cyprus Minerals Co., 158

day care, 35, 45–49
definitions: of abduction, 64–68;
    commonsense versus loose,
    58–59; of domestic violence,
    60–61; of rape, 61–64
Dembosky, Jacob W., 138
domestic violence, vii–viii,
    xiii–xiv, 57–58, 60–61;
    reporting of, 59
Donley, Alex, 123–24
Dow Corning, 154–57
dual–definition strategy, 66–67
Dumanoski, Diane, 41

Eberstadt, Nicholas, 74, 171–73
education: school choice, 97,
    99–101; school quality, vii,
    xi–xiii
electromagnetic fields, 71–72,
    81–83
environmental coverage: air
    quality regulations, 180–82;
    global warming, 35, 49–52,
    117, 147, 157–59, 190–91
*Environmental Health
    Perspectives,* 181, 194
Environmental Protection Agency,
    118, 180–81
epidemiology, viii–ix; bias against
    negative studies in, 150–51
Epstein, William, 150
Equal Employment Opportunity
    Commission, 95
Escherichia coli, 115, 123–28
explanation. *See* interpretation

Fakhrai, Habib, 159–60
Fallows, James, 12, 176
family structures, 85, 87–88
family violence, surveys on, 110–12
Federal Bureau of Investigation,
    133, 135–37

federal government: employment of
    minorities, 85–86, 93–96;
    funding for breast cancer
    research, 119; funding for public
    television, 97, 102–4; needle
    exchange programs, 183–85
Federal Register, 124
Federal Reserve Bank, 17, 23, 85
Fenton, David, 53
Ferree, G. Donald, Jr., 106
filtering, 17–34
Fischhoff, Baruch, 118
Fleischmann, Martin, 36
Food Nutrition Science Alliance,
    148
Food Research and Action Center
    (FRAC), 71, 74–77
Freeman, Neal B., 151
frog deformities, 115, 128–29
Fumento, Michael, 134

Garrett, Laurie, 25
gatekeeping, 3–4
Gelles, Richard J., 60–61, 110–12,
    142
gene therapy, 147–48, 159–60
Gilbert, Neil, 62
global warming, 35, 49–52, 117,
    147, 157–59, 190–91
Gore, Al, 41
Graham, John, 116, 128
Greenberg, Elin Bank, 120

Halloween sadists, vii, x–xi
Hancock, Dale, 125
Hasselmann, K., 191
hedgehog interpretations, 163–74
hemolytic uremic syndrome, 125
Hennekens, Charles H., 139,
    154–57
Herbert, Bob, 123–24
Heritage Foundation, 177
Hiatt, Fred, 190–91

Holocaust, belief in, 97–98, 107–8
Hoppe, David, 128
hunger, 71–77

illegitimacy, 18, 26–27; and child
mortality, 170–73
Immune Response Corporation,
159–60
income inequality, 163, 165–68
infectious diseases, 85, 90–92,
163, 168–70; tuberculosis,
17–18, 24–26
information: ambiguity of, 86;
versus news, 3
Intergovernmental Panel on
Climate Change, 157
interpretation, 85–96; motives
and, 147–61; tunnel vision in,
163–74

Jencks, Christopher, 78–80, 93, 137
Jennings, Peter, 182
journalism. *See* media
*Journal of Epidemiology and
Community Health,* 152
Journal of Legal Studies, 156
*Journal of the American Medical
Association:* on breast implants,
133, 139–41, 154; on coffee,
viii; on infectious diseases, 25,
85, 90–92, 168–69; peer review
in, 151
Joyce Foundation, 104–5

Karoly, Lynn A., 166–67
Kastenberg, William, 40
Kaus, Mickey, 75
Kelly, Michael, 134
Kerr, Richard, 191
Kleck, Gary, 105–7
Koss, Mary P., 58, 61–64
Kotowski, Dan, 156
Kuttner, Robert, 167

Ladd, Everett Carll, 102
Lane, Earl, 193–95
left-of-center tilt, 28
Leo, John, 93
leukemia, electromagnetic fields
and, 81–82
Lindsey, Lawrence, 24
Lindzen, Richard S., 157, 179
Los Angeles Times, 33; on AIDS in
women, 90; on day care, 45; on
gene therapy, 159; on hunger,
76; on infectious diseases, 170;
on sperm counts, 41; on teen
risk of violence, 106
Lott, John R., 156
Louis Harris, 97, 104–7
Lowe, C. R., 169
Lundberg, George, 151

Maddox, John, 179
Mayer, Jean, 77
Mayer, Susan E., 80, 93
McCaffrey, Barry, 184
McCurry, Michael, xiv
McKeown, Thomas, 169
McMurry, Dan, 73, 76
Meadows, Donella H., 41
measurement: ambiguity in,
57–69, 71–84; interpretation
of, 85–96
meat safety, 115, 123–28
media: and advocacy, 117–18;
culture of, 185–89; functions
of, ix–x, 3–4, 7–13;
heterogeneity of, 33; pessimism
in, 27–29; process of, 1–13;
and public policy, 175–95; and
scientific research, 1, 35–54;
and story coverage, 17–34
media bias: toward bad news,
28–29; toward bizarre, 116, 128
mediation, 8

medical coverage: AIDS, 17, 19–21, 85, 88–90, 183–85; breast cancer, 115, 119–23, 147, 152–54; breast implants, 133, 139–41, 154–57; electromagnetic fields, 81–82; infectious diseases, 85, 90–92, 163, 168–70; meat safety, 115, 123–28; tuberculosis, 17–18, 24–26

Michaels, Patrick, 157–58
misunderstandings, 3
morality, media and, 188–89
Morin, Richard, xi, 102–3
mortgages, minorities and, 17, 23–24, 85, 92–93
Moss, A. R., 185
motives, 147–61
Ms. Foundation, 58, 61–64
Murray, Charles, 26–27
Mustard, David, 156
Myers, John Peterson, 41
mythos, 187–89

National Academy of Sciences, 125–26, 184
National Association of Social Workers, 150
National Breast Cancer Coalition, 119
National Cancer Institute, 119–20, 195
National Center for Health Statistics (NCHS), 18, 26–27, 30–31, 172
National Center for Infectious Diseases, 163
National Crime Victimization Survey (NCVS), 17, 22, 31, 97–98, 105–6, 108–9, 136–37
National Education Association, 100

National Incidence Studies of Missing, Abducted, Runaway, and Thrownaway Children (NISMART), 58, 65–68
National Institute of Child Health and Human Development (NICHD), 45–48
National Institutes of Health (NIH), 85–86, 93–96, 154
National Research Council, 71, 81–82
natural science, proxies in, 72, 81–83
Nature, 49
NCHS. See National Center for Health Statistics
NCVS. See National Crime Victimization Survey
needle exchange programs, 183–85
New England Journal of Medicine, viii
The New Republic, xv
news, 1–13; bad, 27–29; mythos of, 187–89; nature of, 6; on scientific research, 1, 35–54
news consumers, 4, 8–9; and lack of coverage, 32–34
Newsday, 193–95; on infectious diseases, 170; on teen sexual activity, 182; on tuberculosis, 25
news stories: coverage of, 17–34; culture of, 185–89; definitions in, 58–59; interpretation of, 85–96
New Yorker, 81
New York Times, 32–33; on abduction, 66–68; on AIDS, 20–21; on breast cancer risk, 119; on breast implants, 141; on child abuse, 112; on day care, 45; on electromagnetic fields, 71–72; on global warming, 50;

on Holocaust beliefs, 107; on
    income inequality, 163,
    165–66; on mortgages for
    minorities, 23–24, 92–93; on
    nuclear waste explosions, 35,
    37–40; on rape, 58, 62–63,
    109; on teens, 107, 182
NICHD. *See* National Institute of
    Child Health and Human
    Development
NIH. *See* National Institutes of
    Health
NISMART. *See* National
    Incidence Studies of Missing,
    Abducted, Runaway, and
    Thrownaway Children
Novello, Antonia, xiv
Nuclear Energy Institute, 195
nuclear radiation, and child
    mortality, 194–95
nuclear waste explosions, 35,
    37–40

Olin Corporation, 147, 156
Olin Foundation, 156
Opinion Research Corp., 102
Orshansky, Mollie, 78
Ozone Action, 157

Park, Robert, 83
Parkinson's disease, viii
Parmesan, Camille, 49–52
peer review, 148–52, 160–61
Pergament, Eugene, 120
pessimism: causes of, 28; media
    and, 27–29
Phi Delta Kappa, 97, 99–100
Philadelphia Inquirer, 147,
    152–54
Physician Task Force on Hunger,
    75–76
Pinner, Robert W., 168–69
Pittsburgh Post-Gazette, 23
Plain Dealer, 102

Plotkin, David, 120, 122
Pollak, Tom, 170–71
polls. *See* surveys
Pons, Stanley, 36
possible links, ix
poverty, 71–74, 77–81; and child
    mortality, 163, 170–73; income
    inequality and, 163, 165–68
press releases, and news coverage,
    30–32
Price, David Andrew, 23
*Proceedings of the National
    Academy of Sciences,* 160
proxies, 71–84
Public Agenda Foundation, 100
public policy, media and, 175–95
public television funding, 97,
    102–4

questions: direct versus oblique,
    108–10; in-person versus
    phone, 110–12

race relations: and education, xiii;
    and employment, 85–86,
    93–96; and mortgages, 17,
    23–24, 85, 92–93
Radiation Public Health Project,
    194
radiation workers, 4–6
radon, 116–17
rape, 98; incidence of, 17;
    questioning on, 108–10;
    reporting of, 58–59, 61–64
Rather, Dan, 71
Rauch, Jonathan, 8
Reader's Digest, 97, 103–4
reality, 7–8; versus reporting,
    133–43
reality industry, 1, 7–13. *See also*
    media
Rector, Robert, 76–77
referee bias, 150–51

reporting: of abductions, 59; of child abuse, 133, 138–39, 141–42; and crime rates, 133, 135–37; of domestic violence, 59; of rape, 58–59, 61–64; versus reality, 133–43; of risk, 115–31; self-reporting, 139–41; underreporting, 59
Reuters, 194
rheumatoid arthritis, ix
Rind, David, 191
risk reporting, 115–31
Roper, Burns W., 99, 108
Roper Organization, 107
Rosenbaum, Donna, 127–28

Safe Tables Our Priority (STOP), 123, 127–28
Sagan, Carl, 189
Samuelson, Robert, 167–68
San Diego Union-Tribune, 112, 147–48, 159–60
San Francisco Chronicle, 107
Santer, Benjamin, 191
Scanlan, James P., 95
Scarborough, Melanie, 75
Schneider, Stephen H., 117
school choice, 97, 99–101
schools, in Texas, vii, xi–xiii
Schudson, Michael, 6–7
Schumer, Charles E., 156
Science, 40, 184, 191, 195
scientific research, 9–11; bias against negative studies in, 150–51; community of, 9; evaluation of, 160–61; media and, 1, 35–54; motives in, 147–61; proxies in, 71–84; and public policy, 175–95; reputation of, 176–78
self-reporting, 139–41
self-righteousness of media, 28–29
sexual activity, of teenagers, 182–83

sexual violence, 22–23. *See also* rape
Shalala, Donna, 133, 138, 176–77, 183
Shaw, David, 33, 119, 122
SIDS, 181–82
Singer, S. Fred, 157, 159
Slate, 138
Slovic, Paul, 118
Smith, Ted J., III, 75
social sciences, proxies in, 72–81
social work, 150
Sondik, Edward J., 120
sperm counts, 35, 41–45
STAR Foundation, 194
Star Tribune, 99–100
statistics: ambiguity in, 57–69; interpretation of, 85–96; versus reality, 133–43
Stein, Gertrude, 84, 98
Stein, Herbert, 168
STOP. *See* Safe Tables Our Priority
Strange Situation, 46–47
Straus, Murray A., 60–61, 110–12, 142
sudden infant death syndrome (SIDS), 181–82
surveys, 59, 97–113; direct versus oblique questioning in, 108–10; in-person versus phone, 110–12; sample in, 99; wording in, 62, 97–98, 100–102, 105–6
Szymanski, Jerry S., 39

Taylor, Michael R., 126
teenagers: sexual activity of, 182–83; risk of violence, 97, 104–7
Teeter, Robert, 106
template theory, 29–30, 53
Texas, schools, vii, xi–xiii
Thibodeau, Tracy M., 66

Thurman, Sandra, 183
Toklas, Alice B., 98
Toledo Blade, 63
tuberculosis, 17–18, 24–26
tunnel vision, 163–74

underreporting, 59
Uniform Crime Reports (UCR), 17, 21–22, 137
United States Department of Agriculture (USDA), 123–26
USA Today, xii, 87–88, 134, 141, 159
U.S. News & World Report, 41–42

Venneri, Francesco, 37–38
violent crime, 17; teenagers and, 97, 104–7. *See also* crime rates
Virginia schools, xiii

Wall Street Journal, 12, 23, 100, 156
Ward, John, 19

Washington Post, 33, 188; on AIDS, 20; on breast implants, 141; on child mortality, 170; on crime rates, 21–22, 133, 135–37; on day care, 45; on domestic violence, xiv, 57–58; on federal funding for public television, 102; on frog deformities, 115, 128–29; on global warming, 157, 190–91; on needle exchange programs, 183; on NIH employment, 94; on poverty, 71; on radiation, 4, 6
Washington Times, 87–88
Wattenberg, Ben, 28
Western Fuels Association, 158
Whelan, Elizabeth M., Jr., 126–27
Whitman, David, 79
Winchester Inc., 156
wire codes, 82
Woodruff, Tracey, 181
World Health Organization, 18, 24–25, 31

ABOUT THE AUTHORS

David Murray is director of the Statistical Assessment Service in Washington, D.C., and an adjunct professor at Georgetown University.

Joel Schwartz is senior adjunct fellow at the Hudson Institute.

S. Robert Lichter is president of the Center for Media and Public Affairs in Washington, D.C.